NEW PLAYS USA 3

New Plays USA Series

New Plays USA 1

Lee Breuer, *A Prelude to Death in Venice*
Tom Cole, *Dead Souls*
David Henry Hwang, *FOB*
Emily Mann, *Still Life*
OyamO, *The Resurrection of Lady Lester*
Adele Edling Shank, *Winterplay*

New Plays USA 2

Donald Freed and Arnold M. Stone, *Secret Honor*
Gary Leon Hill, *Food from Trash*
Franz Xaver Kroetz, *Mensch Meier,* translated by Roger Downey
Ronald Ribman, *Buck*
James Yoshimura, *Mercenaries*

NEW PLAYS USA 3

Edited by
JAMES LEVERETT
and M. ELIZABETH OSBORN

THE PLAYS

Morocco
Allan Havis

Execution of Justice
Emily Mann

The Incredibly Famous Willy Rivers
Stephen Metcalfe

Between East and West
Richard Nelson

Cold Air
Virgilio Piñera
translated and adapted by *Maria Irene Fornes*

Theatre Communications Group New York 1986

Contents

Selection Committee for
New Plays USA 3

New Plays USA 3 was supported in part by a generous grant from Home Box Office, Inc.

The playwrights whose plays appear in this volume are recipients of Playwrights USA Awards, also funded by Home Box Office, Inc.

NEW PLAYS USA 3

Introduction

James Leverett

How much less needs to be explained about the third volume of the *New Plays USA* series than was necessary for the first one when it appeared in 1982! Then it had to be made clear that the book was a selection of the best dramatic writing produced at a group of American theatres variously labeled regional, resident and repertory—designations never adequately explaining their multifarious natures. Now the "Copernican Revolution" is an accomplished fact. The historical center of new American dramatic writing has moved from the central Broadway marketplace out into a network of professional theatres operating, not on ticket sales alone, but by virtue of individual, corporation, foundation and government support. This network is our true National Theatre, and it extends to nearly every state.

We can be proud of having begun to place theatres on an equal footing with libraries, museums and orchestras as necessary enhancements of community life, deserving of civic backing. Yet, at the time this introduction is being written, the survival of none of these "permanent" institutions is sure. Theatre is among the most ancient of arts and, because of its communal nature, the art that requires the longest time to mature within a culture. Yet subsidized theatre, as distinguished from commercial show business, is the youngest art in this young nation, having come into being for all practical purposes during the 1960s. Having only the most fragile roots, it is most vulnerable to the outcome of the great debate now happening throughout our society over the proper concerns of the public and private sectors—who should pay for what, in other words. As an art, theatre cannot exist in any sort of large, meaningful way on what comes in at the box office. On what will it exist, then?

Ultimately of much more import than economics is theatre's aesthetic predicament. It is caught squarely in the middle of the century-long realignment of human attention brought about by film and the most powerful attention-getter of all time, television. Very likely this redefinition will not be complete even when the calendar rolls up 2000, or for years thereafter. The questions are basic: Will there be theatre? What will theatre be?

No theatre is secure. Not the kind that hedges its bets by presenting comfortable, formulaic material, no more than the kind that experiments, challenges and provokes. What the plays of the *New Plays USA* series say in chorus is, "If there is no safety anywhere in this ancient art in this new country in this new age, then we will be dangerous and respond to the world as creatively and directly as we know how. If the majority seems content to put itself to sleep in one way or another, we will cast our lots with the minority that chooses otherwise—and possibly rouse some of the sleepers in the process. And if crushing economic forces seem bent on hemming in our art, they will not shrink our subjects as well. Those will remain large, vital and expressive."

It is folly to superimpose some thematic, aesthetic or other unity on a group of plays assembled, as this one was, with no program in mind besides presenting what pleased and excited the presenters most. But it is interesting, even irresistible, to observe how the collections have changed over the years in this, the only publishing project devoted solely to works produced in American non-profit professional theatres. What you can opine from these changes is your own invention.

New Plays USA 1—containing the work of one black, one Asian-American, and two women, and including a new translation/adaptation of a Russian comic masterpiece, a Joycean performance text, a documentary about the aftermath of Vietnam and a hyperreal family drama (see the front of this book for the authors and titles in both previous collections)—seemed to Michael Feingold, who introduced it, "like a good tank of tropicals, wildly colored and varied." It was both a Noah's Ark, containing representatives of most major species, and a "spontaneous manifesto" (again Feingold's words), at once demonstrating and espousing the diversity of a nation of playwrights working in a national theatre. That manifesto nature has been enriched by each succeeding volume.

Published in 1984, *New Plays USA 2* included a monodrama on the abuses of power in the highest places, a Boschian vision of environmental and spiritual dissolution, a bitter account of idealism brought down by rapacity in the television marketplace, a translation of a contemporary German work presenting citizens dehumanized by an uncaring society, and a melodrama of America causing a Third-World crisis and then getting trapped in it. Richard Gilman, introducing this volume, found the plays shared no subject or theme but a "common state of mind or morale." In them, he said, "the psychic and the social fuse, the private and public merge; in them the political takes on its widest, most useful implications for dramatic vision, the organization of life, the communal arena of values, and so goes beyond program or indictment."

The works in *New Plays USA 3* continue this political and social engagement. Indeed, this factor seems to be even more of a "given" in the consciousnesses of the authors, something they can deal with more securely but with no less passion or commitment. Perhaps, just two years later, they are more worldly as a breed and more clearly determined to make the *whole* world their stage. What the plays in all three volumes belie most certainly is the bromide that American playwrights have no range beyond kitchen tiffs and living-room spats. The *New Plays USA* manifesto lies in the diversity of the plays and in the insistence that our playwrights have something to say.

Drawn with an elliptical spareness that makes its ancient landscape all the more mysterious and evocative, Allan Havis's *Morocco* takes place in an Orient of the mind and of the passions. Three characters—a wealthy American architect, his exotically alluring wife and her Arab jailer—encounter one another in circumstances that are fraught but far from clear. Understanding and human sympathy appear where one expects corruption and turpitude, madness and violence where there should be reason and civility. Sexuality and power are part of the same undertow in what seems to be a parable of East-West relations but which refuses to divulge a moral.

In *Execution of Justice,* Emily Mann brings to the stage the trial of Dan White for the murders of San Francisco Mayor George Moscone and Harvey Milk, that city's first openly gay Supervisor. The courtroom is one of the theatre's oldest settings and the author uses it to examine the effect on society, victims and victimizers alike, of a collapse of a sense of social justice and the failure of due process of law. By doing so, she also questions deeply the habits of entrenched power in this country and the fundamental myth of the American hero, who learned his morals on the streets of Dodge City and now can only react by shooting it out.

If this century has an emblematic figure, it is surely the outsider, the one standing apart for whatever reason of race, religion, nationality, gender, sexual orientation—and suffering, frequently dying, from that separation. In our time, the political emigre is most evident, driven from one state but never really at home in another. Much of our best art, in all forms, has that subject and, ironically but not unexpectedly, many of our best artists are emigres. In Richard Nelson's *Between East and West,* a Czech theatre director and actress, husband and wife, try to start a life in this country. The pain and difficulty of their uprooted situation is measured in tiny, often comic but inevitably heartrending details of cultural collision and in the one great thing that is both their means of survival and their nemesis: their language. The chasm separating them from their native land divides them from their livelihood and art, from the new world in which they are trying to settle, and ultimately from each other.

The world of Stephen Metcalfe's *The Incredibly Famous Willy Rivers* is propelled from excess to excess by its own noise. The rock star Willy is shot, nearly killed, on stage during a concert. The attempted assassination is the "artistic" act of a fan, trapped in an existence that barely grants him an identity and crazed by a media-hyped notion of instant fame. Willy recovers but his comeback is a hellish journey through his past—his personal life left in shambles by notoriety and his public career bloated into amoral meaninglessness by its own success. Metcalfe's canvas, splashed with dissonant and raucous color, is surreal; but one senses that the marketplace of art, sex and death he depicts is absolutely accurate and mirrors a world even larger than the hyperbolic one of rock and roll.

Part of the *New Plays USA* manifesto is the publication in each volume of a new translation. The point is to recognize the translator's art, always crucial to the theatre, as no less exacting and difficult than any other kind of writing. Behind that premise, there must always be an original work worth translating, of course, and in this case it is *Cold Air* by Virgilio Piñera, one of Cuba's foremost modern writers. In what is surely a perfect match of talent and temperament, the translator/adapter is Maria Irene Fornes, whose own plays have been fundamental to the growth of theatre in this country over the past generation. For the work's translation and presentation at INTAR in New York, Fornes received a Hispanic Translation Commission, part of Theatre Communications Group's project for acquainting this country with the riches of Hispanic theatre from throughout the world. The play, always teetering between comedy and tragedy, is redolent of Cuban life between the end of World War II and the rise of Fidel Castro. This volume's only real family play, it is a tapestry of human longing, feelings of impasse and capacity to endure, which seems to map the spiritual terrain of a country that is so near to us and so far away.

Surely what most invites speculation about that which the *New Plays USA* volumes are trying to communicate, to make manifest, is the manner by which their contents are chosen. Like no other system, this process makes use of the creative energies of that National Theatre discussed earlier. The plays in this volume were selected from the 24 issued as manuscripts during the 1983-84 and 1984-85 seasons of *Plays in Process*, Theatre Communications Group's script distribution project, and from the first plays published in TCG's *American Theatre* magazine. Both *Plays in Process* and *American Theatre* depend for their material on the national network of nonprofit professional theatres, which now sustain and produce nearly all of our dramatic writers and translators.

So, the plays in this volume have come a long way. First, a theatre selected each of them from the literally thousands making the rounds every year to become part of the season's roster of presentations. Probably that theatre, and very likely others as well, had already been focusing its material resources and creative energies on the writer and his or her work for some time. In the case of the *PIP* scripts in this volume, once they were scheduled for production, the theatres' artistic directors or literary managers nominated them for further consideration by a distinguished selection committee. There were 225 nominations in all. *New Plays USA 3*, then, is the pinnacle of a pyramid with a very broad base. Fortunately for our theatre, it does *not* contain all of the good plays to appear in this country over the past two years. It does contain an excellent and, for the future of the art whatever it be, encouraging representation of them.

Also hopeful for the future is the fact that all of the writers in this volume are recipients of Playwrights USA Awards. These substantial grants, begun in 1984 with *New Plays USA 2*, are made possible by Home Box Office, Inc. as an investment, no strings attached, not only in what has been written in this country, but also in what will be written.

All of the directors, dramaturgs, actors, designers, management personnel and the many others who have taken part in bringing new work to this country's stages are part of what makes this book possible and deserve our thanks. But most of all thanks to the writers, present and absent in these pages, by whom our theatre lives.

At Theatre Communications Group, I direct the Literary Services department, which is responsible for *Plays in Process*, the Hispanic Translation Project, and publication of plays in *American Theatre*, and I serve as general editor for the *New Plays USA* series. This all means that I generally skim the cream off the top of these fascinating, rewarding activities, while others keep them operating smoothly. Betty Osborn edits many of the plays for *Plays in Process* and all of them for the magazine. Her exemplary work with writers in getting their creations on paper is a resource unto itself for a whole profession. And it is she who really brings the diverse parts of this book together into one coherent piece. Gillian Richards, my other associate in the department, keeps the intricate machinery of *Plays in Process* and the Hispanic Translation Project operating smoothly, types all of the manuscripts for PIP and edits an increasing number of them as well. She was the original editor of *Morocco*. Ray Sweatman, our intern-in-the-nick-of-time, helps on all of the projects in ways that I only dimly but gratefully glimpse. He began his editing career by working on *Between East and West*. To these three my deepest thanks.

And special gratitude to those stalwart, generous readers who took time out of their lives, so crowded with vital work for the theatre, to serve on the *Plays in Process* committee, which provided the first stage of selection for this volume: George Ferencz, resident director of La Mama E.T.C. and project director of INTAR's Hispanic American Musical Theatre Lab; Elinor Fuchs, theatre critic and author of the prizewinning play *Year One of the Empire*; David Henry Hwang, award-winning author, a collection of whose plays, *Broken Promises*, has been published by Avon Books; Romulus Linney, writer and director, whose plays have been produced on and Off Broadway and in theatres throughout the U.S., Canada and Europe; Robert Marx, former theatre program director for the New York State Council on the Arts, currently co-producer of Theatre Festival, Inc., which will present an international festival in New York in 1987-88; Robert Moss, artistic director of the Hangar Theatre in Ithaca, N.Y. and founding producing director of Playwrights Horizons; Amy Saltz, director, whose work has been seen in theatres throughout the U.S., including numerous seasons at the O'Neill Center's National Playwrights Conference; Michelle Shay, actor, who has been featured in new plays on and Off Broadway, as well as classical repertory across the country; Catherine Slade, actor, teacher, director and founding artistic director of the Manhattan Bridge Company; Alisa Solomon, freelance dramaturg and theatre critic for *The Village Voice*.

Morocco
Allan Havis

About Allan Havis

Born in New York City in 1951, Allan Havis holds degrees from City College of New York, Hunter College and Yale School of Drama. His plays, including *Oedipus Again, Heinz, Interludes, Family Rites, Heaven and Earth* and *Mink Sonata*, have received readings and productions at American Repertory Theatre, Virginia Stage Company, Playwrights Horizons, Ensemble Studio Theatre, Second Stage, Ark Theatre, Case Western Reserve University, Hunter Playwrights and Yale School of Drama. A reading of his most recent play *Haut Goût* at Virginia Stage Company and a production of his one-act *Duet for Three* at New York's West Bank Cafe took place early in 1986.

Havis is the author of *Albert the Astronomer*, a children's novel published by Harper & Row. The recipient of the 1976 Marc A. Klein Playwriting Award and two John Golden Awards, he is the winner of a 1985-86 National Endowment for the Arts playwriting fellowship.

About the Play

In the spring of 1984 a one-act version of *Morocco* was produced by American Repertory Theatre, along with a second Havis one-act *The Road from Jerusalem*, under the umbrella title *Holy Wars*. The full-length *Morocco*, chosen by Norfolk's Virginia Stage Company as its winner of the FDG/CBS New Play Award, opened there on February 27, 1985, under the direction of Christopher Hanna. *Morocco* was circulated by *Plays in Process* later that year.

Playwright's Note

As if in a dream, *Morocco* travels an irregular path between things of certainty and doubt. The traditional notion of plot, admittedly, has fallen by the wayside. Time may be truncated or stretched in a particular subjected manner. Logic bends to one's displeasure. During moments of anxiety, reality fools us. Something may seem unreal, or far worse—hyperbolic. To inhabit a Max Ernst canvas for a day, a week, a month, would be most frightening. And yet, there is a comic afterthought to this cold clammy sweat.

An American discovers that he is in a foreign land, without clear purpose or credentials, and in growing conflict with his better instincts. He pretends that, perhaps, the next morning will be brighter. Naked, his speech is distilled and terse. He stands at a threshold.

Characters

MR. KEMPLER, an architect in his late thirties working for a New York firm with clandestine contracts overseas. He is punctual, fastidious, and somewhat arrogant. His anger is slow to surface, although he manages to go through the motions. He is affluent, with experience in business kickbacks. He has been married for ten years and travels with his wife.

COLONEL, a much older man of Arab nationality. He has never seen foreign duty. Overweight and a chain smoker, he gives the appearance of an anxious man about to retire. His position is senior officer at a Moroccan jail for women. His sense of irony is broad and he cannot stifle a bad joke. He thinks his life could improve with a little luck. He deals with whores, drug dealers and thieves. He takes pride in his difficult exterior. He has yet to arrest an American in his city.

MRS. KEMPLER, an unusually alluring woman in her mid-thirties. She is part Latin, part Arabian. Educated in England, she has only a slight Mediterranean accent. She hides very little about herself, but answers all pointed questions as though she were a day-born child. The cleverness inside her is unassuming and soft, and emerges in casual tones.

WAITER

Time

The present year.

Place

Act One   Fez, Morocco.
Act Two   Malaga, Spain.
Act Three Fez, Morocco.

The Play

Morocco

ACT ONE

Fez, Morocco. The COLONEL's *office inside the jailhouse.*

Day One

COLONEL: Is this a picture of your wife?
KEMPLER: Yes, I believe so.
COLONEL: And her wardrobe?
KEMPLER: I don't recognize it.
COLONEL: And have you seen these? *(More photos)*
KEMPLER: I don't quite understand.
COLONEL *(Pause)*: Please, have a seat.
KEMPLER: Is she here?
COLONEL: Yes. *(Offering a cigarette)*
KEMPLER: No, thanks. I don't smoke.
COLONEL: I understand you are an architect.
KEMPLER: Yes.
COLONEL: That's very impressive. Working very hard?
KEMPLER: Yes.
COLONEL: Work is wonderful for the spirit.
KEMPLER: I'm sure.

COLONEL: It says in my report that your wife is a banker.

KEMPLER: That is correct.

COLONEL: An executive?

KEMPLER: Yes.

COLONEL: We treat bankers very well.

KEMPLER: How kind of you.

COLONEL: Do I cause you great embarrassment, Mr. Kempler?

KEMPLER: Not at all.

COLONEL: Wives sometime misbehave.

KEMPLER: You must have confused her with someone else.

COLONEL: I don't believe so.

KEMPLER: Are you head of staff?

COLONEL: Colonel, yes.

KEMPLER: Perhaps you can tell me why she was apprehended.

COLONEL: Certainly. *(Pause)* Prostitution, disorderly conduct, drunkenness.

KEMPLER: That's absurd.

COLONEL *(Amused)*: Of course. *(Pause)* And you wish to post bail?

KEMPLER: Yes, naturally.

COLONEL: I think we can arrange something. *(Pause)* Your wife spent last night sleepless.

KEMPLER: Is she all right?

COLONEL: Reasonably well.

KEMPLER: When may I see her?

COLONEL: Shortly. She's now with our medics.

KEMPLER: She was kept in a cell last night?

COLONEL: Yes.

KEMPLER: Why wasn't I phoned earlier?

COLONEL: She was in no condition to be released. Our buildings are sanitary, Mr. Kempler.

KEMPLER: May I use your telephone?

COLONEL: I'd rather you didn't.

KEMPLER: Colonel, I find these charges incredible to believe.

COLONEL: Yes, I can sympathize.

KEMPLER: Abril doesn't drink.

COLONEL: Perhaps there is more about her?

KEMPLER: I think not.

COLONEL: May I ask you something, Mr. Kempler? *(Pause)* Why are you here?

KEMPLER: In Morocco?

COLONEL: Yes.

KEMPLER: Our jobs brought us here.

COLONEL: Please make it clear to me.

KEMPLER: You have our papers.

COLONEL: Is it that you like foreign food?

KEMPLER: Our work coincides often, and so we travel. My firm is building the industrial park outside your city.

COLONEL: Yes, I know that.

KEMPLER: Abril is with the affiliate bank.

COLONEL: Does she dress this way at the office?

KEMPLER: Obviously not.

COLONEL: Do they not pay her enough?

KEMPLER: Please don't sound ridiculous.

COLONEL: Do I?

KEMPLER: It is a gross distortion.

COLONEL: There is a serious epidemic in my country, and some precautions are needed.

KEMPLER: I can understand.

COLONEL: Not that we don't want foreign investors.

KEMPLER: Then why pick on my wife?

COLONEL: May I recite a parable? *(Phone rings; answering)* Na-on? [Yes?] *(Listening)* Sho-kun. [Thank you.] *(To KEMPLER)* Your wife had been checked for a contagion. She will be detained.

KEMPLER: You must let me see her.

COLONEL: For now that must wait.

KEMPLER: I insist.

COLONEL: You should make a friend of me, Mr. Kempler. I am in a position to help you.

KEMPLER: I'm listening.

COLONEL: First, have a cigarette. *(KEMPLER accepts one)* You needn't inhale to enjoy.

KEMPLER: What can I do for you?

COLONEL *(Ignoring KEMPLER)*: The tobacco is excellent. Almost sweet.

KEMPLER: Yes, very mild.

COLONEL: I keep them in a humidor.

KEMPLER: Very wise.

COLONEL: And yet my wife worries for me. Cancer scares.

KEMPLER: Can I write a check?

COLONEL: No, no, no. I wasn't looking for a gift, Mr. Kempler. First of all, my commander would expect a percentage. Secondly, I would feel compromised and obligated. You might send other things in the mail. I could not in good conscience accept anything in this context. No, no, keep your checks. You are in the company of an honest officer.

KEMPLER: That is reassuring.

COLONEL: Furthermore, a bribe is a direct insult to Morocco.

KEMPLER: Colonel, I was not suggesting anything of the kind.

COLONEL: Bribes make soldiers complacent. Am I repeating myself? *(Pause)* Please, put aside your checkbook. We will do this the proper way.

KEMPLER: Fine.

COLONEL: Do you play chess?

KEMPLER: Why do you ask?

COLONEL: I am quite skillful at the game. And backgammon. Do you play backgammon, Mr. Kempler?

KEMPLER: No.

COLONEL: Four-handed bridge?

KEMPLER: No, Colonel.

COLONEL: Did you play with little buildings as a boy?

KEMPLER: Please, we're wasting time.

COLONEL: Yes, I am sorry. *(Pause)* How is it that you married a whore?

KEMPLER: I will call the U.S. Consulate. *(Standing)*

COLONEL: But of course. *(Rising)* Thank you for stopping by, Mr. Kempler.

Day Two

COLONEL: Good day, Mr. Kempler.

KEMPLER: I have a letter from my Ambassador.

COLONEL: Is that so?

KEMPLER: Please . . . *(Handing it over)*

COLONEL: It's addressed to myself. And in his hand. *(Pause)* Why didn't he call? *(Pause)* Very well. *(Puts letter down without reading)* What more can I do for you?

KEMPLER: Damn it, you can read the letter.

COLONEL *(Obliging KEMPLER)*: Yes, all right then. *(Pause)* But he makes no mention of venereal disease.

KEMPLER: Venereal disease?

COLONEL: Syphilis, yes.

KEMPLER: You will either release her, or let my doctor see her.

COLONEL: Bring in your doctor, Mr. Kempler.

KEMPLER: I shall.

COLONEL: But I doubt that he will contest our reports.

KEMPLER: I hope this will cost you your rank.

COLONEL: Are you Jewish, Mr. Kempler?

KEMPLER: What?

COLONEL: What is your religion?

KEMPLER: How does that matter?

COLONEL: Not in the slightest. But tell me.

KEMPLER: I've been overseas for fifteen years and have never experienced such idiocy.

COLONEL: I won't let you flatter me, Mr. Kempler.

KEMPLER: Colonel, you are an idiot of some caliber.

COLONEL: We will become better friends in time.

KEMPLER: What do you hope to gain from this?

COLONEL: Perhaps your imagination is running away. I am not a sinister man. Look, here is a picture of my family. *(Shows photo on his desk)* I am hardworking. This office takes the worse abuse. Come now, have a cigarette.

KEMPLER: Why have you abducted my wife?

COLONEL: I have already told you.

KEMPLER: You dressed her and photographed her. It's all very entertaining. Who are you trying to hurt?

COLONEL: No one.

KEMPLER: Her bank has received complaints.

COLONEL: Yes, I have spoken directly with her officers.

KEMPLER: You are committing crimes against Americans.

COLONEL: I happen to like your nation.

KEMPLER: Then why this punishment?

COLONEL: Your wife was fraternizing with our army.

KEMPLER: This is very wrong.

COLONEL (*Removing a sack from inside his desk*): I have some of her personal things. You may wish to take them with you. (*Opening sack*) She wears contact lenses. Have you a pair of glasses for her? (*Pause*) Perhaps you can bring them tomorrow.

KEMPLER: Please let me see her for one minute.

COLONEL: And suppose I should let you. What then? You would want her released on the spot. You would raise your voice and get in more difficulties with us. It is better to follow procedures.

KEMPLER: You're detaining an innocent woman.

COLONEL: What is your wish, Mr. Kempler? Do you want her free? Do you want her well? Really, we can straighten this out with remarkable civility.

KEMPLER: I doubt it.

COLONEL: Then what do you suggest? I don't want you wife here. I am embarrassed to see you here. I don't want letters from your Embassy. Do you hear me clearly? Do you think we can try, Mr. Kempler?

KEMPLER: I don't know.

COLONEL: You must at least trust me in this matter.

KEMPLER: I'd like to see my wife.

COLONEL: And you will.

KEMPLER: What did she do to warrant this?

COLONEL: Mrs. Kempler was arrested for soliciting on the streets.

KEMPLER: Is it because she works at the bank?

COLONEL: I don't think so.

KEMPLER: You know of course it is an international bank.

COLONEL: Yes.

KEMPLER: It is a powerful bank.

COLONEL: I realize that.

KEMPLER: Is it my work then?

COLONEL: You put yourself in a curious position, Mr. Kempler.

KEMPLER: My company's policies are very liberal here.

COLONEL: What are your company's policies?

KEMPLER: We hire locally. At least two-thirds.

COLONEL: Are you Jewish, Mr. Kempler?

KEMPLER: Why do you continue on that?

COLONEL: Because I don't like Jews.

KEMPLER: We appreciate the constructions in Fez.

COLONEL: Tell me what you are.

KEMPLER: Yes, I am Jewish.

COLONEL: I am not surprised.

KEMPLER: But my wife is not.

COLONEL: I am not an anti-Semite, Mr. Kempler. My opinions are rather mild. *(Pause)* Is your architectural firm from New York?

KEMPLER: Yes.

COLONEL: But the names are not Jewish? *(Pause)* Somehow we're always doing business with Jews.

KEMPLER: We'll build more with time.

COLONEL: It is an interesting arrangement.

KEMPLER: Why did you stage those photographs?

COLONEL: What?

KEMPLER: They were staged.

COLONEL: Shall we discuss architecture? Are we really in store for American skyscrapers? What beautiful dreams have you waiting for us?

KEMPLER: The designs are very exciting.

COLONEL: Are we making you fat and bored? Why do you architects put bathrooms in the oddest of places? *(Pause)* Don't be silent with me.

KEMPLER: What would you like to hear?

COLONEL: What would I like to hear? Anything you care to say.

KEMPLER: You seem to know enough.

COLONEL: Then you should go back to your hotel and rehearse.

KEMPLER: Rehearse what?

COLONEL: Stories. Make up a story.

KEMPLER: I will.

COLONEL: That's good to hear. *(Pause)* Let us talk tomorrow. Good afternoon.

Day Three

COLONEL: I see that you have brought your physician.

KEMPLER: With your permission.

COLONEL: Yes, but of course.

KEMPLER: Is he with her now?

COLONEL: Yes.

KEMPLER: How is she?

COLONEL: Fine.

KEMPLER: Has she slept?

COLONEL: Yes.

KEMPLER: And eating?

COLONEL: I believe so.

KEMPLER: I will see her today.

COLONEL: You will wait.

KEMPLER: I have some of her things.

COLONEL: Leave them with me.

KEMPLER: And her glasses.

COLONEL: Thank you.

KEMPLER: I must have her home.

COLONEL: We will try.

KEMPLER: We are seldom apart.

COLONEL: I sympathize.

KEMPLER: Will there be a formal arraignment?

COLONEL: It has already occurred. (Pause) You will receive notice of the trial.

KEMPLER: How soon?

COLONEL: Perhaps in a few weeks.

KEMPLER: Must it go to trial?

COLONEL: I'm afraid so.

KEMPLER: Why is she being set up?

COLONEL: I cannot answer that.

KEMPLER: Our country has good relations with yours.

COLONEL: Yes.

KEMPLER: There must be a way to resolve this.

COLONEL: Return to your Consulate, Mr. Kempler.

KEMPLER: Surely you could intervene?

COLONEL: I could not.

KEMPLER: And what if the doctor says that she is fine?

COLONEL: But she is not.

KEMPLER: God help you if you cause her pain.

COLONEL: She is being given penicillin.

KEMPLER: You better not fuck around with her.

COLONEL: Go home and get some sleep.

KEMPLER: I'll wait for the doctor.

COLONEL: Go home, Mr. Kempler.

Day Four

COLONEL: Did you know that our currency has been devalued?

KEMPLER: I heard this morning.

COLONEL: It is unfortunate. Nothing keeps stable.

KEMPLER: Many countries have the same problem.

COLONEL: It is cheap to see Morocco.

KEMPLER: Yes, it is.

COLONEL: How are your hotel accommodations?

KEMPLER: Sufficient.

COLONEL: We have remarkably fine hotels.

KEMPLER: Yes, I would agree.
COLONEL: Did your physician report back to you?
KEMPLER: Yes.
COLONEL: He corroborated with our doctors?
KEMPLER: Yes.
COLONEL: It needn't be a mystery.
KEMPLER: My wife is in your jail.
COLONEL: Only temporarily.
KEMPLER: The doctor said it is an early infection.
COLONEL: Yes, we caught it quickly.
KEMPLER: Your medics gave it to her.
COLONEL: No, Mr. Kempler.
KEMPLER: She told me they did.
COLONEL: Out of embarrassment, no doubt.
KEMPLER: You son-of-a-bitch.
COLONEL: Sit down, Mr. Kempler.
KEMPLER: Your fucking medics gave it to her.
COLONEL: Whyever should they?
KEMPLER: I demand to see her.
COLONEL: Let me tell you something, my friend. I met your wife on two oc-
    casions. She is quite beautiful. I would like to sleep with her myself.
KEMPLER: We should be able to strike a deal.
COLONEL: Not in that tone of voice.
KEMPLER: I don't understand you, Colonel.
COLONEL: Whisper to me, Mr. Kempler.
KEMPLER: Go screw yourself.
COLONEL: You're not whispering.
KEMPLER: There's a limit to this business.
COLONEL: Why don't you contact Amnesty International?
KEMPLER: I have.
COLONEL: And the Red Cross.
KEMPLER: I have.
COLONEL: And your Ambassador calls me every day.
KEMPLER: I know why you're doing this.
COLONEL: Tell me, Mr. Kempler.
KEMPLER: You're crazy.
COLONEL: Yes.
KEMPLER: Very crazy.
COLONEL: It's become a sporting thing.
KEMPLER: You find some prosperous Americans . . .
COLONEL: Please go on.
KEMPLER: And you play with their lives.
COLONEL: I am an officer in the King's army.
KEMPLER: How did you ever get to be Colonel!
COLONEL: I speak English.

KEMPLER: You are causing me great inconvenience.

COLONEL: That's putting it mildly. Why be so kind?

KEMPLER: Then you admit it.

COLONEL: Admit what?

KEMPLER: What you're doing to my wife.

COLONEL: Your wife is very well educated.

KEMPLER: What is that supposed to mean?

COLONEL: Our women are hardly schooled.

KEMPLER: Are you punishing her for that?

COLONEL: No.

KEMPLER: Then why bring it up?

COLONEL: My wife stays home with our children.

KEMPLER: Your nation is very backward.

COLONEL: My nation is based on tradition.

KEMPLER: Your people are illiterate.

COLONEL: I cannot argue that.

KEMPLER: But why snap at my wife?

COLONEL: Mr. Kempler, I told you. I like your wife. *(Silence)* Tomorrow you may see her.

Day Five

COLONEL: You are the first person I see each day.

KEMPLER: The privilege is mutual.

COLONEL: Did I make a promise to you?

KEMPLER: I believe so.

COLONEL: Then I won't keep you any further.

KEMPLER: Thank you.

COLONEL: You needn't thank me. *(Pause)* I see you decided to shave. *(Pause)* You look very presentable.

KEMPLER: How much time do I get?

COLONEL: As long as you want. *(Pause)* Go right ahead, Mr. Kempler.

Day Six

COLONEL: How good to see you, Mr. Kempler. *(Pause)* We have the trial date.

KEMPLER: When?

COLONEL: Three weeks.

KEMPLER: Why so long?

COLONEL: It is the best we can do.

KEMPLER: What about bail?

COLONEL: No, I'm sorry.

KEMPLER: My Ambassador says there is no precedent for this detention.

COLONEL: Well, I think we shall work around it.

KEMPLER: My wife needs to see a dentist.

COLONEL: Did she request that?

KEMPLER: Yes.

COLONEL: All right then.

KEMPLER: She would like unsoiled clothes.

COLONEL: The wash is done weekly.

KEMPLER: I would like to give her some reading material.

COLONEL: She has magazines in her quarters.

KEMPLER: Please make her feel comfortable.

COLONEL: Yes, Mr. Kempler.

KEMPLER: There are insects in her bed. *(Pause)* I would appreciate anything you can do.

COLONEL: Of course. She will get another bed.

KEMPLER: And paper for the lavatory.

COLONEL: Certainly.

KEMPLER: My Ambassador will be stopping by sometime today.

COLONEL: Thank you for telling me.

KEMPLER: And an American journalist.

COLONEL: Fine.

KEMPLER: How long will this go on?

COLONEL: Be patient if you can.

KEMPLER: It is wrong.

COLONEL: How are things at the Industrial Park?

KEMPLER: All right.

COLONEL: On schedule?

KEMPLER: Yes.

COLONEL: Do you walk around with a little lunch pail?

KEMPLER: I do.

COLONEL: Sit, Mr. Kempler. Today let's make it a social visit.

KEMPLER: No, thank you.

COLONEL: When was the last time you slept with Mrs. Kempler?

KEMPLER: Go to hell.

COLONEL: I'm only suggesting your good health.

KEMPLER: I've been examined.

COLONEL: That was prudent.

KEMPLER: No, my attorney suggested it.

COLONEL: Then you will appear in court.

KEMPLER: If need be.

COLONEL: The men in my command have had relations with Mrs. Kempler.

KEMPLER: Of course.

COLONEL: Take me seriously.

KEMPLER: Army life must suit you.

COLONEL: It is respectable.

KEMPLER: The stench permeates the uniform.

COLONEL: It is the King's army.

KEMPLER: How many women do you have locked away?

COLONEL: Not as many as Iran.

KEMPLER: But quite a bit.

COLONEL: A fair share.

KEMPLER: For solicitation?

COLONEL: In many instances.

KEMPLER: Do the convictions hold?

COLONEL: Ask your attorney.

KEMPLER: I'm asking you.

COLONEL: They hold.

KEMPLER: She's willing to leave the country.

COLONEL: Invariably.

KEMPLER: She's not like other women.

COLONEL: I hope not.

KEMPLER: They live on the streets.

COLONEL: There's a reflex in Moroccan life which attempts what I like to call human betterment. Penal life is part of that reflex.

KEMPLER: You don't care about these women.

COLONEL: But I do. I am a humanitarian.

KEMPLER: You are a racist, Colonel.

COLONEL: Am I?

KEMPLER: You know what I mean.

COLONEL: We are all children of Abraham.

KEMPLER: I think not.

COLONEL: One would like to believe it. *(Pause)* How do you reconcile yourself, Mr. Kempler, spending your talents in the Arab world.

KEMPLER: I don't have to.

COLONEL: Certainly you have principles.

KEMPLER: Thank you for your time. *(About to leave)*

COLONEL: Your wife is of Arab descent, Mr. Kempler. Did you know that?

Day Seven

COLONEL: How are you today?

KEMPLER: Fine.

COLONEL: There will be a dentist coming this afternoon.

KEMPLER: How is she today?

COLONEL: In good spirits.

KEMPLER: Is she in a private cell?

COLONEL: Yes.

KEMPLER: My Ambassador said there will be some developments in the next few hours.

COLONEL: Did he say that?

KEMPLER: Yes.

COLONEL: He seems to be very influential in our city.

KEMPLER: It would be a good thing.

COLONEL: The Ambassador is a close acquaintance of the Commissioner.

KEMPLER: Is that a fact?

COLONEL: You have used your leverage, Mr. Kempler.

KEMPLER: She's had enough of your hospitality.

COLONEL: And you're getting to be a nuisance. *(Pause)* There are some women here waiting for several years.

KEMPLER: I'm tired of waiting.

COLONEL: Go listen to some music. Leave, please.

KEMPLER: You will hear more from us.

COLONEL: A paperback about Morocco?

KEMPLER: You know, every dirty restaurant has a bit of you inside it. I see many men with your face.

COLONEL: Pehaps you ought to see a doctor.

KEMPLER: I'd like to see my wife now.

COLONEL: Yes, go right ahead.

KEMPLER: Thank you.

COLONEL: Today your wife confessed.

KEMPLER: Confessed?

COLONEL: To the charges.

KEMPLER: Why should she?

COLONEL: Because she is guilty.

KEMPLER: This is terribly wrong.

COLONEL: Would you like me to read her affidavit?

KEMPLER: No.

COLONEL: It's very short.

KEMPLER: I can imagine how you worded it.

COLONEL: Yes, well . . . I'll leave a copy with you. This should expedite things.

KEMPLER: Did you bargain with her?

COLONEL: Why don't you ask your wife?

KEMPLER: I will.

COLONEL: And ask her if she was treated with respect.

KEMPLER *(Takes the affidavit from the desk):* Any other matter to settle?

COLONEL: You can see your wife now.

KEMPLER: Fine.

COLONEL: How is your building project?

KEMPLER: Why do you ask?

COLONEL: When is ribbon-cutting?

KEMPLER: Fairly soon.

COLONEL: Please do invite me.

KEMPLER: You are on my list.

COLONEL: How thoughtful.

KEMPLER: Aren't you ever given a day off?

COLONEL: It's a ten-day shift.
KEMPLER: You could stand a change of clothes.
COLONEL: Yes, forgive me.
KEMPLER: It's quite all right.
COLONEL: My wife is to blame. *(Pause)* She works very hard, Mr. Kempler.
KEMPLER: Perhaps we could get together some afternoon for tea?
COLONEL: A very kind suggestion.
KEMPLER: Then after Abril is released.
COLONEL: If luck so has it.
KEMPLER: For a moment you can pretend that I'm not a Jew.
COLONEL: For a moment.

Day Eight

KEMPLER: Renovation?
COLONEL: They're bringing indoor plumbing into the dormitories.
KEMPLER: It's a nice touch to the facility.
COLONEL: Yes, we think so.
KEMPLER: My country is beginning extradition proceedings.
COLONEL: God's speed to you.
KEMPLER: Her confession is void.
COLONEL: Is it?
KEMPLER: She copied it from your steno.
COLONEL: It is in plain English, and in her hand.
KEMPLER: She had no choice. *(Pause)* I hope you will stop annoying her.
COLONEL: You exasperate me, Mr. Kempler.
KEMPLER: I expect this affair to end without further pain.
COLONEL: You will get your wish.
KEMPLER: I speak for my wife as you know.
COLONEL: You are a hero in my eyes. A cigarette?
KEMPLER: This time next week we will be in New York.
COLONEL: Be careful with us.
KEMPLER: Our memories of Fez will fall into the nearest sewer.
COLONEL: Her looseness is no reflection on my city.
KEMPLER: It is fiction.
COLONEL: Be careful that Mrs. Kempler does not repeat herself in some other town.
KEMPLER: I don't think so. *(Pause)* I wish my country could extend to you the same hospitality you have shown to us.
COLONEL: That would be welcoming. We are both Semitic, in a manner of speaking.
KEMPLER: I wouldn't be cheerful about it.
COLONEL: Why not?
KEMPLER: Because it is a depressing picture.

COLONEL: Only if you think so.

KEMPLER: Your people have so many resources.

COLONEL: Your people too.

KEMPLER: But I'm talking about your natural resources, your lands.

COLONEL: You may build for us. I think that is fair.

KEMPLER: It isn't.

COLONEL: But it is American. Labor for contract.

KEMPLER: With good will.

COLONEL: If there is any . . .

KEMPLER: Someone ought to build a real facility instead of keeping this stable.

COLONEL: Why not bid for it?

KEMPLER: Next year.

COLONEL: Yes, when you visit us next year. *(Pause)* You and I make conversation easily.

KEMPLER: It is marvelous, Colonel.

COLONEL: I never know when you're joking, Mr. Kempler.

Day Nine

COLONEL: Sit down, Mr. Kempler. I have the recent medic's report. *(Pause)* Her treatment is going accordingly and should cure her totally. No allergic reaction from the patient. Eating habits are normal. Her blood pressure is good. The dental work begun earlier in the week has been completed. Apparently they built a cap around one of the teeth. And that is our report. *(Pause)* Any questions?

KEMPLER: No.

COLONEL: Good.

KEMPLER: She'll be leaving tomorrow?

COLONEL: Luck is on your side.

KEMPLER: It is too long.

COLONEL: Think, in a few hours this will be over and you and your wife will be together.

KEMPLER: You're right.

COLONEL: You don't look happy, Mr. Kempler.

KEMPLER: I am very happy.

COLONEL: How about smiling a little?

KEMPLER: I am smiling.

COLONEL: Let's have a celebration drink. *(Brings out bottle from desk)* These times are brief.

KEMPLER: Just a short one, thanks.

COLONEL: L'chaim.

KEMPLER: Same to you.

THEY *drink.*

COLONEL: Another?

KEMPLER: No.

COLONEL: Must you hate me every morning?

KEMPLER: Yes.

COLONEL (*Pours himself a second drink*): You would like to cheat me?

KEMPLER: How could I cheat you?

COLONEL: You make more money than I. You dress well. You have a very exciting wife. You travel around the world.

KEMPLER: And you can rot in your jail.

COLONEL: Yes, exactly. I can rot in my jail.

KEMPLER: You elicit sympathy, Colonel.

COLONEL: Yes, I know. (*Laughing*) It's a jail full of fugitive women. Half of them were found on their back. I am their warden. I am their shepherd. (*Pause*) They have sad lives. You can understand.

KEMPLER: I'd like to see my wife now.

COLONEL: Let her wait a moment. (*Pause*) You won't be allowed physical contact with her for six weeks. You must be patient with her problem.

KEMPLER: Thank you for the advice.

COLONEL: You may hug her all you want.

KEMPLER: Thanks.

COLONEL: Kissing is at your discretion. (*Pause*) Have you any children?

KEMPLER: No.

COLONEL: I have six. My oldest is fourteen. He has my features. My son is very important to me. He has a temper like the devil.

KEMPLER: We wish your family well.

COLONEL: Do you plan to have a family?

KEMPLER: Perhaps.

COLONEL: Do you like baseball, Mr. Kempler?

KEMPLER: Not too much.

COLONEL: It is a popular thing?

KEMPLER: Yes.

COLONEL: We have races here.

KEMPLER: What sort of races?

COLONEL: Dog races.

KEMPLER: I thought this was a religious city.

COLONEL: Would you like to join me for a race?

KEMPLER: What do you expect me to say?

COLONEL: Why do you always answer me with another question?

KEMPLER: I'd rather you show me a few of your mosques.

COLONEL: Unfortunately that is not permitted.

KEMPLER: I've seen the one in Meknes.

COLONEL: You must be Moslem to see the mosques.

KEMPLER: Why not arrange something for me?

COLONEL: Would you like an armband?

KEMPLER: No.

COLONEL: Why did you marry a Gentile?

KEMPLER: I have no answer.

COLONEL: Aren't you religious, Mr. Kempler? I'm told that you are.

KEMPLER: No.

COLONEL: You get strident like a foolish zealot.

KEMPLER: No, not at all.

COLONEL: Have I created a zealot then?

KEMPLER: No.

COLONEL: Is it good to be a Jew?

KEMPLER: It is.

COLONEL: I can only wonder, Mr. Kempler. *(Pause)* You seem to tell me so little. *(Pause)* Is this secrecy Jewish?

Day Ten

COLONEL: Good day, Mr. Kempler. *(Long silence)* Your wife is waiting for you in the next room.

END OF ACT ONE

ACT TWO

Some days later. Evening. An expensive restaurant in Malaga, Spain. Tables on the terrace. Lights rise. Perhaps there is Spanish guitar music. KEMPLER *is downstage lighting a cigarette.* HE *sees* MRS. KEMPLER *entering.* HE *joins her, perhaps at a wishing well. A silence.*

KEMPLER *(Smiling at his wife)*: You were gone a long time.
MRS. KEMPLER: I couldn't find the lavatory.
KEMPLER: I've ordered for you. *(Pause)* Clams.
MRS. KEMPLER: Excellent.
KEMPLER: Salad. Local wine.
MRS. KEMPLER: And you?
KEMPLER: Chateaubriand.
MRS. KEMPLER: Is Ralph coming?
KEMPLER: No.
MRS. KEMPLER: Really?
KEMPLER: He canceled.
MRS. KEMPLER: That's strange.
KEMPLER: He's under the weather. Left word with the hotel desk.
MRS. KEMPLER: I'm disappointed.
KEMPLER: So am I, darling.
MRS. KEMPLER: Then shall we phone him afterwards?
KEMPLER: If you like.
MRS. KEMPLER: Is it cool out here?
KEMPLER: Yes, take my jacket.
MRS. KEMPLER: No, darling. I'll be all right.
KEMPLER: A cocktail?
MRS. KEMPLER: No, I think not. What are you drinking?
KEMPLER: Vodka.
MRS. KEMPLER: May I? *(Sipping)* How long are we going to stay?
KEMPLER: At the hotel?
MRS. KEMPLER: It's a lovely hotel.
KEMPLER: A few more days. It's up to you.
MRS. KEMPLER: Won't you need to get back this week?
KEMPLER: No, I made arrangements.
MRS. KEMPLER: Still . . .
KEMPLER: Don't worry your little head.
MRS. KEMPLER: I know your deadline, Charles.

A WAITER *enters. serves* KEMPLER *and* MRS. KEMPLER *wine, exits.* THEY *hold up their glasses.*

KEMPLER: Shall we toast?
MRS. KEMPLER: What will it be tonight?

KEMPLER: To good living.

MRS. KEMPLER: Cheers.

THEY *touch glasses, drink. A moment of awkwardness before* THEY *seat themselves at a set table.*

I'm having the worst difficulty with my makeup this evening. Does it show?

KEMPLER: No, no.

MRS. KEMPLER: But my mascara, Charles?

KEMPLER: Perhaps it's perspiration.

MRS. KEMPLER: Not so loud.

KEMPLER: Aren't you feeling well?

MRS. KEMPLER: Yes, I think so.

KEMPLER: Are you having chills?

MRS. KEMPLER: Earlier. I'm fine now.

KEMPLER: We can stay in tonight.

MRS. KEMPLER: Let's see, darling.

KEMPLER: Am I doting over you?

MRS. KEMPLER: Of course not.

THEY *hold hands briefly.*

KEMPLER: It becomes second nature for me.

MRS. KEMPLER: A model husband you are.

KEMPLER: An inept model.

MRS. KEMPLER: Are you fishing for sympathy?

KEMPLER *(Playful)*: Yes.

MRS. KEMPLER: You can have anything from me, but sympathy.

KEMPLER: You're looking healthier, Mrs. Kempler.

MRS. KEMPLER: It's the wine.

KEMPLER: What would you like to do tomorrow?

MRS. KEMPLER: The gardens at the Alcazaba?

KEMPLER: And afterwards?

MRS. KEMPLER: Let's picnic and get drunk silly.

KEMPLER: I see you're feeling back in stride.

MRS. KEMPLER: Some have jet lag. Perhaps it was jail lag. *(Touching her tooth)*

KEMPLER: The cap again?

MRS. KEMPLER: The dental work was done by a gorilla.

KEMPLER: We could always have the work checked. *(Pause)* At least they didn't charge for it.

MRS. KEMPLER: Oh, but they did.

KEMPLER: One cannot sue a foreign government.

MRS. KEMPLER: Not if I could have my way.

KEMPLER: They were getting to me through you.

MRS. KEMPLER: Why?

KEMPLER: I had no business being there.

MRS. KEMPLER: Darling, nothing was illegal.

KEMPLER: They knew my firm was Jewish.

MRS. KEMPLER: Morocco is not Syria, Charles.

KEMPLER: Are you upset with me?

MRS. KEMPLER: No.

KEMPLER: My ambition is rather tempered. At least, I'd like to think so. *(Pause)* Where is the waiter?

MRS. KEMPLER: It's a three-star kitchen, Charles. When they're ready.

KEMPLER: Did you hear about your transfer?

MRS. KEMPLER: Not yet.

KEMPLER: Will it be any problem?

MRS. KEMPLER: Hardly.

KEMPLER: What's your preference? *(Pause)* You needn't work everything around me.

MRS. KEMPLER: Whatever, darling.

KEMPLER: We can stay in Europe.

MRS. KEMPLER: Fine.

KEMPLER: Or Japan.

MRS. KEMPLER: I really don't care.

KEMPLER: Well, I'd just as soon stay in this area.

MRS. KEMPLER: One telegram would suffice.

KEMPLER: You do have more flexibility.

MRS. KEMPLER: We just have to buy more winter clothes.

KEMPLER: I'm so hungry this evening.

MRS. KEMPLER: Have another drink.

KEMPLER: Why do you encourage me?

MRS. KEMPLER *(Sweetly)*: Because you're different when you drink.

KEMPLER: Different than what?

MRS. KEMPLER: Different than sober. *(Kisses her fingertip, touches his lip)*

KEMPLER: Why can't I be sober?

HE *sees* WAITER, *signals.* WAITER *brings another drink.*

It's peculiar how Arabs drink everywhere but in public sight.

MRS. KEMPLER: It's a veiled society, you know very well.

KEMPLER: And they know how to protect their women.

MRS. KEMPLER: I don't want to discuss the inanities of the Arab world.

KEMPLER: Yes, darling.

MRS. KEMPLER: To find women displaced under the peasants, who are under the merchants and militia, who are under the politically affluent . . . makes me very ashamed of my background. This casual degradation has become all too embarrassing, particularly when it hits home, Charles.

KEMPLER: I'll never forget his odor.

MRS. KEMPLER: The Colonel?

KEMPLER: His wonderfully cheap tobacco and dank-mold carpets. He knew I found him abhorrent. For his dirtiness, above all.

MRS. KEMPLER: Yes, darling, you see—cleanliness is looked upon as a very alien characteristic. Grounds for suspicion and deportation. Unless one is very religious.

KEMPLER: They all say they're religious.

MRS. KEMPLER: Even peasants want respect.

KEMPLER: He was a peasant.

MRS. KEMPLER: For a peasant he spoke excellent English. *(Long pause)* I really believed he liked you, Charles.

KEMPLER: Liked me?

MRS. KEMPLER: He was a little crazy. You can understand that. When he talked to me in Arabic he forgot his rank. You didn't cause him offense.

KEMPLER: He told you so?

MRS. KEMPLER: Yes.

KEMPLER: What else did he tell you?

MRS. KEMPLER: Very little else.

KEMPLER: They've kept the photographs.

MRS. KEMPLER: I really don't know.

KEMPLER: How many were there?

MRS. KEMPLER: Men? *(Pause)* I thought we weren't going to discuss this another time.

KEMPLER: Everything you told me in jail was contradictory.

MRS. KEMPLER: I had a terrible fever then.

KEMPLER: Why do you bring up inconsistencies?

MRS. KEMPLER: Talk to my doctor, Charles.

KEMPLER: I have talked with him.

MRS. KEMPLER: Wonderful.

KEMPLER: What am I to think?

MRS. KEMPLER: About what?

KEMPLER: About you.

MRS. KEMPLER: Think what you want. Thank God I survived Morocco.

KEMPLER: I have thanked God.

MRS. KEMPLER: I wish I could believe you.

KEMPLER: I have thanked God.

MRS. KEMPLER: I know exactly what you went through.

KEMPLER: Do you?

MRS. KEMPLER: I do.

KEMPLER: Doubts don't comfort me.

MRS. KEMPLER: I don't sleep around anymore, Charles.

KEMPLER: That's not the issue.

MRS. KEMPLER: What is the issue?

KEMPLER: I don't know, Abril.

MRS. KEMPLER: Look at me, Charles. *(HE does, intently)* Our marriage is very strong. *(Long pause)* The photographs continue to bother you.

KEMPLER: Yes.

MRS. KEMPLER: You know what choice they gave me.

KEMPLER: What choice did they give you?

MRS. KEMPLER *(Dryly)*: Use your imagination, darling.

KEMPLER: I'd rather not.

MRS. KEMPLER: Then I have little else to say about this.

KEMPLER: You don't have to defend yourself.

MRS. KEMPLER: Thank you.

KEMPLER: Everything was divisive.

MRS. KEMPLER: Perhaps that was the point.

KEMPLER: Why were you at the bar?

MRS. KEMPLER: Drinking, of course.

KEMPLER: Couldn't you have waited for a girlfriend?

MRS. KEMPLER: I was working late that evening.

KEMPLER: I'd like a better explanation.

MRS. KEMPLER: Do I take an oath before answering?

KEMPLER: Please . . .

MRS. KEMPLER: Sleep with cockroaches for a month, then ask me any question you want.

KEMPLER: Don't make a game of it.

MRS. KEMPLER *(Seriously)*: It was not a game, Charles.

KEMPLER: The photographs don't show an inhibited woman.

MRS. KEMPLER: What did they show?

KEMPLER: Did they drug you? *(Pause)* Why was it so difficult to see you?

MRS. KEMPLER: You know the jails. Maybe I was unconscious. Do you think you married a prostitute?

KEMPLER: Don't be absurd.

MRS. KEMPLER: Does it give you a vicarious thrill?

KEMPLER: I don't like punishment.

MRS. KEMPLER: Nor do I. Why are you staring at me?

KEMPLER: I'm not the one to comment on moral conduct.

MRS. KEMPLER: Why don't you?

KEMPLER: Because I'm more caught up on your motives. *(Pause)* You'll always be promiscuous. Since the first day I've known you.

MRS. KEMPLER: I did not sleep with the Moroccan army. Even at gunpoint.

KEMPLER: Then my thinking is very twisted.

MRS. KEMPLER: No vaccine in the world could withstand a Moroccan soldier. They were very considerate, Charles. Think of the bright side. We can have relations again.

KEMPLER: Yes, it's remarkably accommodating of them. *(Spills drink)* Damn it.

MRS. KEMPLER: Have another then.

KEMPLER: It's just as well.

MRS. KEMPLER: You believe I was whoring, Charles.

KEMPLER: Yes, I do.

MRS. KEMPLER: To what purpose?

KEMPLER: Kicks.

MRS. KEMPLER: Like taking drugs?

KEMPLER: Like fucking soldiers.

MRS. KEMPLER: My breeding is better than yours. I was at Oxford, darling.

KEMPLER: You're part Arab.

MRS. KEMPLER: We're supreme racehorses and mythmakers.

KEMPLER: I tip my hat to you.

MRS. KEMPLER: And I'm part Spanish. I'm from both sides of the Mediterranean. *(Pause)* How long do you intend to chaff?

KEMPLER: How long do you intend to embarrass us?

MRS. KEMPLER: Indefinitely.

KEMPLER: Wonderful.

MRS. KEMPLER: What sort of guarantee are you looking for?

KEMPLER: Fidelity being outside your vocabulary, any guarantee could only extend ninety days at best.

MRS. KEMPLER: You're really not being fair to me. They gave me the strain my first day in prison.

KEMPLER: Do you know what the Ambassador asked me?

MRS. KEMPLER: Yes, you told me.

KEMPLER: "Mr. Kempler, wives overseas often need mad money. Does your wife indulge herself after hours?" *(Pause)* "Mr. Kempler, your wife is . . . charming." *(Pause)* "Mr. Kempler, do you think you can keep an eye on her for the weeks ahead?"

WAITER *enters with entrees.*

MRS. KEMPLER: Are you looking for a moral, Charles? What exactly is the point?

WAITER *leaves.*

KEMPLER: If we lived in a small town, gossip would dampen your spirits.

MRS. KEMPLER: Haven't you had an affair in the last year or two?

KEMPLER: No.

MRS. KEMPLER: You wouldn't tell me anyway.

KEMPLER: You'd know the moment I do.

MRS. KEMPLER: Are we going to dine, or argue?

KEMPLER: I have no appetite. You've made me a laughingstock.

MRS. KEMPLER: No one is laughing at you.

KEMPLER: They are laughing at me.

MRS. KEMPLER: Charles . . . *(Touches his hand)*

KEMPLER *(Softly)*: I'm very much in love with you.

MRS. KEMPLER: Keep telling me that.

KEMPLER: You can be so beautiful.

MRS. KEMPLER: And so can you. I will behave better, darling.

KEMPLER: With each promise there is a false star overhead.

MRS. KEMPLER: Are you now counting stars?

KEMPLER: I am.

MRS. KEMPLER: Count sheep, Charles. *(Soft giggle)* You were once extremely romantic.

KEMPLER: In the Peace Corps.

MRS. KEMPLER: Not that many years ago.

KEMPLER: Before I started balding.

MRS. KEMPLER: Success has affected you, darling.

KEMPLER: Why do you say that?

MRS. KEMPLER: There was a time when you gave me special attention.

KEMPLER: Fatigue is a very human thing.

MRS. KEMPLER: Is it really fatigue? *(Pause)* I can't have children. You know that pains me.

KEMPLER: As well as me.

MRS. KEMPLER: Perhaps it's harder for the woman. We can go to all the expensive doctors in the world. It won't remedy the situation.

KEMPLER: Wanting children can be an act of will, Abril.

MRS. KEMPLER: Which puts the onus on me.

KEMPLER: No.

MRS. KEMPLER: Isn't it better that we spend money on ourselves?

KEMPLER: We don't need money.

MRS. KEMPLER: What a pity not to be broke and hungry, without a prayer in all hell. *(Pause)* My head is full of nonsense. Charles, are you going to make love to me tonight?

KEMPLER: Do I need a reservation?

MRS. KEMPLER *(Laughing)*: Oh, yes.

KEMPLER: Is there a room assignment?

MRS. KEMPLER: You know the room.

KEMPLER: Did you speak to the Colonel like that?

MRS. KEMPLER: Charles, piss on your obsessions. *(Pause)* I think we ought to establish some rules between us. Either we are on holiday, or revisiting *Judgment at Nuremberg*.

KEMPLER: We are on holiday.

MRS. KEMPLER: Glory be to heaven.

KEMPLER: I told Ralph.

MRS. KEMPLER: You told Ralph what?

KEMPLER: About the arrest.

MRS. KEMPLER: He must have had a good laugh.

KEMPLER: He did.

MRS. KEMPLER: Wasn't Ralph's wife arrested?

KEMPLER: Yes, cocaine.

MRS. KEMPLER: You and Ralph ought to start a club.

KEMPLER: We're working on it.

MRS. KEMPLER: Do you want a divorce, Charles?

KEMPLER: No.

MRS. KEMPLER: Are you certain?

KEMPLER: I'm in love with you.

MRS. KEMPLER: Do you think I'm schizophrenic?

KEMPLER: Yes.

MRS. KEMPLER: My problem is not hopeless.

KEMPLER: I could always rent you out to parties.

MRS. KEMPLER: Charles, are you in a good mood today?

KEMPLER: Yes, I think so.

MRS. KEMPLER: That's good. When you're in a good mood, I'm in a good mood.

KEMPLER: Then we should leave right now.

MRS. KEMPLER: I haven't touched my plate.

KEMPLER: We should pack and fly out tonight.

MRS. KEMPLER: Leave Spain?

KEMPLER: Let's buy a house in Massachusetts.

MRS. KEMPLER: That is so dull, Charles.

KEMPLER: You owe me this.

MRS. KEMPLER: There are limits.

KEMPLER: Why the hell do we have to live like gypsies?

MRS. KEMPLER: Because I'm part gypsy.

KEMPLER: You're a little of everything.

MRS. KEMPLER: I really wish Ralph were here tonight. He would arbitrate for us. Every couple needs an arbitrator.

KEMPLER: Shall we ask the waiter?

MRS. KEMPLER: Do what you want, darling.

KEMPLER: How do they let you stay on at the bank?

MRS. KEMPLER: I'm very good there.

KEMPLER: But they're reserved people.

MRS. KEMPLER: And so am I.

KEMPLER: And the Pope is Jewish.

MRS. KEMPLER: Is he, Charles? *(Pause)* I never know when you're joking. *(Pause)* Are we candidates for therapy?

KEMPLER: Exemplary candidates.

MRS. KEMPLER: I'm willing, if you are.

KEMPLER: You would end up sleeping with the psychiatrist.

MRS. KEMPLER: Darling, are we a vaudeville?

KEMPLER: It seems so. Have you slept with Ralph?

MRS. KEMPLER: Once.

KEMPLER: Is that all?

MRS. KEMPLER: I believe so.

KEMPLER (*Understated*): Then what am I getting all worked up about?

MRS. KEMPLER: I've no idea.

KEMPLER: Why don't you get out your appointment calendar and tell me the nights you're free.

MRS. KEMPLER: Be a sport, Charles. You know my sense of humor.

KEMPLER: You make me cry inside.

MRS. KEMPLER: You're very touching when you cry.

KEMPLER: Do you pity me?

MRS. KEMPLER: Whatever for?

KEMPLER: For my masochism.

MRS. KEMPLER: You?

KEMPLER: Me.

MRS. KEMPLER: No, I don't pity you.

KEMPLER: Are we competing with each other?

MRS. KEMPLER: These are too many questions for one night, darling.

KEMPLER: Then I give up.

MRS. KEMPLER: Have another drink.

KEMPLER: There was a time in my life when I had tremendous discipline. Do you remember?

MRS. KEMPLER: Are you over the hill now?

KEMPLER: It occurred to me.

MRS. KEMPLER: Can I tell the truth, Charles? (*Pause*) You are no longer modern.

KEMPLER: What is that supposed to mean?

MRS. KEMPLER: I think you're closer to the last century. Strange, an architect driven by innovation lives with those from the distant past. You are a bit of a relic. An antique. A very vulnerable heart.

KEMPLER: You're just as vulnerable.

MRS. KEMPLER: In some ways.

KEMPLER: I can bruise you.

MRS. KEMPLER: Yes, you could.

KEMPLER: Yet I'm no crueler than you. Why must we hurt each other like this?

MRS. KEMPLER: I don't know, darling.

KEMPLER: Your time in jail has softened you. You seem to have acquired something useful.

MRS. KEMPLER: Have I?

THEY *kiss slowly.*

KEMPLER: I'll return in a matter of days. The complex is planned to open shortly.

MRS. KEMPLER: We can both go back to Fez.

KEMPLER: You remember what the State Department said.

MRS. KEMPLER: All right. I'll stay here, darling. I've no desire to cause you more trouble.

KEMPLER: Our luck has been perverse all year. *(Pause)* Call Ralph for me.

MRS. KEMPLER: And say what?

KEMPLER: That I'll be out of town.

MRS. KEMPLER: Are you being provocative?

KEMPLER: No.

MRS. KEMPLER: You view Ralph as a rival.

KEMPLER: Not at all.

MRS. KEMPLER: I know you better.

KEMPLER: Call Ralph and say that I know more than I should.

MRS. KEMPLER: But why?

KEMPLER: Let's save our marriage as though our lives were at stake.

MRS. KEMPLER: As you wish.

KEMPLER: I can't do it alone.

MRS. KEMPLER: No one is expecting you to.

KEMPLER: You're so exceptionally bright and gifted, dearest. I can't fault you for certain excesses, and who am I to make rules for a spirit such as yours.

MRS. KEMPLER: Why, Charles. That is so sweet of you to say.

KEMPLER: Therefore, I beg you to feign a little modesty for the next few months. Perhaps you'll get addicted to it. Something glorious might come of it. What do you think?

MRS. KEMPLER: I think you are very generous.

KEMPLER: Do you love me, Abril?

MRS. KEMPLER: Yes.

KEMPLER: Should I believe you?

MRS. KEMPLER: Yes.

KEMPLER: Is the future bright?

MRS. KEMPLER: The future is always bright.

KEMPLER: Things in the past are forgiven?

MRS. KEMPLER: Best they are.

KEMPLER: I was never shocked.

MRS. KEMPLER: I could swear that you were.

KEMPLER: No. I was never shocked. *(Takes out wallet)*

END OF ACT TWO

ACT THREE

A week later. The COLONEL'S *office in Morocco. It is late afternoon.* KEMPLER *is at the door, waiting for the* COLONEL'S *attention.*

KEMPLER *(Abruptly, rudely)*: Excuse me, I thought you were free for the evening.

COLONEL: Yes, I thought so as well. Come in, Mr. Kempler. I really didn't expect you to drop by. When you phoned, I was quite surprised.

KEMPLER: I thought it best to phone.

COLONEL: I'm honored that you called. You've been in my thoughts for several days. Come in, come in. *(KEMPLER approaches him)* Tell me, what are you doing here?

KEMPLER: Details.

COLONEL: I thought you left the country?

KEMPLER: Yes, for a short while. We were in Spain.

COLONEL *(Patronizing)*: And how was Spain?

KEMPLER: Quite charming actually. May I sit? *(The* COLONEL *gestures)* I see you've painted the office.

COLONEL: Can you tell?

KEMPLER: A fine improvement.

COLONEL: Thank you. My wife chose the color. *(Pause)* Are you here strictly on business?

KEMPLER: The park has opened.

COLONEL: I was waiting for your invitation.

KEMPLER: You didn't miss a thing.

COLONEL: And now what, Mr. Kempler?

KEMPLER: Plans on the continent. Too early to tell. *(Long pause. Awkward)* My office forwarded your letter.

COLONEL: What letter?

KEMPLER: I should say, your little note.

COLONEL: I sent no note.

KEMPLER: Is that right, Colonel? It was prison stationary.

COLONEL: Mr. Kempler, I have no cause to do such thing.

KEMPLER: I'm sure you had your reasons.

COLONEL: Reasons?

KEMPLER: Why belabor an unfortunate situation?

COLONEL: You must be dreaming.

KEMPLER: Not at all. My wife must also be dreaming.

COLONEL: I've had a very long day, Mr. Kempler.

KEMPLER: My wife had me see a psychiatrist in Malaga.

COLONEL: Bravo!

KEMPLER: He was quite expensive. Three hundred dirhams a session. I didn't even get full hours.

COLONEL: Why are you telling me this?

KEMPLER: May I smoke?

COLONEL: By all means.

KEMPLER: Colonel, stop these little games.

COLONEL: Mr. Kempler, I've no idea what the hell you're talking about. What games?

KEMPLER: Perhaps I've no tolerance for these things.

COLONEL: I'm a very busy man, from early in the morning. I try to make it easy for myself, and for others. If your building project is finished, why be here at all? Why imagine things that are not so? Why make faces at me, Mr. Kempler? Why not just have a drink with me? *(Pause)* You look terrible. Are you well?

KEMPLER: Yes, of course.

COLONEL: Is your wife with you?

KEMPLER: Yes, she is.

COLONEL: How is she?

KEMPLER: Fine. Lovely as ever.

COLONEL: I didn't expect you to return to Fez. I thought you had made that clear to me.

KEMPLER: Perhaps I came back on principle.

COLONEL: Excuse me. *(Takes out liquor)* A drink?

KEMPLER: Please.

COLONEL: What can I do for you then?

KEMPLER: Tell me who my wife is?

COLONEL: Your wife is your wife.

KEMPLER: Why not amplify that for me?

COLONEL: Don't be ridiculous, Mr. Kempler. You know your wife much better than I.

KEMPLER: In your note you had no trouble expressing yourself.

COLONEL: Was this note signed by me?

KEMPLER: I'm certain it was yours, Colonel.

COLONEL: And if it was mine, why would you be upset?

KEMPLER: Do I look upset?

COLONEL: What did this note say?

KEMPLER *(Temper rising)*: I worked very hard in Fez. Everyone knows that. I made time for her. We had more than enough time for each other. I know how to be generous.

COLONEL: Are you in trouble?

KEMPLER: Can I have another drink?

COLONEL: Take the bottle.

KEMPLER *(Pouring from the bottle)*: I trust your judgment. Did you know that?

COLONEL: My judgment, Mr. Kempler?

KEMPLER: Tell me, just friend to friend, how would you continue with Abril?

COLONEL: I?

KEMPLER: Would you let her stay the way she was?

COLONEL: Your wife is a gypsy. I don't understand gypsies.

KEMPLER: But you speak her language.

COLONEL: I'm sure she speaks many languages.

KEMPLER: You know her for what she is. A woman like Abril can live without shame. I cannot.

COLONEL: Did you catch her again?

KEMPLER: Yes. Now I can tell by which earrings she has on. Isn't that something? The drop pearls are her little neon lights.

COLONEL: Are you being facetious?

KEMPLER: My wife is an anomaly. Hardly an asset. What would you do in this instance?

COLONEL: What instance?

KEMPLER: You found her with a . . .

COLONEL *(Interrupting)*: I cannot say.

KEMPLER: Shall I read your mind, Colonel?

COLONEL: Please.

KEMPLER: You would take down your saber. You would torture her, as you did in your jail.

COLONEL: Torture is arcane. You have a strange imagination, Mr. Kempler.

KEMPLER: You would humiliate her beyond need or satisfaction. You would bond her, and brand her like cattle, keep her on a straw mattress without clothes. You would beat her and taunt her with your black riding crop. I know what you really can do, Colonel. Arabs dominate these bitches very well.

COLONEL: You watch too many movies, Mr. Kempler.

KEMPLER: But it's true. These are your priorities. Two Arab brothers would sooner kill a woman, than let her come between them. That is your culture since creation.

COLONEL: Why overpraise my people? We're all thieves and beggars, addicts and murderers. *(Amused)* And you are Dagwood Bumstead. Isn't that so?

KEMPLER: Yes, I am.

COLONEL: It's a comic strip. You sleep on the couch, and the dog barks, and your wife Blondie has purchased a new dress with your seventeen credit cards. *(Pause)* Would you care for another drink? *(Pours two glasses)* Yet your wife Blondie loves you very much. You must know that.

KEMPLER: I don't think so.

COLONEL: You are fooling yourself. Believe me, you are. My religion believes in duty with regard to the wife. She is not a kitchen appliance. She is not disposable as such. But training is expected, and you must do the training. How is that for wisdom?

KEMPLER: Uninspiring.

COLONEL: Yes, forgive me. I am not Mohammed.

KEMPLER: Your advice is late in coming.

COLONEL: And so is the Messiah.

KEMPLER: I cannot afford a shattered marriage. Can you understand that?

COLONEL: You are very gifted, Mr. Kempler. I think you could sustain injury. You have plenty of nerve.

KEMPLER: Do you think so?

COLONEL: If you Jews charade with Gentile names and Gentile faces and Gentile firms, I call that nerve. Nerve to appear unquestionably Jewish. That you worked on your diction and that you admire our mosques and restaurants and women. Nerve to marry one of us, in fact. Yes, you have this incredible trait every waking day. It makes you successful, Mr. Kempler. It's in your every step.

KEMPLER: Thank you for the ridicule.

COLONEL: It is a bouquet to you. *(Pause)* Where is your wife, Mr. Kempler?

KEMPLER: I left her in Spain.

COLONEL: Is she well?

KEMPLER: I don't really care.

COLONEL: You do care.

KEMPLER: No, it's over.

COLONEL: Infidelity can be treated.

KEMPLER: I don't have a claim to her any longer.

COLONEL: Even whores have a state of grace.

KEMPLER: She's another species altogether.

COLONEL: Have children. That is my recommendation. Make babies. A half a dozen to start. *(Pause. Studied look)* It is heartfelt, Mr. Kempler.

KEMPLER: We can't have children.

COLONEL *(Sympathetic)*: I'm sorry. *(Distracted, perhaps with papers on the desk)* How many men do you think have been with her?

KEMPLER: There were a good many.

COLONEL: Fifty? A hundred?

KEMPLER: Have you a bet with someone?

COLONEL: I'm only trying to get a grasp.

KEMPLER: She's not for hire. She never was.

COLONEL: I didn't insinuate anything.

KEMPLER: I'm not old-fashioned, Colonel.

COLONEL: You're simply a husband.

KEMPLER: Yes, I'm simply a husband. *(Long pause)* I threatened to kill her the night before leaving Malaga.

COLONEL: Did you?

KEMPLER: Our sex life stopped dead.

COLONEL: Was there a sex life at all, Mr. Kempler?

KEMPLER: Yes.

COLONEL: No, no, you can tell me the truth . . .

KEMPLER: I am.

COLONEL: Are you faithful?

KEMPLER: She cheats. I do not cheat.

COLONEL: We all cheat. *(Pause)* Your wife is from Gibraltar. Once a crazy place. I wish I could be more helpful, Mr. Kempler.

KEMPLER: Actually, you've been very helpful.

COLONEL: Have I?

KEMPLER: I thought you knew that.

COLONEL: I know very little.

KEMPLER: You know me like a glove. I admire you, Colonel. I admire your sense of resolve, and your polite manner. You have a circumspect mind too, and that has not gone by unnoticed. *(Pause)* I would like the photographs back, Colonel.

COLONEL: Yes, as you wish. I will mail them to you.

KEMPLER: Colonel . . . *(Hand extended)*

The COLONEL *gives* KEMPLER *photographs.*

COLONEL: Why don't we go into the city tonight? You did invite me out. I know a very fine restaurant, Mr. Kempler, with a Sephardic menu. We'll pretend we're two bachelors.

KEMPLER: Why pretend?

COLONEL: You are in a humor. *(Rising)* I'll get my coat. Has your wife been to see the project?

KEMPLER: She was reluctant to go. Sometimes she is superstitious.

COLONEL: Really?

KEMPLER: Women are superstitious, Colonel. You know that. I hope to carry on another project or two. Tangier. You know how good steady work can be.

COLONEL: I do.

KEMPLER: What would you say if I told you . . .

COLONEL: Tell me what.

KEMPLER: If I told you that Mrs. Kempler has disappeared.

COLONEL: Has she? Where has she gone?

KEMPLER: Don't you know? *(Perhaps sitting down)*

COLONEL: Shall I notify the police?

KEMPLER: You are the police.

COLONEL: If the woman has disappeared . . .

KEMPLER: Don't be clever.

COLONEL: Is she in this city?

KEMPLER: I don't know. We came back together.

COLONEL: That wasn't wise to bring her back, Mr. Kempler.

KEMPLER: I had no choice. *(Pause)* She told the chambermaid in Malaga that I was incontinent. That she had to throw away the sheets. This is her sense of humor. A luxury hotel, no less.

COLONEL *(Nearing the door)*: Are you incontinent?

KEMPLER: I have never wet a bed in my life.

COLONEL: Why did you marry this woman?

KEMPLER: I don't know. It was from love.

COLONEL: She is an instrument of your daily embarrassment. Is this American, Mr. Kempler? Mixing success with the best cow manure? You have magnificent dreams of erecting buildings and parks and monuments, dignity very few men achieve. But in all the time I have known you I cannot see your dignity.

KEMPLER: Look harder, Colonel. It is there.

COLONEL: You're a stubborn man. As stubborn as she.

KEMPLER: No one spotted her as you had. No one at her office suspected.

COLONEL: They are all whores at the bank.

KEMPLER: I always thought of her as my princess.

COLONEL: Yes, my dear friend. You married an enchanting storybook princess. Such youth at your age is quite damaging. You will go home, find your wife, and begin again. Forget your lunch pail. Philosophy can only make a man alcoholic.

KEMPLER: If God were only so kind.

COLONEL: God barters.

KEMPLER: God is barbaric.

COLONEL *(Patting* KEMPLER's *shoulder)*: Only in the movies.

KEMPLER: Do you go to the movies, Colonel?

COLONEL: Yes, on occasion.

KEMPLER: I only like sad movies.

COLONEL: I like the cowboy movies. We all like the cowboy movies, Mr. Kempler. You ought to try acting like a cowboy. You can make campfire at night, and kiss your horse sweet dreams. You put me in a strange mood today. One more drink for the road?

KEMPLER: Thank you.

COLONEL: I like you without your necktie.

KEMPLER: Do you?

COLONEL: But you sit like you have a rifle up your trousers.

KEMPLER: It's the overtime at the drafting table.

COLONEL: Drink up. It might be hard to buy drinks outside.

KEMPLER: After you.

THEY *drink in unison.*

It occurred to me that Abril might be possessed.

COLONEL: Possessed?

KEMPLER: That the Devil has entered her.

COLONEL: You don't believe things like that?

KEMPLER: No, of course not.

COLONEL: It is a stupid belief.

KEMPLER: Many people believe otherwise.

COLONEL: Surely not you.

KEMPLER: Only the Devil can alter someone.

COLONEL: Please, no ghosts stories this evening. Your wife is not possessed. It is out of the question. She is too intelligent to be possessed. *(Pause)* Where is your wife, Mr. Kempler?

KEMPLER: I killed her.

COLONEL: Where is your wife?

KEMPLER: You should know.

COLONEL: Where is she, Mr. Kempler?

KEMPLER: Hell, for all I care. You needn't act bewildered.

COLONEL: Why do you persist with this joke?

KEMPLER: Take down my confession, Colonel. I'll make it easy for you. Friend to friend.

COLONEL: Don't make a fool of me.

KEMPLER: Her body is still warm in the hotel room.

COLONEL: Here in Fez?

KEMPLER: Yes.

COLONEL: Very amusing. *(Pause)* You never told me how you met your wife.

KEMPLER: We met a dozen years ago at a building project. She represented the banking committee. She was different then. Very chaste. Very supportive. Very soft and fragile. I fell for her at once. When I started courting her I did miraculous things. Expenses meant nothing to me. We acted like schoolchildren on holiday. She was so pristine in daylight. So open to my clumsiness. Patient with my faults. What little faults I had. Things were simpler then.

COLONEL: As for us all.

KEMPLER *(Pause)*: Sex alone cannot destroy my wife.

COLONEL: I don't know what does destroy a woman. Perhaps it is rich living. Perhaps she has taken the worst your world has provided for her. Perhaps she is possessed by your Devil. She cannot be taught to be another way. Not her. That is plain. Devil or no Devil. *(Long pause)* How did you murder Mrs. Kempler?

KEMPLER: I picked up a clothes iron.

COLONEL: Was death instantaneous?

KEMPLER: I think so.

COLONEL: Any struggle?

KEMPLER: None.

COLONEL: Did you actually have the courage to do it?

KEMPLER: Does it matter?

COLONEL: As long as you're confessing . . .

KEMPLER: It was as though I were sleepwalking. I paced the hotel room afterwards looking for loose coins that I had thrown at her. I unwrapped all of the hotel soap, showered vigorously, lunched on the balcony alone, and then dressed to go out.

COLONEL: Why do you patronize me? You don't have the courage to kill a housefly, Mr. Kempler. I doubt that you would even raise a hand to your wife.

KEMPLER: I would agree with you, but the truth is . . .

COLONEL: But the truth is that you are impotent to act.

KEMPLER: Believe what you want.

COLONEL: That is all I can do.

KEMPLER: I am not a coward. I would gladly do it again.

COLONEL: Mr. Kempler, your concerns are dear to me. I wish I had medicine for you. This isn't pity. You should have married a Jew as you were no doubt instructed since birth. You would be happier today. Yes, I'm certain of it. Some things are incorrect. I think you are incorrect. I think your blindness is in very poor taste. I don't think you can help yourself either. Do not try to impress me. I pray for you and your wife. If you have done something wrong, do not make me an accomplice.

KEMPLER: I don't need an accomplice.

COLONEL: But you are pointing at me.

KEMPLER: I don't need an accomplice, Colonel. I did everything alone. I stained the bedsheets with her blood, and poured her liquid mascara over the head wounds. It was the best that I could do. I couldn't hear her cry. I couldn't explain to her the meaning of her punishment. I couldn't express myself to my wife with more urgency than with a shot to the head. It really was the best that I could do. She sat in the hotel lobby all evening, and there were complaints from the management. I had to carry her upstairs. Yes, she was drunk. Some men were following her. Conversation was impossible. I dropped her over the hotel bed. She kicked off her shoes. *(Long pause)* And then I killed her.

COLONEL: Must you spoil my evening?

KEMPLER: No, I had no intention of spoiling your evening.

COLONEL: I did not hear any of this.

KEMPLER: There is nothing you did not hear. And there is nothing that you did not see. You can't hurt me anymore.

MRS. KEMPLER *is at the door, seen only by the* COLONEL.

MRS. KEMPLER: Charles? *(KEMPLER turns around)* I want you home. Please come home with me. *(Short pause. Eye contact)* Darling?

KEMPLER: Go. I'll soon join you.

MRS. KEMPLER: Only if you come with me.

KEMPLER: Why did you come?

COLONEL: Go home, Mr. Kempler. It's time I closed the office.

MRS. KEMPLER: Did you get the photographs, Charles?

KEMPLER: Yes.

MRS. KEMPLER: Any further business?

KEMPLER *(Slowly)*: No further business.

KEMPLER *crosses to exit.* MRS. KEMPLER *and the* COLONEL *are downstage.*

MRS. KEMPLER *(After a pause)*: Wash kolti l-rajali shi hashi halba? [Did you say anything wrong to my husband?]

COLONEL: La abadan. [No, never.]

MRS. KEMPLER: Wakha. Kul shi mezyen. [Fine. Everything is all right.]

COLONEL: Ma kaynsh sabab. Barakallafikum. [There would be no reason. God's blessings on you.]

MRS. KEMPLER: Charles? *(Signalling to* KEMPLER, *ready to leave)*

COLONEL *(Near bowing, deference)*: Do visit us again?

MRS. KEMPLER *(Smiling pleasantly)*: As far as I'm concerned, we never met.

COLONEL: As you wish.

MRS. KEMPLER *(Lingering moment)*: Maa-sa-lama. [Goodbye.]

COLONEL *(Stirring to best posture)*: Maa-sa-lama, Mrs. Kempler. *(After a moment, facing* KEMPLER*)* Mr. Kempler . . .

END OF PLAY

Execution of Justice
Emily Mann

About Emily Mann

Born in Boston in 1952, Emily Mann received a B.A. from Harvard and an MFA from the University of Minnesota. Her first play, now titled *Annulla, An Autobiography*, premiered at The Guthrie Theater's Guthrie 2 under her direction in 1977. In 1985 a revised version of the play was presented by The Repertory Theatre of St. Louis and selected for TCG's *Plays in Process* series. Mann's second play, *Still Life*, premiered at the Goodman Studio Theatre in 1980 and was then produced at American Place Theatre in New York under the author's direction, winning Obies for playwriting, direction and all three performers as well as for best production. Also a *Plays in Process* selection, *Still Life* was later published in TCG's *New Plays USA 1* and *Coming to Terms: American Plays & the Vietnam War* anthologies, and has been performed around the world. Mann has also written for television and film. Current projects include a rhythm-and-blues opera co-authored with Ntozake Shange and a translation of Pierre Laville's *Nights and Days*.

Mann's other directorial credits include the BAM Theater Company's productions of *He and She* and *Oedipus the King*, the Guthrie's *The Glass Menagerie* and ATL's *A Weekend near Madison*, which subsequently ran Off Broadway. A member of New Dramatists, she has been the recipient of a CAPS grant, a Guggenheim fellowship, a National Endowment for the Arts associateship, and a McKnight fellowship, and is the winner of a 1985-86 NEA playwriting fellowship. In 1983 Mann received the Rosamond Gilder Award from the New Drama Forum for "outstanding creative achievement in the theatre."

About the Play

Execution of Justice was commissioned by San Francisco's Eureka Theatre in 1982, and developed over the next 18 months in collaboration with dramaturg Oskar Eustis, artistic director Anthony Taccone and the company's actors. A co-winner of Actors Theatre of Louisville's 1984 Great American Play Contest, the play received its premiere there in March of that year, under the direction of Eustis and Taccone. *Execution of Justice* has also been staged by the Alley Theatre in Houston, Arena Stage in Washington, Center Stage in Baltimore, The Empty Space in Seattle, The Guthrie Theater in Minneapolis, and by Eureka in association with Berkeley Repertory Theatre and San Jose Repertory Company. The director of the Guthrie production, Mann is also directing the Broadway production scheduled to open in March 1986. *Execution of Justice* was originally published in the November 1985 issue of TCG's *American Theatre* magazine.

Playwright's Note

The words come from trial transcript, interview, reportage, the street.

This play is dedicated to Oskar Eustis, dramaturg, who understood the trials. Many thanks to the Eureka Theatre and artistic director Tony Taccone, who risked the verdict.

The author also thanks the John Simon Guggenheim Memorial Foundation for its fellowship to research and write the play.

Thanks to the following people for their help and information: Scott Smith and the Harvey Milk Archives, Harry Britt, Rob Epstein and Richard Schmiechen, Supervisor Carol Ruth Silver, Russ Cone, Gene Marine, Corey Busch, Gwenn Craig, Randy Shilts, Mike Weiss, Daniel Nicoletta, Jim Denman, Mel Wax, Marilyn Waller, Warren Hinckle, Bill Bathurst, Edward Mycue, Joseph Freitas, Jim Nicola and New Playwrights' Theatre, Stuart Ross, Bonnie Ayrault, Bill Block.

Special thanks to Jon Jory, Julie Crutcher and Actors Theatre of Louisville; Stan Wojewodski and Center Stage; Susan Gregg, David Feldshuh and Theatre Cornell; Tom Creamer, M. Burke Walker and The Empty Space; Doug Wager and Arena Stage; Sharon Ott and Berkeley Repertory Theatre; Liviu Ciulei, Mark Bly, Michael Lupu and The Guthrie Theater; Gail Merrifield Papp.

A San Francisco Chronology

1975

San Francisco is in flux. The great port that had sprung up to handle the Gold Rush, that had built thousands of ships and processed millions of servicemen in two world wars, is in decline. Piers that once held freight now hold tourist attractions. Tourism becomes a billion-dollar-a-year industry. Downtown develops as a corporate headquarters, and white-collar jobs open up. Blue-collar jobs are lost, are outnumbered by service-industry jobs. Working-class neighborhoods, both black and Irish Catholic, deteriorate. Some are torn down as downtown and superhighways expand. Some fill up with Asian and Hispanic immigrants. Others undergo "gentrification." San Francisco's homosexual community grows strong and becomes a mecca for thousands of gays from across the country, long attracted to the city by its "open" reputation. Many settle in one of the city's changing neighborhoods, along Castro Street.

Officeseekers adapt to the realignment of political power.

Two young women try to kill President Ford.

November 4, 1975
A coalition of racial minorities, labor rank and file, and neighborhood activists breaks down the decades-long control of City Hall by the Irish political machine. George Moscone is elected Mayor.

Among the new Mayor's appointments is the Reverend Jim Jones, whom Moscone names chairman of the city's Housing Authority.

1976
An attempt is made, with a bomb, to kill Supervisor Dianne Feinstein.

November 2, 1976
Voters approve a new system for electing the Board of Supervisors, San Francisco's equivalent of a city council; the city is divided into 11 districts, each of which will select its own Supervisor.

1977
An attempt is made, with a bomb, to kill District Attorney Joseph Freitas.

Spring 1977
Dan White decides to run for Supervisor from District 8, a heavily Catholic working-class neighborhood in southeast San Francisco. White is a native San Franciscan, a high school sports star, a Vietnam vet, an ex-police officer, and a fireman. A prime issue in White's campaign is his opposition to the Youth Campus, a home for juvenile offenders located in his district.

Harvey Milk, a small businessman and leader of the Castro Street gay community, will run for Supervisor in District 5. Milk is a native New Yorker and part of the recent gay migration to San Francisco, having settled in the city in 1972.

November 8, 1977
Harvey Milk, "The Mayor of Castro Street," wins a seat on the Board of Supervisors. He is the first openly gay elected official in the United States. Dan White, who in his campaign had pledged to "eradicate the malignancies which blight our beautiful city," also wins election to the Board.

March 1978
A Board of Supervisors committee, chaired by White, meets to consider Milk's first legislative proposal: a ban on all forms of discrimination against gays in the city. The committee votes 3-0 to recommend approval to the full Board. The following Monday, the Board considers whether or not to approve the Youth Campus. White believes he has Milk's support to give him the 6-5 majority he needs to close the Youth Campus. When the vote is taken, however, Milk votes for the Youth Campus, and the issue White had campaigned on is defeated by one vote. When the gay rights legislation is brought up before the entire Board a week later, White is the one Supervisor to vote against it.

Fall 1978

Harvey Milk campaigns statewide against the Briggs Initiative, a ballot proposition championed by archconservative State Senator John Briggs. It would ban homosexuals from teaching in California schools. Dan White contributes $100 to Milk's anti-Briggs campaign, saying "Everyone has the right to earn a living."

Harassed by press investigations into irregularities at the People's Temple, Jim Jones moves his congregation to Jonestown, the jungle refuge he is building in Guyana.

Tuesday, November 7

The Briggs Initiative is defeated. Another initiative sponsored by Briggs, Proposition 7, passes. Proposition 7 enacts a tougher death penalty and includes a clause invoking an automatic death penalty for anyone convicted of murdering a public official in an effort to prevent that official from carrying out his public duties. Milk and Moscone strongly opposed Proposition 7. White supported its passage.

Friday, November 10

Dan White resigns from the Board of Supervisors. He cites financial difficulties as the reason. Upon his election he had been forced to resign from the Fire Department; the Supervisor's salary is only $9,600. The previous spring he had sought extra income by signing a lease to operate a fast-food stand, the Hot Potato.

Harvey Milk extracts a promise from Mayor Moscone that White's replacement will be sympathetic to the needs of the gay community.

Tuesday, November 14

Challenged by his disappointed aides and supporters, White reconsiders his decision. He calls Moscone and asks for his resignation back.

Wednesday, November 15

Moscone meets with White and tells him that as long as there are no legal impediments he will consider the resignation rescinded. He adds that if there is a legal question, he will simply reappoint White to the Board. White goes to the City Attorney's office to ask about the legal question and overhears a phone call from Harvey Milk asking the same information.

Congressman Leo Ryan arrives in Guyana to investigate a constituent's charges that his grandson is being held in Jonestown against his will.

Thursday, November 16

Dan White appears at a public rally organized to oppose his reappointment to the Board. He fails to win the crowd to his side and is literally booed off the stage. Hearing of this, Moscone begins to have second thoughts about reappointing White.

Saturday, November 18
The City Attorney tells Moscone that White cannot rescind his resignation, it's up to the Mayor to reappoint him. Moscone tells White he needs concrete proof of support for White from the citizens of District 8.

Sunday, November 19
Congressman Ryan is killed in Guyana and the first news of the massacre reaches San Francisco.

Tuesday, November 21
Moscone meets with Don Horanzey, a candidate backed as a replacement for White. White's aides seek a temporary restraining order to prevent the Mayor from appointing someone else.
    The body count in Guyana tops 500. Rumors of a People's Temple hit squad are given credence by the police. Security measures are implemented at City Hall.

Thursday, November 23
Thanksgiving. Moscone receives two death threats connected with the People's Temple.

Friday, November 24
Dianne Feinstein, President of the Board of Supervisors, meets with the City Attorney, who tells her that White intends to take his seat when the Board convenes on Monday the 27th. Feinstein says that although she favors White regaining his seat, she will not recognize him unless he has been reappointed by the Mayor. That evening, Moscone learns that the restraining order has been turned down in court. He is free to appoint whom he wants.
    The body count in Guyana is up to 780.

Saturday, November 25
Moscone offers Horanzey the District 8 seat on the Board of Supervisors. Horanzey asks for time to consider. White hears the rumor that someone will be appointed to his seat on Monday.

Sunday, November 26
The morning paper puts the body count in Guyana at 910.
    Horanzey calls Moscone to accept the seat. Moscone tells him to be at City Hall for a press conference at 10:30. When the Board convenes at 2·00 Horanzey will be sworn in. The Mayor tells his press secretary to send telegrams to the other candidates informing them they have not been selected. White's name is not on the list, and the press secretary assumes the Mayor will call White personally. Moscone neglects to do this.
    That evening, White receives a phone call from KCBS News asking for his reaction to Moscone's decision to appoint someone else to his seat.

Monday, November 27

Dan White enters the Mayor's Office in City Hall and shoots George Moscone four times. He reloads his gun, enters the Supervisors' office, and shoots Harvey Milk five times. He meets his wife Mary Ann at St. Mary's Cathedral, then surrenders to the police. That evening a tremendous crowd moves down Market Street from the Castro district in a candlelight procession and gathers outside City Hall.

Dianne Feinstein, as President of the Board of Supervisors, becomes Acting Mayor.

May 1, 1979

The trial of Dan White, on two counts of first-degree murder, begins.

May 21, 1979

Dan White is convicted on two counts of the reduced charge of voluntary manslaughter. Maximum sentence: seven years and eight months. A mob of thousands, led by the city's gay community, attacks City Hall, shattering windows and burning police cars. 150 are injured. Later that night, the police riot on Castro Street, clubbing down homosexuals on the sidewalks and in the gay bars.

November 1979

Dianne Feinstein is elected Mayor of San Francisco.

1980

Voters repeal district elections for the Board of Supervisors and reinstate citywide, at-large elections.

The California penal code is amended to prevent arguing the "diminished capacity" defense, which attorney Douglas Schmidt used in the trial of Dan White.

January 6, 1984

Dan White is paroled from Soledad Prison. He begins life outside in Los Angeles.

October 21, 1985

Dan White is found dead of carbon monoxide poisoning at his wife's home in San Francisco.

Adapted from Tom Creamer's notes for The Empty Space program, incorporating additional facts from Warren MacIsaac's notes for the Center Stage program.

Characters

DAN WHITE
MARY ANN WHITE, his wife
COP
SISTER BOOM BOOM

Chorus of Uncalled Witnesses

JIM DENMAN, ex-undersheriff, White's jailer immediately following the shooting
YOUNG MOTHER, late 30s, mother of three
MOSCONE'S FRIEND, old political crony, 50s
MILK'S FRIEND, 30s
GWENN CRAIG, black lesbian leader, 40s
HARRY BRITT, City Supervisor, 40s, Milk's successor
JOSEPH FREITAS, JR., ex-D.A., speaking in 1983

Trial Characters

COURT, the judge
CLERK
DOUGLAS SCHMIDT, defense lawyer
THOMAS F. NORMAN, prosecuting attorney
JOANNA LU, TV reporter
3 PROSPECTIVE JURORS
FOREMAN

Witnesses for the People

STEPHENS, the coroner
RUDY NOTHENBERG, Deputy Mayor
BARBARA TAYLOR, KCBS reporter
OFFICER BYRNE, policewoman in charge of records
WILLIAM MELIA, JR., civil engineer
CYR COPERTINI, appointment secretary to the Mayor
CARL HENRY CARLSON, aide to Milk
RICHARD PABICH, assistant to Milk
FRANK FALZON, Chief Inspector of Homicide
EDWARD ERDELATZ, Inspector

Witnesses for the Defense

FIRE CHIEF SHERRATT
POLICE OFFICER SULLIVAN

CITY SUPERVISOR LEE DOLSON
FIREMAN FREDIANI
PSYCHIATRISTS JONES, BLINDER, SOLOMON, LUNDE, DELMAN
DENISE APCAR, aide to White

In Rebuttal for the People

CAROL RUTH SILVER, City Supervisor
DR. LEVY, psychiatrist

Characters on Tape

Dianne Feinstein, City Supervisor, later Mayor
George Moscone, Mayor
Harvey Milk, City Supervisor

PEOPLE OF SAN FRANCISCO, JURORS, CAMERAMEN, MOURNERS, RIOTERS, RIOT POLICE

The play can be performed by as few as 18 actors.

Time

1978 to the present.

Place

San Francisco.

The Play

Execution of Justice

For my father,
Arthur Mann

ACT ONE: Murder

A bare stage. White screens overhead. Screen: Images of San Francisco, punctuated with images of Milk and Moscone. Hot, fast music. PEOPLE *enter. A maelstrom of urban activity.*
    Screen: Without warning, documentary footage of Dianne Feinstein (Almost unable to stand): As president of the Board of Supervisors, it is my duty to make this announcement: Mayor George Moscone . . . and Supervisor Harvey Milk . . . have been shot . . . and killed. *(Gasps and cries. A long moment)* The suspect is Supervisor Dan White.
    The CROWD *in shock.* THEY *cannot move. Then* THEY *run. In the chaos,* MARY ANN WHITE *enters, trying to hail a cab; exits. Screen: A crucifix fades up. Shaft of light. A church window.* DAN WHITE *prays. Audio: Hyperreal sounds of mumbled Hail Marys; of high heels echoing, moving fast; of breathing hard, running.* MARY ANN WHITE *enters, breathless.* WHITE *looks up.* SHE *approaches him.*

WHITE: I shot the Mayor and Harvey.

MARY ANN WHITE *crumples. Lights change.*

CLERK: This is the matter of the People versus Daniel James White.

Amplified gavel. Lights change.

COP (*Quiet*): Yeah, I'm wearing a "Free Dan White" T-shirt.
You haven't seen what I've seen—
my nose shoved into what I think stinks.
Against everything I believe in.
There was a time in San Francisco when you knew a guy
by his parish.

SISTER BOOM BOOM *enters. Nun drag; white face, heavily made up; spike heels.*

Sometimes I sit in church and I think of those disgusting drag queens dressed
    up as nuns and I'm a cop,
and I'm thinkin',
there's gotta be a law, you know,
because they're makin' me think things I don't want to think
and I gotta keep my mouth shut.

BOOM BOOM *puts out cigarette.*

Take a guy out of his sling—fist-fucked to death—
they say it's mutual consent, it ain't murder,
and I pull this disgusting mess down, take him to the morgue,
I mean, my wife asks me, "Hey, how was your day?"
I can't even tell her.
I wash my hands before I can even look at my kids.

The COP *and* BOOM BOOM *are very aware of each other but never make eye contact.*

BOOM BOOM: God bless you one. God bless you all.
COP: See, Danny knew—he believes in the rights of minorities. Ya know, he just
    felt—we are a minority, too.
BOOM BOOM: I would like to open with a reading from the Book of Dan. *(Opens
    book)*
COP: We been workin' this job three generations—my father was a cop—
    and then they put—Moscone, Jesus, Moscone put this
    N-Negro-loving, faggot-loving Chief telling us what to do—
    he doesn't even come from the neighborhood,
    he doesn't even come from this city!
    He's tellin' us what to do in a force that knows what to do.
    He makes us paint our cop cars faggot blue—
    he called it "lavender gloves" for the queers,
    handle 'em, treat 'em with "lavender gloves," he called it.
    He's cuttin' off our balls.
    The city is stinkin' with degenerates—
    I mean, I'm worried about my kids, I worry about my wife,
    I worry about me and how I'm feelin' mad all the time.

You gotta understand that I'm not alone—
It's real confusion.

BOOM BOOM: "As he came to his day of reckoning, he feared not for he went unto the lawyers and the doctors and the jurors, and they said, 'Take heart, for in this you will receive not life but three to seven with time off for good behavior.' " *(Closes book reverently)*

COP: Ya gotta understand—
Take a walk with me sometime.
See what I see every day . . .

BOOM BOOM: Now we are all faced with this cycle.

COP: Like I'm supposed to smile when I see two bald-headed,
shaved-head men with those tight pants and muscles,
chains everywhere, french-kissin' on the street,
putting their hands all over each other's asses,
I'm supposed to smile,
walk by, act as if this is *right??!!*

BOOM BOOM: As gay people and as people of color and as women we all know the cycle of brutality which pervades our culture.

COP: I got nothin' against people doin' what they want, if I don't see it.

BOOM BOOM: And we all know that brutality only begets more brutality.

COP: I mean, I'm not makin' some woman on the streets for everyone to see.

BOOM BOOM: Violence only sows the seed for more violence.

COP: I'm not . . .

BOOM BOOM: And I hope Dan White knows that.

COP: I can't explain it any better.

Pause.

BOOM BOOM: Because the greatest, most efficient information gathering and dispersal network is the Great Gay Grapevine.

COP: Just take my word for it—

BOOM BOOM: And when he gets out of jail, no matter where Dan White goes, someone will recognize him.

COP: Walk into a leather bar with me some night—
they—they're—
there are queers who'd agree with me—it's disgusting.

BOOM BOOM: All over the world, the word will go out. And we will know where Dan White is.

COP: The point is: Dan White showed you could fight City Hall.

Pause.

BOOM BOOM: Now we are all aware, as I said,
of this cycle of brutality and murder.

And the only way we can break that horrible cycle is with
love, understanding and forgiveness.
And there are those who were before me here today—gay brothers and
   sisters—
who said that we must somehow learn
to love, understand and forgive
the sins that have been committed against us
and the sins of violence.
And it sort of grieves me that some of us are not
understanding and loving and forgiving of Dan White.
And after he gets out,
after we find out where he is . . . *(Long, wry look)*
I mean, not, y'know,
with any malice or planning . . . *(Long look)*
You know, you get so depressed and your blood sugar goes up
and you'd be capable of just about *anything!*
(Long pause. Smiles)
And some angry faggot or dyke who is not
understanding, loving and forgiving—
is going to perform a horrible act of violence and brutality
against Dan White.
And if we can't break the cycle before somebody gets Dan White,
somebody will get Dan White
and when they do,
I beg you all to
love, understand and *for-give. (Laughs)*

Lights fade to black.

CLERK: This is the matter of the People versus Daniel James White and the
record will show that the Defendant is present with his counsel and the
District Attorney is present and this is out of presence of the jury.

Courtroom being set up. TV lights.

JOANNA LU *(On camera)*: The list of prospective witnesses that the defense has
presented for the trial of the man who killed the liberal Mayor of San Francisco, George Moscone, and the first avowedly gay elected official, City
Supervisor Harvey Milk, reads like a Who's Who of City Government *(Looks
at list)* . . . Judges, Congressmen, current and former Supervisors, and even
a State Senator. The D.A. has charged White with two counts of first-degree
murder, invoking for the first time the clause in the new California capital
punishment law that calls for the gas chamber for any person who has
assassinated a public official in an attempt to prevent him from fulfilling

his official duties. Ironically, Harvey Milk and George Moscone vigorously lobbied against the death penalty while Dan White vigorously supported it. This is Joanna Lu at the Hall of Justice.

Gavel. Spotlight on CLERK.

CLERK: Ladies and gentlemen, this is the information in the case now pending before you: the People of the State of California, Plaintiff, versus Daniel James White, Defendant. Action Number: 98663, Count One.

Gavel. Lights up. Trial in progress. Screen: "Jury Selection."

COURT: Mr. Schmidt, you may continue with your jury selection.
SCHMIDT: Thank you, Your Honor.
CLERK: It is alleged that Dan White did willfully, unlawfully and with malice aforethought murder George R. Moscone, the duly elected Mayor of the City and County of San Francisco, California.
SCHMIDT: Have you ever supported controversial causes, like homosexual rights, for instance?
JUROR #1 *(Woman)*: I have gay friends . . . I, uh . . . once walked with them in a Gay Freedom Day Parade.
SCHMIDT: Your Honor, I would like to strike the juror.
JUROR #1: I am str . . . I am heterosexual.
COURT: Agreed.

Gavel.

CLERK: The Defendant Daniel James White is further accused of a crime of felony to wit: that said Defendant Daniel James White did willfully, unlawfully and with malice aforethought, murder Harvey Milk, a duly elected Supervisor of the City and County of San Francisco, California.
SCHMIDT: With whom do you live, sir?
JUROR #2: My roommate.
SCHMIDT: What does he or she do?
JUROR #2: *He* works at the Holiday Inn.
SCHMIDT: Your Honor, I ask the court to strike the juror for cause.
COURT: Agreed.

Gavel.

CLERK: Special circumstances: it is alleged that Daniel James White in this pro-ceeding has been accused of more than one offense of murder.
JUROR #3: I worked briefly as a San Francisco policeman, but I've spent most of my life since then as a private security guard.
SCHMIDT: As you know, serving as a juror is a high honor and responsibility.

JUROR #3: Yes, sir.

SCHMIDT: The jury serves as the conscience of the community.

JUROR #3: Yes, sir. I know that, sir.

SCHMIDT: Now, sir, as a juror you take an oath that you will apply the laws of the state of California as the judge will instruct you. You'll uphold that oath, won't you?

JUROR #3: Yes, sir.

SCHMIDT: Do you hold any views against the death penalty no matter how heinous the crime?

JUROR #3: No, sir. I support the death penalty.

SCHMIDT: Why do you think Danny White killed Milk and Moscone?

JUROR #3: I have certain opinions. I'd say it was social and political pressures . . .

SCHMIDT: I have my jury.

COURT: Mr. Norman?

No response. Fine with him. Gavel.

LU *(On camera)*: The jury has been selected quickly for the Dan White trial. It appears the prosecution and the defense want the same jury. Assistant D.A. Tom Norman exercised only 3 out of 27 possible peremptory challenges. By all accounts, there are no blacks, no gays, and no Asians. One juror is an ex-policeman, another the wife of the county jailer, four of the seven women are old enough to be Dan White's mother. Most of the jurors are working- and middle-class Catholics. Speculation in the press box is that the prosecution feels it has a law-and-order jury. In any case, Dan White will certainly be judged by a jury of his peers. *(Turns to second camera)* I have with me this morning District Attorney Joseph Freitas, Jr. *(TV lights on* FREITAS*)* May we ask sir, the prosecution's strategy in the trial of Dan White?

FREITAS: I think it's a clear case. . . . We'll let the facts speak for themselves. . . .

FALZON *enters, sits at prosecutor's table.*

CLERK: And the Defendant, Daniel James White, has entered a plea of not guilty to each of the charges and allegations contained in this information.

WHITE *enters.* MARY ANN WHITE *enters with infant in arms, sees him.* THEY *sit.*

COURT: Mr. Norman, do you desire to make an opening statement at this time?

NORMAN: I do, Judge.

COURT: All right. You may proceed.

Lights change. Screen: "Act One: Murder." Gavel. Screens go to white.

NORMAN *(Opening statement, prosecution)*: Your Honor, members of the jury—

and you *(Takes in audience)* must be the judges now, counsel for the defense: *(To audience)*

Ladies and Gentlemen: I am Thomas F. Norman and I am the Assistant District Attorney, and I appear here as trial representative to Joseph Freitas Jr., District Attorney. Seated with me is Frank Falzon, Chief Inspector of Homicide for San Francisco.

George R. Moscone was the duly elected Mayor of San Francisco. *(Screen: Portrait of Moscone)* Harvey Milk was the duly elected Supervisor or City Councilman of District 5 of San Francisco. *(Screen: Portrait of Milk)*

The defendant in this case, Mr. Daniel James White, had been the duly elected Supervisor of District 8 of San Francisco, until for personal reasons of his own he tendered his resignation in writing to the Mayor on or about November the 10th, 1978, which was approximately 17 days before this tragedy occurred.

Subsequent to tendering his resignation he had the feeling that he wanted to withdraw that resignation, and that he wanted his job back.

George Moscone, it appears, had told the accused that he would give him his job back or, in other words, appoint him back to the Board if it appeared that there was substantial support in District Number 8 for that appointment.

Material was received by the Mayor in that regard, and in the meantime, Mr. Daniel James White had resorted to the courts in an effort to withdraw his written resignation.

It appears that those efforts were not met with much success.

Screen: "The Defense, Douglas Schmidt."

SCHMIDT: Ladies and Gentlemen, the prosecutor has quite skillfully outlined certain of the facts that he believes will be supportive of his theory of first-degree murder.

I intend to present *all* the facts, including some of the background material that will show, not so much *what* happened on November 27th, but *why* those tragedies occurred on November 27th.

The evidence will show, and it's not disputed, that Dan White did, indeed, shoot and kill George Moscone and I think the evidence is equally clear that Dan White did shoot and kill Harvey Milk.

Why then should there be a trial?

The issue in this trial is properly to understand *why* that happened.

Lights. Screen: "Chief Medical Examiner and Coroner for the City and County of San Francisco."

STEPHENS *(Holding photo)*: In my opinion and experience, Counsel, the larger tattoo pattern at the side of the Mayor's head is compatible with a firing distance of about one foot, and the smaller tattoo pattern within the larger tattoo pattern is consistent with a firing distance of a little less than one foot.

That is: The wounds to the head were received within a distance of one foot when the Mayor was already on the floor incapacitated.

NORMAN *looks to jury. Screen: Image of figure shooting man in head from a distance of one foot, leaning down. Lights.*

SCHMIDT: Why? . . . Good people, fine people, with fine backgrounds, simply don't kill people in cold blood, it just doesn't happen, and obviously some part of them has not been presented thus far. Dan White was a native of San Francisco. He went to school here, went through high school here. He was a noted athlete in high school. He was an army veteran who served in Vietnam, and was honorably discharged from the army. He became a policeman thereafter, and after a brief hiatus developed, again returned to the police force in San Francisco, and later transferred to the fire department.

He was married in December of 1976, and he fathered his son in July 1978.

Dan White was a good policeman and Dan White was a good fireman. In fact, he was decorated for having saved a woman and her child in a very dangerous fire, but the complete picture of Dan White perhaps was not known until some time after these tragedies on November 27th. The part that went unrecognized was—for the past ten years Daniel White was suffering from a mental disease. The disease that Daniel White was suffering from is called "depression," sometimes called "manic depression."

Lights.

NORMAN: Doctor, what kind of wound was that in your opinion?

STEPHENS: These are gunshot wounds of entrance, Counsel.

The cause of death was multiple gunshot wounds . . . particularly the bullet that passed through the base of the Supervisor's brain. This wound would cause instant or almost instant death. I am now holding People's 30 for identification. In order for this wound to be received, Counsel . . . the Supervisor's left arm has to be in close to the body with the palm up. The right arm has to be relatively close to the body with the palm turned away from the body and the thumb in towards the body.

NORMAN: Can you illustrate that for us?

STEPHENS: Yes, Counsel. The left arm has to be in close to the body and slightly forward with the palm up. The right hand has to be palm away with the thumb pointed towards the body and the elbow in slightly to the body with the arm raised. In this position, all of these wounds that I have just described in People's 30 and 29 line up.

Freeze. Lights.

SCHMIDT *(Talking to jury)*: Dan White came from a vastly different lifestyle than Harvey Milk, who was a homosexual leader and politician. Dan White was an idealistic young man, a working-class young man. He was deeply endowed with and believed very strongly in the traditional American values, family and home, like the District he represented. *(Indicates jury)* Dan White believed people when they said something. He believed that a man's word, essentially, was his bond. He was an honest man, and he was fair, perhaps too fair for politics in San Francisco.

Screen: WHITE *campaigning, American flag behind him. Audio:* Rocky *theme song, crowd response throughout his speech.*

WHITE *(To crowd)*: Do you like my new campaign song?
CROWD *(Audio; cheering)*: Yeah!
WHITE *(To camera; TV lights)*: For years, we have witnessed an exodus from San Francisco by many of our family members, friends and neighbors. Alarmed by the enormous increase in crime, poor educational facilities and a deteriorating social structure, they have fled to temporary havens. . . . In a few short years these malignancies of society will erupt from our city and engulf our tree-lined, sun-bathed communities that chide us for daring to live in San Francisco. That is, unless we who have remained can transcend the apathy which has caused us to lock our doors while the tumult rages unchecked through our streets. Individually we are helpless. Yet you must realize there are thousands and thousands of angry frustrated people such as yourselves waiting to unleash a fury that can and will eradicate the malignancies which blight our beautiful city. I am not going to be forced out of San Francisco by splinter groups of radicals, social deviates, and incorrigibles. UNITE AND FIGHT WITH DAN WHITE.

Crowd cheers. Lights change. Screens go to white.

SCHMIDT: I think Dan White saw the city deteriorating as a place for the average and decent people to live.
COURT: Mr. Nothenberg, please be seated.
SCHMIDT: The irony is . . . that the young man with so much promise in seeking the job on the Board of Supervisors actually was destined to construct his downfall. After Dan White was elected he discovered there was a conflict of interest if he was a fireman and an elected official. His wife, Mary Ann, was a schoolteacher and made a good salary. But after their marriage, it was discovered that the wife of Dan White had become . . . pregnant and had to give up her teaching job. So the family income plummeted from an excess of $30,000 to $9,600 which is what a San Francisco Supervisor is paid. I believe all the stress and the underlying mental illness culminated in his resignation that he turned in to the Mayor on November 10th, 1978.

Screen: "Mr. Nothenberg, Deputy Mayor." Lights.

NORMAN: Would you read that for us?

NOTHENBERG: "Dear Mayor Moscone: I have been proud to represent the people of San Francisco from District 8 for the past ten months, but due to personal responsibilities which I feel must take precedent over my legislative duties, I am resigning my position effective today. I am sure that the next representative to the Board of Supervisors will receive as much support from the People of San Francisco as I have. Sincerely, Dan White." It is so signed.

SCHMIDT *(To jury)*: Some days after November the 10th pressure was brought to bear on Dan White to go back to the job that he had worked so hard for, and there was a one-way course that those persons could appeal to Dan White, and that was to appeal to his sense of honor: Basically—Dan you are letting the fire department down, letting the police department down. It worked. That type of pressure worked, because of the kind of man Dan White is.

He asked the Mayor for his job back.

NORMAN: Mr. Nothenberg, on or about Monday the 27th of November last year, do you know whether Mayor Moscone was going to make an appointment to the Board of Supervisors, particularly for District No. 8?

NOTHENBERG: Yes, he was.

SCHMIDT: The Mayor said: We have political differences, but you are basically a good man, and you worked for the job and I'm not going to take you to fault. The letter was returned to Dan White.

NORMAN: Do you know whom his appointee to District 8 was going to be?

NOTHENBERG: Yes, I do.

NORMAN: Who was that please?

NOTHENBERG: It was going to be a gentleman named Don Horanzey.

SCHMIDT: As I said, Dan White believed a man's word was his bond. *(HE moves down to the jury)*

Mayor Moscone had said: If there was any legal problem he would simply reappoint Dan White. Thereafter it became: Dan White there is no support in District 8 and unless you can show some broad-base support, the job will not be given to you, and finally, the public statement coming from the Mayor's office: It's undecided. But you will be notified, prior to the time that any decision is made. They didn't tell Dan White. But they told Barbara Taylor.

Lights change.

TAYLOR *(Audio; on phone)*: I'm Barbara Taylor from KCBS. I'd like to speak to Dan White.

WHITE *(Audio)*: Yuh.

TAYLOR *(Audio)*: I have received information from a source within the Mayor's office that you are not getting that job. I am interested in doing an interview to find out your reaction to that. Mr. White?

Long pause. Spotlight on WHITE.

WHITE *(Audio)*: I don't know anything about it.

Audio: Click, busy signal. Lights change.

TAYLOR *(Live)*: The Mayor told me: "The only one I've talked to who is in favor of the appointment of Dan White is Dan White."
NORMAN: Thank you, Miss Taylor.
SCHMIDT: After that phone call, Denise Apcar, Dan's aide, told Dan White that there were going to be supporters down at City Hall the next morning to show support to the Mayor's office. In one day they had collected 1100 signatures in District 8 in support of Dan White.

But the next morning, Denise called Dan and told him the Mayor was unwilling to accept the petitioners.

Screen: "Denise Apcar, Aide to Dan White."

APCAR: Yes. I told Danny—I don't remember my exact words—that the Mayor had "circumvented the people."
NORMAN: Did you believe at that time that the Mayor was going to appoint someone other than Dan White?
APCAR: Oh, yes.
NORMAN: At that time, were your feelings such that you were angry?
APCAR: Definitely. Well the Mayor had told him . . . and Dan always felt that a person was going to be honest when they said something. He believed that up until the end.
NORMAN: You felt and believed that Mr. Milk had been acting to prevent the appointment of Mr. Dan White to his vacated seat on the Board of Supervisors?
APCAR: Yes. I was very much aware of that.
NORMAN: Had you expressed that opinion to Mr. White?
APCAR: Yes.
NORMAN: Did Mr. White ever express that opinion also to you?
APCAR: He wasn't down at City Hall very much that week so I was basically the person that told him these things.

Pause.

NORMAN: Did you call Mr. White and tell him that you had seen Harvey Milk come out of the Mayor's office after you had been informed the Mayor was not in?

APCAR: Yes, I did. Then he called me back and said, "Denise, come pick me up. I want to see the Mayor."

NORMAN: When you picked him up, did he do anything unusual?

APCAR: Well . . . he didn't look at me and normally he would turn his body a little bit towards the driver and we would talk, you know, in a freeform way, but this time he didn't look at me at all. He was squinting hard. He was very nervous, he was agitated. He was blowing a lot. He was rubbing his hands, blowing into his hands and rubbing them like he was cold, like his hands were cold. He acted very hurt. Yes. He was, he looked like he was going to cry. He was doing everything he could to restrain his emotion.

NORMAN: Did you ever describe him as acting "all fired up"?

APCAR: Yes, yes I—I believe I said that.

NORMAN: Did he mention at that time that he also was going to talk to Harvey Milk?

APCAR: Yes, he did.

NORMAN: Did he ever say he was going to "really lay it on the Mayor"?

APCAR: It's been brought to my attention I said that, yes.

NORMAN: When you were driving Mr. White downtown, was there some discussion relative to a statement you made. "Anger had run pretty high all week towards the Mayor playing pool on us, dirty, you know?"

APCAR: I believe I was describing my anger. At the time I made those statements I was in shock and I spoke freely and I'm sure I've never used those terms before.

NORMAN: When you made those statements it was 40 minutes after noon on November 27th, was it not?

APCAR: Yes.

NORMAN: Miss Apcar—When you were driving Mr. White to City Hall did you know he was carrying a loaded gun?

APCAR: No. I did not.

NORMAN: Thank you.

Lights.

SCHMIDT: Dan White went to City Hall and he took a .38 caliber revolver with him, and that was not particularly unusual for Dan White.

Dan White was an ex-policeman, and as a policeman one is required to carry, off-duty, a gun, and as an ex-policeman—well, I think it's common practice.

And additionally, remember, there was the atmosphere created by the Jonestown People's Temple tragedy *(Screens flood with Jonestown imagery. Music)* which had occurred a few days before November 27th, and at that time there were rumors that there were hit lists that had been placed on public officials in San Francisco. Assassination squads. And in hindsight of course we can all realize the fact did not happen, but at the time there were 900 bodies laying in Guyana to indicate, that indeed people were bent on murder.

Screen: "Officer Byrne, Department of Records." Lights.

NORMAN: Officer Byrne, do persons who were once on the police force who have resigned their positions, do they have a right to carry a concealed firearm on their person?

SCHMIDT: And I think it will be shown that Jim Jones himself was directly allied to the liberal elements of San Francisco politics and not to the conservative elements.

BYRNE: No, a resigned person would not have that right.

SCHMIDT: And so, it would be important to understand that there were threats directed towards conservative persons like Dan White.

NORMAN: Officer, have you at my instance and request examined those particular records to determine whether there is an official permit issued by the Chief of Police to a Mr. Daniel James White to carry a concealed firearm?

BYRNE: Yes, I have.

NORMAN: What have you found?

BYRNE: I find no permit.

NORMAN: Thank you.

Lights.

SCHMIDT: Yes, it's a violation of the law to carry a firearm without a permit, but that firearm was *registered* to Dan White.

NORMAN: Mr. Melia, please be seated.

SCHMIDT: Upon approaching the doors on Polk Street White observed a metal-detection machine.

Knowing that he did not know the man that was on the metal-detection machine, he simply went around to the McAllister Street well, where he expected to meet his aide.

He did not find Denise Apcar there. She'd gone to put gas in her car. He waited for several moments, but knowing that it was imminent, the talk to the Mayor, he stepped through a window at the Department of Public Works. *(Screen: Slide of windows with man in front demonstrating procedure)* Which doesn't require any physical prowess, and you can step through those windows, and the evidence will show that though now they are barred, previously it was not uncommon for people to enter and exit there. They are very large windows, and are large, wide sills, *(Screen shows windows he stepped through—small, high off the ground, now barred)* and it's quite easy to step into the building through these windows. *(Screen: Slide of man in three-piece suit trying to get leg up)*

Screen: "William Melia, Jr., Civil Engineer."

MELIA: At approximately 10:35 I heard the window open. I heard someone jump to the floor and then running through the adjoining room. I looked up and caught a glance of a man in a suit running past the doorway of my office into the City Hall hallway.

NORMAN: What did you do?

MELIA: I got up from my desk and called after him: "Hey, wait a second."

NORMAN: Did that person wait or stop?

MELIA: Yes, they did.

NORMAN: Do you see that person here in this courtroom today?

MELIA: Yes, I do.

NORMAN: Where is that person?

MELIA: It's Dan White. (Pause) He said to me: "I had to get in. My aide was supposed to come down and let me in the side door, but never showed up." I had taken exception to the way he had entered our office, and I replied: "And you are?" And he replied: "I'm Dan White, the City Supervisor." He said, "Say, I've got to go," and with that, he turned and ran out of the office.

NORMAN: Did you say that he ran?

MELIA: Right.

Pause.

NORMAN: Mr. Melia—had you ever seen anyone else enter or exit through that window or those windows along that side?

MELIA: Yes, I had. It was common for individuals that worked in our office to do that.

NORMAN: Were you alarmed when you learned that a Supervisor crawled or walked through that window, or stepped through that window?

MELIA: Was I alarmed?

NORMAN: Yes.

MELIA: Yes. I was . . . alarmed.

NORMAN *looks to jury.*

SCHMIDT (Annoyed): I think it's significant at this point—also because the fact that he crawled through the window *appears* to be important—it's significant to explain that people *often climb through that window*, and indeed, on the morning of the 27th, Denise had the key to the McAllister Street well door.

So, Dan White stepped through the window, identified himself, traveled up to the second floor. (Screen: "Mrs. Cyr Copertini, Appointment Secretary to the Mayor") And then approached the desk of Cyr Copertini and properly identified himself, and asked to see the Mayor.

Lights.

CYR: I am the appointment secretary to Mayor Feinstein.

NORMAN: In November of last year and particularly on November 27th what was your then occupation?

CYR: I was appointment secretary to the elected Mayor of San Francisco, George Moscone. (SHE *is deeply moved*)

NORMAN: Mrs. Copertini—were you aware that there was anything that was going to happen that day of November 27th of interest to the citizens of San Francisco, uh . . . I mean, such as some public announcement?

Pause.

CYR: . . . There was to be a news conference to announce the new Supervisor for the Eighth District, at 11:30.

NORMAN: Mrs. Copertini, at approximately 10:30 A.M. when you saw Mr. Daniel White, he appeared in front of your desk . . . do you recall what he said?

CYR: He said, "Hello, Cyr. May I see the Mayor?" I said: "He has someone with him, but let me go check with him." I went in to the Mayor and told him that Supervisor White was there to see him. He was a little dismayed. He was a little uncomfortable by it and said: "Oh, all right. Tell him I'll see him, but he will have to wait a coupla minutes."

I asked the Mayor, "Shouldn't I have someone in there with him," and he said: "No, no, I'll see him alone."

I said, "Why don't you let me bring Mel Wax in?" And he said: "No, no, I'll see him alone." And then I went back.

NORMAN: Who was Mel Wax?

CYR: The press secretary.

NORMAN: When you went out to your office, did you then see Mr. Daniel White?

CYR: Yes. I said it will be a few minutes. He asked me how I was and how things were going. Was I having a nice day.

NORMAN: Was there anything unusual about his tone of voice?

CYR: No. I don't think so. He seemed nervous. . . .

I asked him would he like to see the newspaper while he was waiting? He said: "No, he wouldn't," and I said: "Well, that's all right. There's nothing in it anyway unless you want to read about Caroline Kennedy having turned 21."

And he said: "21? Is that right." He said: "Yeah, that's all so long ago. It's even more amazing when you think that John John is now 18."

Lights change. Funeral Mass: Gregorian chant; boys' choir. Pause.

DENMAN: The only comparable situation I ever remember

CYR: It was about that time he was admitted to the Mayor's office.

Pause.

DENMAN: was when JFK was killed.
NORMAN: Did you tell Mr. Daniel White that he could go in?
CYR: Yes.
DENMAN: I remember that in my bones, in my body.
NORMAN: Did he respond in any way to that?
DENMAN: Just like this one
CYR: He said: "Good girl, Cyr."
NORMAN: Good girl, Cyr?
CYR: Right.
DENMAN: when Camelot all of a sudden turned to hell.
NORMAN: Then what did he do?
CYR: Went in.

Pause.

NORMAN: After he went in there did you hear anything of an unusual nature
that was coming from the Mayor's office?
CYR: After a time I heard a . . . commotion.

Lights change.

YOUNG MOTHER: I heard it on the car radio, I literally gasped.
NORMAN: Explain that to us, please.
YOUNG MOTHER: I wanted to pull over to the side of the road and scream.
CYR: Well, I heard—a series of noises—a group and then one—
YOUNG MOTHER: Just scream.
CYR: I went to the window to see if anything was happening out in the street,
YOUNG MOTHER: Then I thought of my kids.
CYR: and the street was rather extraordinarily calm.
DENMAN: I noticed when I walked outside that there was an unusual quiet.
CYR: For that hour of the day there is usually more—there wasn't really anything
out there.
DENMAN: I went to the second floor and started walking toward the Mayor's
office.
YOUNG MOTHER: I wanted to get them out of school and take them home,
NORMAN: Could you describe these noises for us?
YOUNG MOTHER: I wanted to take them home and *(Makes a hugging gesture)* lock
the door.
CYR: Well, they were dull thuds rather like—
DENMAN: And there was this strange combination of panic and silence that you
rarely see,
CYR: I thought maybe it was an automobile door that somebody had tried to
shut, by, you know, pushing, and then finally succeeding.

DENMAN: it was like a silent slow-motion movie of a disaster.

NORMAN: Do you have any recollection that you can report with any certainty to us as to how many sounds there were?

CYR: No. As I stood there I—I thought I ought to remember—(SHE *breaks down*)

DENMAN: There was this hush and aura, people were moving with strange faces, (CYR *sobs*) as if the world had just come to an end.

MOSCONE'S FRIEND: George loved this city, and felt what was wrong could be fixed.

NORMAN: Do you want a glass of water?

CYR *sobs*.

DENMAN: And I asked someone what had happened and he said: "The Mayor has been shot."

CYR: I ought to remember that pattern in case it is something, but I—

MOSCONE'S FRIEND: He knew—it was a white racist town. A Catholic town. But he believed in people's basic good will.

CYR *sobs*.

COURT: Just a minute. Do you want a recess?

MOSCONE'S FRIEND: He never suspected, I bet, Dan White's psychotic behavior.

NORMAN: Do you want a recess?

MOSCONE'S FRIEND: That son of a bitch killed someone I loved. I mean, I loved the guy.

CYR: No. I'm all right.

COURT: Are you sure you are all right?

CYR: Yes.

YOUNG MOTHER: I just thought of my kids.

Long pause.

MOSCONE'S FRIEND: I loved his idealism. I loved his hope.

CYR: Then what happened was Rudy Nothenberg left to tell the press that the conference would start a few minutes late.

MOSCONE'S FRIEND: I loved the guy.

CYR: And then he came back to me right away and said: "Oh, I guess we can go ahead. I just saw Dan White leave."

MOSCONE'S FRIEND: I loved his almost naive faith in people.

CYR: So then he went into the Mayor's office and said: "He isn't here." And I said: "Well, maybe he went into the back room."

MOSCONE'S FRIEND: I loved his ability to go on.

CYR: Then he just gave a shout saying: "Gary, get in here. Call an ambulance. Get the police."

MOSCONE'S FRIEND: See, I got too tired to stay in politics and do it. George and I were together from the beginning. Me, Phil Burton, Willy Brown. Beatin' all the old Irishmen.

DENMAN: I heard right away that Dan White had done it.

MOSCONE'S FRIEND: But George believed, as corny as this sounds, that you do good for the people. I haven't met many of those and George was one of those. Maybe those are the guys that get killed. I don't know.

Pause. CYR *crying.*

NORMAN: All right. All this you told us about occurred in San Francisco, didn't it?

Pause.

CYR *(Deeply moved)*: Yes.

SCHMIDT: Dan White, as it was quite apparent at that point, had *cracked* because of his underlying mental illness. . . .

Screen: "Carl Henry Carlson, Aide to Harvey Milk."

CARLSON: I heard Peter Nardoza, Dianne Feinstein's aide, say "Dianne wants to see you," and Dan White said: "That'll have to wait a couple of minutes, I have something to do first."

NORMAN: I have something to do first?

CARLSON: Yes.

Pause.

NORMAN: Do you recall in what manner Mr. White announced himself?

SCHMIDT: There were stress factors due to the fact that he hadn't been notified,

CARLSON: He appeared at the door which was normally left open. Stuck his head in and asked: "Say, Harv, can I see you for a minute?"

SCHMIDT: and the sudden emotional surge that he had in the Mayor's office was simply too much for him

NORMAN: What did Harvey Milk do at that time if anything?

CARLSON: He turned around.

SCHMIDT: and he cracked.

CARLSON: He turned around

SCHMIDT: The man cracked.

CARLSON: and said "Sure," and got up and went across the hall . . .

SCHMIDT: He shot the Mayor,

CARLSON: to the office designated as Dan White's office on the chart.

SCHMIDT: reloaded his gun, basically on *instinct*, because of his police training,

NORMAN: After they went across the hall to Mr. White's office . . .

SCHMIDT: and was about to leave the building at that point and he looked down the hall,

NORMAN: Would you tell us what next you heard or saw?

SCHMIDT: he saw somebody that he believed to be an aide to Harvey Milk.

CARLSON: A few seconds later, probably 10, 15 seconds later, I heard a shot, or the sound of gunfire.

SCHMIDT: He went down to the Supervisors' area to *talk* to Harvey Milk.

COURT: Excuse me. Would you speak out. Your voice is fading a bit.

SCHMIDT: At that point, in the same state of rage, emotional upheaval with the stress and mental illness having cracked this man

STEPHENS *(Demonstrates as* HE *speaks)*: The left arm has to be close to the body and slightly forward with the palm up.

SCHMIDT: *ninety seconds* from the time he shot the Mayor, Dan White shot and killed Harvey Milk.

CARLSON: After the shot, I heard Harvey Milk scream. "Oh, no." And then the first—the first part of the second "no" which was then cut short by the second shot.

STEPHENS: The right hand has to be palm away with the thumb pointed towards the body and the elbow in slightly to the body with the arm raised.

NORMAN: How many sounds of shots did you hear altogether, Mr. Carlson?

CARLSON: Five or six. I really didn't consciously count them.

STEPHENS: In this position all of these wounds that I have just described in People's 29 and 30 line up.

Pause.

CARLSON: A few moments later the door opened, the door opened and Daniel White walked out, rushed out, and proceeded down the hall.

NORMAN: Now, Mr. Carlson, when Daniel White first appeared at the office of Harvey Milk and he inquired of Harvey Milk, "Say, Harv, can I see you for a minute?," could you describe his tone of voice in any way?

CARLSON: He appeared to be very normal, usual friendly self. I didn't, I didn't feel anything out of the ordinary. It was just very typical Dan White.

Lights change.

GWENN: I'd like to talk about when people are pushed to the wall.

SCHMIDT: Harvey Milk was against the reappointment of Dan White.

GWENN: In order to understand the riots, I think you have to understand that the Dan White verdict did not occur in a vacuum.

SCHMIDT: Basically, it was a political decision. It was evident there was a liberal wing of the Board of Supervisors, and there was a smaller conservative wing, and Dan White was a conservative politician for San Francisco.

PABICH: My address is 542-A Castro Street.

GWENN: I don't think I have to say what their presence meant to us, and what their loss meant to us—

NORMAN: What did you do after you saw Dan White put the key in the door of his old office, Room 237?

GWENN: The assassinations of our friends Harvey and George were a crime against us all.

PABICH: Well, I was struck in my head, sort of curious as to why he'd been running.

GWENN: And right here, when I say "us," I don't mean only gay people.

PABICH: And he was—it looked like he was in a hurry. I was aware of the political situation.

GWENN: I mean all people who are getting less than they deserve.

PABICH: I was aware that Harvey was taking the position to the Mayor that Mr. White shouldn't be reappointed. Harvey and I had talked earlier that it would be a significant day.

Lights. Subliminal music.

MILK'S FRIEND: After Harvey died, I went into a depression that lasted about a year, I guess. They called it depression, anyway. I thought about suicide, well, I more than thought about it.

SCHMIDT: Mr. Pabich, Mr. Milk had suggested a replacement for Dan White, hadn't he?

PABICH: He had, to my understanding, recommended several people, and basically took the position that Dan White should not be reappointed.

MILK'S FRIEND: I lost my job. I stayed in the hospital for, I would guess, two months or so. They put me on some kind of drug that . . . well, it helped, I guess. I mean, I loved him and it was . . .

SCHMIDT: Was he requesting that a homosexual be appointed?

PABICH: No, he was not. (HE *stares at* SCHMIDT, *stunned*)

Lights change.

MILK'S FRIEND: Well, he was gone and that couldn't change.

SCHMIDT: I have nothing further. Thank you.

MILK'S FRIEND: He'd never be here again, I knew that.

COURT: All right. Any redirect, Mr. Norman?

NORMAN: No. Thank you for coming, Mr. Pabich.

GWENN: It was as if Dan White had given the go-ahead. It was a free-for-all, a license to kill.

MILK'S FRIEND: I had this recurring dream. We were at the opera, Harvey and I.

PABICH *with* JOANNA LU. *TV lights.*

PABICH *(On camera)*: It's over. Already I can tell it's over. He asked me a question, a clear queer-baiting question, and the jury didn't bat an eye.

MILK'S FRIEND: I was laughing. Harvey was laughing.

PABICH *(On camera)*: Dan White's going to get away with murder.

LU *(On camera)*: Mr. Pabich . . .

MILK'S FRIEND: Then Harvey leant over and whispered: When you're watching *Tosca*, you know you're alive. That's when I'd wake up.

PABICH *rushes out, upset.*

GWENN: I remember the moment I heard Harvey had been shot— (SHE *breaks down)*

MILK'S FRIEND: And I'd realize—like for the first time all over again—he was dead.

Blackout. Hyperreal sounds of high heels on marble, echoing, moving fast. Mumbled Hail Marys. Light up slowly on SCHMIDT, NORMAN.

SCHMIDT: From here I think the evidence will demonstrate that Dan White ran down to Denise's office, screamed at his aide to give him the key to her car.

And he left, went to a church, called his wife, went into St. Mary's Cathedral, prayed, and his wife got there, and he told her, the best he could, what he remembered he had done, and then they walked together to the Northern Police Station where he turned himself in; asked the officer to look after his wife, asked the officer to take possession of an Irish poster he was carrying . . . *(Screen: Cover of Uris book* Ireland: A Terrible Beauty. *Desolate, haunting)* and then made a statement, what best he could recall had occurred.

Lights. FALZON *rises from his seat at prosecutor's table.*

FALZON: Why . . . I feel like hitting you in the fuckin' mouth. . . . How could you be so stupid? How?

WHITE: I . . . I want to tell you about it . . . I want to, to explain.

FALZON: Okay, if you want to talk to me, I'm gonna get my tape recorder and read you your rights and do it right.

NORMAN: The People at this time move the tape-recorded statement into evidence.

Screen: "The Confession."

FALZON: Today's date is Monday, November 27th, 1978. The time is presently 12:05. We're inside the Homicide Detail, Room 454, at the Hall of

Justice. Present is Inspector Edward Erdelatz, Inspector Frank Falzon and for the record, sir, your full name?

WHITE: Daniel James White.

Lights.

FALZON: Would you, normally in a situation like this, ah . . . we ask questions, I'm aware of your past history as a police officer and also as a San Francisco fireman. I would prefer. I'll let you do it in a narrative form as to what happened this morning if you can lead up to the events of the shooting and then backtrack as to why these events took place. *(Looks at* ERDELATZ*)*

WHITE: Well, it's just that I've been under an awful lot of pressure lately, financial pressure, because of my job situation, family pressure because of ah . . . not being able to have the time with my family. *(Sob)*

FALZON: Can you relate these pressures you've been under, Dan, at this time? Can you explain it to Inspector Erdelatz and myself.

WHITE: It's just that I wanted to serve (FALZON *nods*) the people of San Francisco well and I did that. Then when the pressures got too great, I decided to leave. After I left, my family and friends offered their support and said, whatever it would take to allow me to go back into office—well, they would be willing to make that effort. And then it came out that Supervisor Milk and some others were working against me to get my seat back on the Board. He didn't speak to me, he spoke to the City Attorney but I was in the office and I heard the conversation.

I could see the game that was being played, they were going to use me as a *scapegoat*, whether I was a good Supervisor or not, was not the point. This was a political opportunity and they were going to degrade me and my family and the job that I had tried to do an, an more or less *hang me out to dry*. And I saw more and more evidence of this during the week when the papers reported that ah . . . someone else was going to be reappointed. The Mayor told me he was going to call me before he made any decision, he never did that. I was troubled, the pressure, my family again, my, my son's out to a babysitter.

FALZON: Dan, can you tell Inspector Erdelatz and myself, what was your plan this morning? What did you have in mind?

WHITE: I didn't have any devised plan or anything, it's, I was leaving the house to talk, to see the Mayor and I went downstairs, to, to make a phone call and I had my gun down there.

FALZON: Is this your police service revolver, Dan?

WHITE: This is the gun I had when I was a policeman. It's in my room an ah . . . I don't know, I just put it on. I, I don't know why I put it on, it's just . . .

FALZON: You went directly from your residence to the Mayor's office this morning?

WHITE: Yes, my, my aide picked me up but she didn't have any idea ah . . . you know that I had a gun on me or, you know, and I went in to see him an, an he told me he wasn't going to, intending to tell me about it. Then ah . . . I got kind of fuzzy and then just my head didn't feel right and I, then he said: "Let's go into the, the back room and, and have a drink and talk about it."

FALZON: Was this before any threats on your part, Dan?

WHITE: I, I never made any threats.

FALZON: There were no threats at all?

WHITE: I, I . . . oh no.

FALZON: When were you, how, what was the conversation, can you explain to Inspector Erdelatz and myself the conversation that existed between the two of you at this time?

WHITE: It was pretty much just, you know, I asked, was I going to be reappointed. He said, no I am not, no you're not. And I said, why, and he told me, it's a political decision and that's the end of it, and that's it.

FALZON: Is this when you were having a drink in the back room?

WHITE: No, no, it's before I went into the back room and then he could obviously see, see I was obviously distraught an then he said, let's have a drink an I, I'm not even a drinker, you know I don't, once in a while, but I'm not even a drinker. But I just kinda stumbled in the back and he was all, he was talking an nothing was getting through to me. It was just like a roaring in my ears an, an then em . . . it just came to me, you know, he . . .

FALZON: You couldn't hear what he was saying Dan?

WHITE: Just small talk that, you know, it just wasn't registering. What I was going to do now, you know, and how this would affect my family, you know, an, an just, just all the time knowing he's going to go out an, an lie to the press an, an tell 'em, you know, that I, I wasn't a good Supervisor and that people didn't want me an then that was it. Then I, I just shot him, that was it, it was over.

FALZON: What happened after you left there, Dan?

WHITE: Well, I, I left his office by one of the back doors an, I was going down the stairs and then I saw Harvey Milk's aide an then it struck me about what Harvey had tried to do an I said, well I'll go talk to him. He didn't know I had, I had heard his conversation and he was all smiles and stuff and I went in and, you know, I, I didn't agree with him on a lot of things, but I was always honest, you know, and here they were devious. I started to say you know how hard I worked for it and what it meant to me and my family an then my reputation as, as a hard worker, good honest person and he just kind of smirked at me as if to say, too bad an then, an then, I just got all flushed an, an hot, and I shot him.

FALZON: This occurred inside your room, Dan?

WHITE: Yeah, in my office, yeah.

FALZON: And when you left there did you go back home?

WHITE: No, no, no I drove to the, the Doggie Diner on, on Van Ness and I called my wife and she, she didn't know, she . . .

FALZON: Did you tell her Dan?

Sobbing.

WHITE: I called up, I didn't tell her on the phone. I just said she was work . . . see, she was working, son's at a babysitter, shit. I just told her to meet me at the cathedral.

FALZON: St. Mary's?

Sobbing.

WHITE: She took a cab, yeah. She didn't know. She had knew I'd been upset and I wasn't even talking to her at home because I just couldn't explain how I felt and she had no, nothing to blame about it, she was, she always has been great to me but it was, just the pressure hitting me an just my head's all flushed and expected that my skull's going to crack. Then when she came to the church, I, I told her and she kind of slumped and she, she couldn't say anything.

FALZON: How is she now do you, do you know is she, do you know where she is?

WHITE: I don't know now. She, she came to Northern Station with me. She asked me not to do anything about myself, you know that she, she loved me and she'd stick by me and not to hurt myself.

FALZON: Is there anything else you'd like to add at this time?

WHITE: Just that I've been honest and worked hard, never cheated anybody or, you know, I'm not a crook or anything an I wanted to do a good job, I'm trying to do a good job an I saw this city as it's going, kind of downhill an I was always just a lonely vote on the Board and try to be honest an, an I just couldn't take it anymore an that's it.

FALZON: Inspector Erdelatz?

ERDELATZ: Dan, right now are you under a doctor's care?

WHITE: No.

ERDELATZ: Are you under any medication at all?

WHITE: No.

ERDELATZ: When is the last time you had your gun with you prior to today?

WHITE: I guess it was a few months ago. I, I was afraid of some of the threats that were made an, I, I, just wanted to make sure to protect myself you know this, this city isn't safe you know and there's a lot of people running around an well I don't have to tell you fellows, you guys know that.

ERDELATZ: When you left your home this morning Dan, was it your intention to confront the Mayor, Supervisor Milk or anyone else with that gun?

WHITE: No, I, I, what I wanted to do was just, talk to him, you know, I, I ah, I didn't even know if I was going to be reappointed or not be reappointed. *Why do we do things, you know, why did I, I don't know. No, I, I* just wanted to talk to him that's all an at least have him be honest with me an tell me why he was doing it, not because I was a bad Supervisor or anything but, you know, I never killed anybody before. I never shot anybody . . .

ERDELATZ: Why did . . .

WHITE: . . . I didn't even, I didn't even know if I wanted to kill him. I just shot him, I don't know.

ERDELATZ: What type of gun is that you were carrying, Dan?

WHITE: It's a .38, a two-inch .38.

ERDELATZ: And do you know how many shots you fired?

WHITE: Uh . . . no I don't, I don't. I, I out of instinct when I, I reloaded the gun ah . . . you know, it's just the training I guess I had, you know.

ERDELATZ: Where did you reload?

WHITE: I reloaded in my office when, when I was I couldn't out in the hall.

Pause.

ERDELATZ: And how many bullets did you have with you?

WHITE: I, I, I don't know, I ah . . . the gun was loaded an, an, I had some ah . . . extra shots you know, I just, I, 'cause, I kept the gun with, with a box of shells and just grabbed some.

ERDELATZ: Inspector Falzon?

FALZON: No questions. Is there anything you'd like to add, Dan, before we close this statement?

WHITE: Well it's just that, I never really intended to hurt anybody. It's just this past several months, it got to the point I couldn't take it and I never wanted the job for ego or, you know, perpetuate myself or anything like that. I was trying to do a good job for the city.

FALZON: Inspector Erdelatz and I ah . . . appreciate your cooperation and the truthfulness of your statement.

Lights change. WHITE *sobbing.* MARY ANN WHITE *sobbing,* JURORS *sobbing.* FALZON *moved.*

NORMAN: I think that is all. You may examine.

COURT: Do you want to take a recess at this time?

SCHMIDT: Why don't we take a brief recess?

COURT: Let me admonish you ladies and gentlemen of the jury, not to discuss this case among yourselves nor with anyone else, nor allow anyone to speak to you about the case, nor are you to form or express an opinion until the matter has been submitted to you.

House lights up. Screen: "Recess."

END OF ACT ONE

ACT TWO: In Defense of Murder

As audience enters, documentary images of Milk and Moscone on screen.

*MOSCONE *(On video)*: My late father was a guard at San Quentin, and who I was visiting one day, and who showed to me, and then explained the function of, the uh, the uh death chamber. And it just seemed inconceivable to me, though I was pretty young at the time, that in this society that I had been trained to believe was the most effective and efficient of all societies, that the only way we could deal with violent crime would be to do the ultimate ourselves, and that's to governmentally sanction the taking of another person's life.

*MILK *(On video)*: Two days after I was elected I got a phone call—the voice was quite young. It was from Altoona, Pennsylvania. And the person said, "Thanks." And you've got to elect gay people so that that young child, and the thousands upon thousands like that child, know that there's hope for a better world. There's hope for a better tomorrow. Without hope, they'll only gaze at those blacks, the Asians, the disabled, the seniors, the us'es, the us'es. Without hope, the us'es give up. I know that you cannot live on hope alone. But without it, life is not worth living. And you, and you, and you, gotta give 'em hope. Thank you very much.

Lights up. Courtroom. FALZON *on witness stand.* DAN WHITE *at defense table sobbing.* MARY ANN WHITE *behind him sobbing.* FIVE JURORS *sobbing.*

WHITE *(Audio)*: Well, it's just that I never really intended to hurt anybody. It's just this past several months, it got to the point I couldn't take it and I never wanted the job for ego or, you know, perpetuate myself or anything like that. I was just trying to do a good job for the city.

FALZON *(Audio)*: Inspector Erdelatz and I ah . . . appreciate your cooperation and the truthfulness of your statement.

FALZON *switches tape off.*

NORMAN: I think that is all. You may examine.

Lights change. Screen: "Inspector Frank Falzon, Witness for the Prosecution." Screen: "Act Two: In Defense of Murder."

SCHMIDT: Inspector Falzon, you mentioned that you had known Dan White in the past, prior to November 27th, 1978?

---

*Monologues by Milk and Moscone excerpted from *The Times of Harvey Milk*, a film by Robert Epstein and Richard Schmeichen.

FALZON: Yes, sir, quite well.

SCHMIDT: About how long have you known him?

FALZON: According to Dan, it goes way back to the days
 we attended St. Elizabeth's Grammar School together, but
 we went to different high schools.
 I attended St. Ignatius, and he attended Riordan.
 He walked up to me one day at the Jackson Playground,
 with spikes over his shoulders, glove in his hand,
 and asked if he could play on my team.
 I told him it was the police team,
 and he stated that he was a new recruit at Northern Station,
 wanted to play on the police softball team,
 and since that day Dan White and I
 have been very good friends.

SCHMIDT: You knew him fairly well then, that is fair?

FALZON: As well as I know anybody, I believed.

SCHMIDT: Can you tell me, when you saw him first on November 27th, 1978,
 how did he appear physically to you?

FALZON: Destroyed. This was not the Dan White I had known, not at all.
 That day I saw a shattered individual,
 both mentally and physically in appearance,
 who appeared to me to be shattered.

 Dan White, the man I knew
 prior to Monday, the 27th of November, 1978,
 was a man among men.

SCHMIDT: Knowing, with regard to the shootings of Mayor Moscone and
 Harvey Milk, knowing Dan White as you did, is he the type of man that
 could have premeditatedly and deliberately shot those people?

NORMAN: Objection as calling for an opinion and conclusion.

COURT: Sustained.

SCHMIDT: Knowing him as you do, have you ever seen anything in his past that
 would lead you to believe he was capable of cold-bloodedly shooting
 somebody?

NORMAN: Same objection.

COURT: Sustained.

SCHMIDT: Your Honor, at this point I have anticipated that maybe there would
 be some argument with regard to opinions not only as to Inspector Falzon,
 but with a number of other witnesses that I intend to call, and accordingly
 I have prepared a memorandum of what I believe to be the appropriate
 law. *(Shows memo)*

COURT: I have no quarrel with your authorities, but I think the form of the
 questions that you asked were objectionable.

SCHMIDT: The questions were calculated to bring out an opinion on the state
 of mind and—I believe that a lay person, if he is an intimate acquaintance,

surely can hazard such an opinion. I believe that Inspector Falzon, as a police officer, has an opinion.

COURT: Get the facts from this witness. I will let you get those facts, whatever they are.

SCHMIDT: All right, we will try that. Inspector Falzon, again, you mentioned that you were quite familiar with Dan White; can you tell me something about the man's character, as to the man that you knew prior to the—prior to November 27th, 1978?

NORMAN: Objection as being irrelevant and vague.

COURT: Overruled. *(To* FALZON) Do you understand the question?

FALZON: I do, basically, Your Honor.

COURT: All right, you may answer it.

NORMAN: Well, Your Honor, character for what?

COURT: Overruled. *(To* FALZON) You may answer it.

FALZON: The Dan White that I knew prior to Monday, November 27, 1978,
was a man who seemed to excel in pressure situations,
and it seemed that the greater the pressure, the more enjoyment that Dan had,
exceeding at what he was trying to do.

Examples would be in his sports life,
that I can relate to,
and for the first time in the history of the State of California,
there was a law enforcement softball tournament held in 1971.

The San Francisco Police Department entered
that softball tournament along with other major departments,
Los Angeles included,
and Dan White was not only named on the All-Star Team
at the end of the tournament,
but named the most valuable player.

He was just outstanding under pressure situations,
when men would be on base and that clutch hit was needed.

At the end of the tournament, a dinner was held,
the umpires were invited,
and one individual had umpired baseball games for over 30 years,
made the comment that Dan White
was the best ballplayer he had ever seen participate
in any tournament in South Lake Tahoe.

Another example of Dan White's attitude toward pressure
was that when he decided to run for the District 8 Supervisor's seat,
and I can still vividly remember the morning

he walked into the Homicide Detail and sat down to—
announced that he was going to run for City Supervisor,

I said: "How are you going to do it, Dan?
Nobody heard of Dan White. How are you going to go out there,
win this election?"

He said: "I'm going to do it the way the people want it to be done,
knock on their doors, go inside, shake their hands,
let them know what Dan White stands for."

And he said: "Dan White is going to represent them.
There will be a voice in City Hall, you watch, I'll make it."

He did what he said he was going to do,
he ran, won the election.

SCHMIDT: Given these things that you mentioned about Dan White, was there anything in his character that you saw of him, prior to those tragedies of the 27th of November, that would have led you to believe that he would ever kill somebody cold-bloodedly?
NORMAN: Objection, irrelevant.
COURT: Overruled.
NORMAN: Let me state my grounds for the record.
COURT: Overruled.
NORMAN: Thank you, Judge. It's irrelevant and called for his opinion and speculation.
COURT: Overruled. *(To* FALZON*)* You may answer that.
FALZON: Yes, Your Honor.

I'm aware—I'm hesitating only because
there was something I saw in Dan's personality
that didn't become relevant to me
until I was assigned this case.

He had a tendency to run, occasionally,
from situations.
I saw this flaw, and I asked him about it,
and his response was that his ultimate goal
was to purchase a boat, just travel around the world,
get away from everybody,
and yet the Dan White that I was talking to
was trying to be involved with people,
constantly being a fireman,
being a policeman, being a Supervisor.

He wanted to be helpful to people,
and yet he wanted to run away from them.
That did not make sense to me.

Today, this is the only flaw in Dan White's character
that I can cite up here, and testify about.

Otherwise, to me, Dan White was an exemplary individual,
a man that I was proud to know and be associated with.

SCHMIDT: Do you think he cracked? Do you think there was something wrong with him on November 27th?

NORMAN: Objection as calling for an opinion and speculation.

COURT: Sustained.

SCHMIDT: I have nothing further. *(Turns back)* Inspector, I have one last question. Did you ever see him act out of revenge the whole time you have known him?

NORMAN: Objection. That calls for speculation.

COURT: No, overruled, and this is as to his observations and contacts. Overruled.

FALZON: The only time Dan White could have acted out in revenge
is when he took the opposite procedure
in hurting himself,
by quitting the San Francisco Police Department.

SCHMIDT: Nothing further. Thank you, sir.

NORMAN: Inspector Falzon, you regard yourself as a close friend to Mr. Daniel White, don't you?

FALZON: Yes, sir.

NORMAN: Do you regard yourself as a *very* close friend of Mr. Daniel White?

FALZON: I would consider myself a close friend of yours, if that can relate to you my closeness with Dan White.

Pause. NORMAN *uncomfortable.*

NORMAN: Of course, you haven't known me as long as you have known Mr. Daniel White, have you, Inspector?

FALZON: Just about the same length of time, Counsel.

Long pause.

NORMAN: Inspector Falzon, while you've expressed some shock at these tragedies, would you subscribe to the proposition that there's a first time for everything?

FALZON: It's obvious in this case; yes, sir.

NORMAN: Thank you. (HE *sits.* FALZON *leaves the witness stand and takes his seat beside him at the prosecutor's table)* The Prosecution rests.

Lights change. Screen: "The Prosecution Rests." Commotion in court.

COURT: Order.

Gavel. Lights. FREITAS alone.

FREITAS: I was the D.A.
Obviously in some respects, the trial ruined me.
This trial . . .

Screen: Pictures of WHITE as fire hero. Screen: "The Defense." Subliminal music. Lights up. FOUR CHARACTER WITNESSES dressed as fire chief, police officer, fireman, City Supervisor (suit).

SHERATT (*Fire chief*): Dan White was an excellent firefighter. In fact, he was commended for a rescue at Geneva Towers. The award hasn't been given to him as yet, uh . . .

FREDIANI (*Fireman*): Dan White was the valedictorian of the Fire Department class. He was voted so by members of the class.

Screen: Still of WHITE as valedictorian.

MILK'S FRIEND: When I was in the hospital, what galled me most was the picture of Dan White as the All-American Boy.

SHERRATT: but a meritorious advisory board and fire commission were going to present Mr. White with a Class C medal.

Screen: Still of WHITE as fire hero.

FREDIANI: Everybody liked Dan.

SCHMIDT: Did you work with Dan as a policeman?

SULLIVAN (*Policeman*): Yes, I did.

MILK'S FRIEND: Maybe as a gay man, I understand the tyranny of the All-American Boy.

Screen: Still of WHITE as police officer.

FREDIANI: He loved sports and I loved sports.

Screen: Still of WHITE as Golden Gloves boxer.

SULLIVAN: Dan White as a police officer, was a very fair police officer on the street.

MILK'S FRIEND: Maybe because I am so often his victim.

GWENN: I followed the trial in the papers.

SCHMIDT: Having had the experience of being a police officer, is it unusual for persons that have been police officers to carry guns?

SULLIVAN: Uh, pardon me, Mr. Schmidt?

GWENN: I thought then something was wrong with this picture.

SCHMIDT: I say, it is uncommon that ex-police officers would carry guns?

GWENN: Something was wrong, we thought, when the Chief Inspector of Homicide became the chief character witness for the defense.

SULLIVAN: No, it is a common thing that former police officers will carry guns.

GWENN: Why didn't the Chief Inspector of Homicide ask Dan White how he got into City Hall with a loaded gun?

SCHMIDT: Without a permit?

SULLIVAN: Yes.

GWENN: White reloaded after shooting the Mayor. If it was "reflex," police training, why didn't he reload again after shooting Harvey Milk?

SCHMIDT: Is there anything in his character that would have led you to believe he was capable of shooting two persons?

NORMAN: Objection.

COURT: Overruled.

SULLIVAN: No, nothing whatever.

GWENN: And what can explain the coup de grace shots
White fired into the backs of their heads as they lay there
helpless on the floor?

DOLSON (*Supervisor*): Dan in my opinion was a person who *saved* lives.

GWENN: Where is the prosecution?

Pause.

FREITAS: I mean, I would have remained in politics. Except for this. I was voted out of office.

SCHMIDT (*To* DOLSON): Supervisor Dolson, you saw him on November 27th, 1978, did you not?

DOLSON: I did.

FREITAS: In hindsight, you know, I would have changed a lot of things.

SCHMIDT: What did you see?

FREITAS: But hindsight is always perfect vision.

Screen: Still of WHITE *as City Supervisor outside City Hall.*

DOLSON: What I saw made me want to cry . . .
Dan was always so neat.
Looked like a marine on parade;
and he made me feel ashamed of the way I usually looked,
and here he was, this kid, who was badly disheveled,
looking like he had been crying.

GWENN: What pressures were you under *indeed*?

DOLSON: and he had his hands cuffed behind him,
   which was something I never expected to see.
   He looked crushed, looked like he was absolutely *devastated*. (Sobs)
GWENN: As the *"victim"* sat in the courtroom
   shielded by bulletproof glass,
   we heard of policemen and firemen sporting
   "Free Dan White" T-shirts
   as they raised 100,000 dollars for Dan White's defense fund,
   and the same message began appearing
   in spray paint on walls around the city.
   FREE DAN WHITE.
DOLSON: I put my arm around him, told him that everything
   was going to be all right,
   but how everything was going to be all right,
   I don't know. (HE *is deeply moved*)

   MARY ANN WHITE *sobs.*

GWENN: And the trial was still happening,
SCHMIDT (*Deeply moved*): Thank you. I have nothing further.

   DOLSON *sobs.*

GWENN: but the tears at the Hall of Justice are all for Dan White.

   ALL *exit. Lights change.* FREITAS *alone in empty courtroom, nervous, fidgeting.*

FREITAS: I was voted out of office.
   (*Screen: "Joseph Freitas, Jr., Former D.A."*)
   Well, I'm out of politics and I don't know whether
   I'll get back into politics
   because it certainly did set back my personal ah . . .
   aspirations as a public figure dramatically.
   I don't know . . .

   You know, there was an attempt to not allow our office to prosecute the case
   because I was close to Moscone myself.
   And we fought against that.
   I was confident—(*Laughs*)
   I chose Tom Norman because he was the senior homicide prosecutor
   for twenty years and he was quite successful at it.
   I don't know . . .

   There was a great division in the city then, you know.
   The city was divided all during that period.

George was a liberal Democrat and Dick Hongisto.
I was considered a liberal Democrat
and George as you'll remember was elected
Mayor over John Barbagelata who was the leader
of what was considered the Right in town.
And it was a narrow victory.
So, after his election, Barbagelata persisted in attacking them
and keeping
I thought—
keeping the city divided.
It divided on emerging constituencies like
the gay constituency.
That's the one that was used to cause the most divisive
emotions more than any other.
So the divisiveness in the city was there.

I mean that was the whole point of this political fight
between Dan White
and Moscone and Milk:
The fight was over who controlled the city.

The Right couldn't afford to lose Dan.
He was their swing vote on the Board of Supervisors.
He could block the Milk/Moscone agenda.
That was why Milk didn't want Dan White on the Board.
So, it was political, the murders.

Maybe I should have,
again in hindsight, possibly Tom,
even though his attempts to do that may have been ruled inadmissable,
possibly Tom should have been a little stronger in that area.
But again, at the time . . . I mean,
even the press was shocked at the outcome . . .

But—
Well, I think that what the jury had already bought
was White's background—
Now that's what was really on trial.
Dan White sat there and waved his little American flag
and they acquitted him.
They convicted George and Harvey.
Now if this had been a poor black or a poor Chicano
or a poor white janitor who'd been fired,
or the husband of an alleged girlfriend of Moscone's
I don't think they would have bought the diminished capacity defense.

But whereas they have a guy who was a member of a
county Board of Supervisors who left the police department,
who had served in the army, who was a fireman,
who played baseball—
I think that's what they were caught up in—
that kind of person *must* have been crazy to do this.
I would have interpreted it differently.
Not to be held to a higher standard, but uh . . .
that he had all the tools to be responsible.

One of the things people said was:
"Why didn't you talk more about George's background, his family life,
    etc.?"
Well . . .
One of the reasons is that Tom Norman did know that,
had he opened up that area,
they were prepared,
yeah—
they were prepared to smear George—
bring up the incident in Sacramento.
With the woman—
(And other things.)
It would be at best a wash,
so why get into it?
If you know they're going to bring out things
that aren't positive.
We wanted to let the city heal. We—
And after Jonestown . . .
Well—it would have been the
city on trial.

If the jury had stuck to the facts alone,
I mean, the confession alone was enough to convict him . . .
I mean, look at this kid that shot Reagan,
it was the same thing. All the way through that,
they said, my friends—
"Well, Christ, look at what the prosecutors went through on this one,
    Joe—
It's tragic that this has to be the kind of experience
that will make you feel better.

And then about White being anti-gay
well . . .
White inside himself may have been anti-gay, but

that Milk was his target . . .
As I say—*Malice was there.*
Milk led the fight to keep White off the Board,
which makes the murder all the more rational.
I know the gay community thinks the murder was anti-gay:
political in that sense. But
I think, they're wrong.

Ya know, some people—in the gay community—
ah—even said I threw the trial.
Before this, I was considered a great friend
to the gay community.
Why would I want to throw the trial,
this trial—
in an election year?

Oh, there were accusations you wouldn't believe . . .

At the trial, a woman . . . it may have been one of the jurors—
I can't remember . . .
Actually said—
"But what would Mary Ann White do without her husband?"
And I remember my outrage.
She never thought,
"What will Gina Moscone do without George?"
I must tell you that it's hard for me to talk about a lot
of these things,
all of this is just the—just
the tip of the iceberg . . .

We thought—Tommy and I—Tom Norman and I—
We thought it was an open-and-shut case
of first-degree murder.

Lights.

NORMAN: It wasn't just an automatic reaction when he fired those last two shots
into George Moscone's *brains* was it, Doctor?
COURT: Let's move on, Mr. Norman. You are just arguing with the witnesses
now.
NORMAN: Your Honor—
COURT: Let's move on.

Screen: "The Psychiatric Defense." Lights up. PSYCHIATRISTS, *conservative dress,
in either separate witness stands or a multiple stand unit.*

SOLOMON: I think he was out of control and in an unreasonable stage. And I think if the gun had held, you know, maybe more bullets, maybe he would have shot more bullets. I don't know.

LUNDE: This wasn't just some mild case of the blues.

SOLOMON: I think that, you know, maybe Mr. Moscone would have been just as dead with one bullet. I don't know.

JONES: I think he was out of control.

DELMAN: Yes.

NORMAN: George Moscone was shot four times, Doctor. The gun had five cartridges in it. Does that change your opinion in any way?

SOLOMON: No. I think he just kept shooting for awhile.

NORMAN *throws his notes down.*

SCHMIDT: Now, there is another legal term we deal with in the courtroom, and that is variously called "malice" or "malice aforethought." And this must be present in order to convict for murder in the first degree.

JONES: Okay, let me preface this by saying I am not sure how malice is defined. I'll give you what my understanding is.

In order to have malice, you would have to be able to do certain things: to be able to be intent to kill somebody unlawfully. You would have to be able to do something for a base and antisocial purpose. You would have to be aware of the duty imposed on you not to do that, not to unlawfully kill somebody or do something for a base, antisocial purpose, that involved a risk of death, and you would have to be able to act, despite having that awareness of that, that you are not supposed to do that, and so you would have to know that you are not supposed to do it, and then also act despite— keeping in mind that you are not supposed to do it.

Is that your answer—your question?

SCHMIDT: I think so.

Pause.

JONES *(Laughs):* I felt that he had the capacity to do the first three:
that he had the capacity to intend to kill,
but that doesn't take much, you know,
to try to kill somebody,
it's not a highfalutin' mental state.

I think he had the capacity to do something for a base and antisocial purpose.
I think he had the capacity to know that there was a duty
imposed on him not to do that,
but *I don't think he had the capacity to hold that notion*

in his mind while he was acting;
so that I think that the depression,
plus the moment, the tremendous emotion of the moment,
with the depression,
reduced his capacity for conforming conduct.
(Pause)
As ridiculous as this sounds, even to the point of instituting
to kill the Mayor,
what he describes is more simply—
is striking out, not intending to kill,
well, obviously, if you have a gun in your hand,
and you are striking out,
you know you are going to cause at least great bodily harm,
if not death,
but as near as I can come to the state of mind at that time,
he was just, you know, striking out.
(Pause)
In fact, I asked him:
"Why didn't you hit them?"
And he was flabbergasted that I asked such a thing,
because it was contrary to his code of behavior,
you know, he was taken aback, kind of—
hit them seemed ridiculous to him—
because it would have been so unfair,
since he could have defeated them so easily
in a fistfight.

SCHMIDT: Thank you. (HE *sits; to* NORMAN) You may examine.

NORMAN: Doctor Jones, when let off at City Hall the accused was let off at the Polk Street entrance and then walked a block and a half to Van Ness Avenue. Why wouldn't he just enter City Hall through the main entrance?

JONES: He got towards the top of the stairs, then looked up, saw the metal detector and thought: "Oh, my goodness, I got that gun."

Pause.

NORMAN: Doctor, why would he care whether there was a metal detector there, and that a gun would have been discovered upon his person?

JONES: Well, I would presume that would mean some degree of hassle. I mean, I presume that the metal detector would see if somebody is trying to bring a weapon in.

NORMAN: That is usually why they have it. *(Pause)* Did he realize at that time that he was unlawfully carrying a concealable firearm?

JONES: I presume so.

NORMAN: Dr. Jones, if it's a fact that Dan White shot George Moscone twice in the body, and that when George Moscone fell to the floor disabled, he shot twice more into the right side of George Moscone's head at a distance of between 12 and 18 inches, he made a decision at that time, didn't he, to either discharge the gun into the head of George Moscone, or not discharge the gun into the head of George Moscone?

JONES: If decision means he behaved in that way, then, yes.

NORMAN: Well, didn't he have to make some kind of choice based upon some reasoning process?

JONES: Oh, no, not based on reasoning necessarily. I think—I don't think that I—you know, great emotional turmoil in context of major mood disorder—he was enraged and anxious and frustrated in addition to the underlying depression, I think that after Moscone says "How's your family?" or "What's your wife going to do?," at that point, I think that it's—it's over.

NORMAN: It's over for George Moscone.

SOLOMON: I think that if you look at the gun as a transitional object, you can see that transitional objects are clung to in—in situations of great—of anxiety and insecurity, as one sees with children—

NORMAN: Doctor, are you telling us that a person who has lived an otherwise law-abiding life and an otherwise moral life could not premeditate and deliberate as is contemplated by the definition of first-degree murder?!

SOLOMON: I'm not saying that absolutely. Obviously, it's more difficult for a person who lives a highly moral life. And this individual, Dan White, had, if you want—a hypertrophy complex. Hypertrophy meaning overdeveloped. Rigidly. Morally. Overdeveloped—

But I would say in general, yes.

I don't think you'd even kill Mr. Schmidt if you lost this case.

NORMAN: It's unlikely.

SOLOMON: You may be very angry, but I don't think you will do it because I think you are probably a very moral and law-abiding citizen, and I think if you did it, I would certainly recommend a psychiatric examination, because I think there would be a serious possibility that you had flipped. *(Pause)* It's most interesting to me how split off his feelings were at this time.

LUNDE: Dan White had classical symptoms that are described in diagnostic manuals for depression and, of course, he had characteristics of compulsive personality, which happens to be kind of a bad combination in those sorts of people.

NORMAN *(Frustrated)*: You are aware that he took a gun with him when he determined to see George Moscone, a loaded gun?

SOLOMON: Yes.

NORMAN: Why did he take that gun, in your opinion, Dr. Solomon?

SOLOMON: I might say that I think there are symbolic aspects to this.

COURT: Let's move on to another question.

NORMAN: Well, Your Honor . . .

COURT: Let's move on.

NORMAN (*Frustrated*): All right. Dr. Delman, after he went in the building armed with a gun through a window and went up to see George Moscone, at the time he came in to see George Moscone, do you feel that he was angry with George Moscone?

DELMAN: Yes.

NORMAN: When George Moscone told him that he wasn't going to appoint him, do you think that that brought about and increased any more anger?

DELMAN: Yes.

NORMAN: All right. Now there was some point in there when he shot George Moscone, isn't that true?

DELMAN: Yes.

NORMAN: Do you know how many times he shot him?

DELMAN: I believe it's four.

NORMAN: Well, Doctor, do you put any significance upon the circumstances that he shot George Moscone twice in the head?

DELMAN: The question is, "Do I put any significance in it?"

NORMAN: Yes.

DELMAN: I really have no idea why that happened.

NORMAN: Well, Doctor, do you think he knew that if you shot a man twice in the head that it was likely to surely kill him?

DELMAN: I'm sure that he knew that shooting a man in the head would kill him, Mr. Norman.

NORMAN: Thank you! (HE *sits*)

SCHMIDT: But, it is your conclusion, Doctor, that Dan White could not premeditate or deliberate, within the meaning we have discussed here, on November 27th, 1978?

DELMAN: That is correct.

NORMAN *slaps hand to head. Lights.*

BLINDER: I teach forensic psychiatry.
I teach about the uses and abuses of psychiatry in the judicial system.
The courts tend to place psychiatry in a position
where it doesn't belong. Where it becomes the sole arbiter
between guilt and innocence.
There is also a tendency in the stresses of the adversary system
to polarize a psychiatric statement so that a psychiatrist finds himself trying
to put labels on normal stressful behavior,
and *everything* becomes a mental illness.
And I think that is an abuse.
(*Refers to his notes*)
Dan White found City Hall rife of corruption.
With the possible exceptions of Dianne Feinstein and Harvey Milk,

the Supervisors seemed to make their judgments, their votes,
on the basis of what was good for them,
rather than what was good for the city.
And this was a very frustrating thing for Mr. White:
to want to do a good job for his constituents and find he
was continually defeated.

In addition to these stresses, there were
attacks by the press
and there were threats of literal attacks on Supervisors.
He told me a number of Supervisors like himself
carried a gun to scheduled meetings.
Never any relief from these tensions.

Whenever he felt things were not going right,
he would abandon his usual program of exercise and good nutrition
and start gorging himself on junk foods:
Twinkies, Coca-Cola.

Soon Mr. White was just sitting in front of the TV.
Ordinarily, he reads. (Mr. White has always been an identifiable Jack
   London adventurer.)

But now, getting very depressed about the fact he would not be reappointed,
he just sat there before the TV
binging on Twinkies.
(Screen: "The Twinkie Defense")
He couldn't sleep.
He was tossing and turning on the couch in the living room
so he wouldn't disturb his wife on the bed.

Virtually no sexual contact at this time.
He was dazed, confused, had crying spells,
became increasingly ill,
and wanted to be left alone.

He told his wife:
"Don't bother cooking any food for me.
I will just munch on these potato chips."

Mr. White stopped shaving
and refused to go out of the house
to help Denise rally support.

He started to receive information that he would not be reappointed
from unlikely sources.
This was very stressing to him.

Again, it got to be cupcakes, candy bars.
He watched the sun come up on Monday morning.

Finally, at 9:00 Denise called.
He decides to go down to City Hall.
He shaves and puts on his suit.
He sees his gun—lying on the table.
Ammunition.
He simultaneously puts these in his pocket.
Denise picks him up.
He's feeling anxious about a variety of things.
He's sitting in the car hyperventilating,
blowing on his hands, repeating:
"Let him tell me to my face why he won't reappoint me.
Did he think I can't take it?
I am a man.
I can take it."

He goes down to City Hall, and I sense that time is short
so let me bridge this by saying that as I believe
it has been testified to,
he circumvents the mental [sic] detector,
goes to the side window,
gets an appointment with the Mayor.
The Mayor almost directly tells him,
"I am not going to reappoint you."

The Mayor puts his arm around him saying:
"Let's have a drink.
What are you going to do now, Dan?
Can you get back into the Fire Department?
What about your family?
Can your wife get her job back?
What's going to happen to them now?

Pause. Lights up low on MARY ANN WHITE.

Somehow this inquiry directed to his family struck a nerve.
The Mayor's voice started to fade out and Mr. White felt

"As if I were in a dream."
He started to leave and then inexplicably turned around
and like a reflex
drew his revolver.
He had no idea how many shots he fired.

The similar event occurred
in Supervisor Milk's office. *[sic]*

He remembers being shocked by the sound of the gun
going off for the second time like a cannon.
He tells me that he was aware that he engaged in a lethal act,
but tells me he gave no thought to his wrongfulness.
As he put it to me:
"I had no chance to even think about it."

He remembers running out of the building,
driving, I think, to church,
making arrangements to meet his wife,
and then going from the church
to the Police Department.

Pause. BLINDER *exhausted.*

SCHMIDT: Doctor, you have mentioned the ingestion of sugar and sweets and that sort of thing. There are certain theories with regard to sugar and sweets and the ingestion thereof, and I'd like to just touch on that briefly with the jury. Does that have any significance, or could it possibly have any significance?

BLINDER *(Turns to jury)*: First, there is a substantial body of evidence that in susceptible individuals, large quantities of what we call junk food, high-sugar-content food with lots of preservatives, can precipitate antisocial and even violent behavior.

There have been studies, for example, where they have taken so-called career criminals and taken them off all their junk food and put them on meat and potatoes and their criminal records immediately evaporate. *(Pause)* It's contradictory and ironic, but the way it works is that for such a person, the American Dream is a Nightmare. For somebody like Dan White.

SCHMIDT: Thank you, Doctor.

Lights fade on PSYCHIATRISTS. *Pause. Blazing white lights up on* MARY ANN WHITE. SHE *is almost blinded.* SHE *comes forward.*

You are married to this man, is that correct?

MARY ANN: Yes.

SCHMIDT: When did you first meet him?

MARY ANN: I met him—*(Sobbing)*

SCHMIDT: If you want to take any time//just let us know.

MARY ANN *(Pulling herself together)*: I met him in April, 1976 . . .

SCHMIDT: And you were married//and you took a trip?

MARY ANN: Yes. Yes, we went to Ireland on our honeymoon
   because Danny just had this feeling that Ireland was like a place
   that was just peaceful.

   He just really likes—loves—everything about Ireland and so we—*(Sobbing)*

SCHMIDT: Excuse me.

MARY ANN: —so we went there//for about five wee—

SCHMIDT: During that period did you notice anything//unusual about his
   behavior?

MARY ANN: Yes, I mean, you know, when we went I thought—went thinking
   it was going to be kind of romantic,
   and when we got there, it was all of a sudden,
   he went into almost like a two-week-long mood,
   like I had seen before, but I had never seen one, I guess,
   all the way through,
   because when we were going out, I might see him for a day,
   and being a fireman, he would work a day,
   and then I wouldn't see him,
   and when we got to Ireland . . .

   I mean, I was just newly married and I thought:
   "What did I do?"

SCHMIDT: After he was on the Board, did you notice these moods//become
   more frequent?

MARY ANN: Yes, he had talked to me about how hard the job was on him.
   You know, from June he started to talk about how it was.
   Obviously you can sense when you are not sleeping together,
   and you are not really growing together,
   and he would say,
   "Well, I can't—I can't really think of anyone else
   when I don't even like myself."
   And I said, "It's just him.
   He's not satisfied with what I'm doing
   and I don't like myself//and so I can't . . . "

SCHMIDT: Did you see him on the morning of . . . November 27th?

MARY ANN: Yes//I did.

Note: // = overlap; next speaker starts, first speaker continues.

SCHMIDT: And at that time did he indicate what he was going to do//that day?
MARY ANN: It was just, he was going **to stay** *home.*
(*With uncharacteristic force*) He wasn't leaving the house.

Beat. SCHMIDT *looks to jury.*

SCHMIDT: Later that morning, did you receive a call//to meet him somewhere?
MARY ANN: Yes. I did. Yes, I went to St. Mary's Cathedral.
 I went
 and I saw him
 and he walked over toward me and I—
 I could see that he had been crying,
 and I, I just kind of looked at him
 and he just looked at me
 and he said,
 he said,
 "I shot the Mayor and Harvey."
SCHMIDT: Thank you.

DAN WHITE *sobs.* SCHMIDT *puts hand on* WHITE*'s shoulder.* MARY ANN WHITE
stumbles off the stand to her husband. WHITE *shields his eyes.* SHE *looks as if* SHE
will embrace him.

The defense is prepared to rest at this time.

MARY ANN WHITE *sobs. Hyperreal sound of high heels echoing on marble. Mumbled
Hail Marys.*

COURT: Let me admonish you ladies and gentlemen of the jury,
 not to discuss this case among yourselves nor with anyone else,
 nor to allow anyone to speak to you about the case,
 nor are you to form or express an opinion until the matter has been
  submitted to you.

ALL *exit. Screen: "The Defense Rests."*

•MILK'S FRIEND (*Enters alone*):
 We got back from the airport the night of the 27th
 And my roommate said:
 There's going to be a candlelight march.
 By now, we thought it had to have reached City Hall.
 So we went directly there. From the airport to City Hall.

*Dialogue from *The Times of Harvey Milk,* a film by Robert Epstein and Richard
 Schmeichen.

And there were maybe 75 people there.
And I remember thinking:
My God is this all anybody . . . cared?

Somebody said: No, the march hasn't gotten here yet.

So we then walked over to Market Street,
which was two or three blocks away.
And looked down it.
And Market Street runs in a straight line out to the Castro area.
And as we turned the corner,
there were people as wide as this wide street
As far as you could see.

Screens flooded with the lights of candles. Documentary footage of the march. We see what MILK'S FRIEND *describes. Music: Barber Adagio. The* ENTIRE COMPANY *enters holding candles.*

• YOUNG MOTHER *(After a long while)*:
Thousands and thousands of people,
And that feeling of such loss.

Music continues.

• GWENN: It was one of the most eloquent expressions of a
community's response to violence
that I have ever seen . . .
A MOURNER *(Black armband)*: I'd like to read from the transcript of Harvey
Milk's political will.
(Reads) This is Harvey Milk speaking on Friday, November 18.
This tape is to be played only in the event of my death
by assassination.
(Screen: Pictures of Milk)
I've given long and considerable thought to this,
and not just since the election.
I've been thinking about this for some time prior to the election
and certainly over the years.
I fully realize that a person who stands for what I stand for—
a gay activist—
becomes a target for a person who is insecure, terrified,
afraid or very disturbed themselves.

WHITE *enters, stops.*

Knowing that I could be assassinated at any moment
or any time,
I feel it's important that some people should understand
my thoughts.
So the following are my thoughts, my wishes, my desires,
whatever.
I'd like to pass them on and played for the appropriate people.
The first and most obvious concern is that
if I was to be shot and killed,
the Mayor has the power,
George Moscone,
(Screen: Pictures of Moscone, the funeral, the mourners, the widow)
of appointing my successor . . .
to the Board of Supervisors.
I cannot prevent some people
from feeling angry and frustrated and mad,
but I hope that they would not demonstrate violently.
If a bullet should enter my brain,
let that bullet destroy every closet door.

Gavel. ALL MOURNERS *blow out candles.* WHITE *sits. Blackout. Screen: "The People's Rebuttal." Screen: "Dr. Levy, Psychiatrist for the Prosecution." Lights up.*

LEVY: I interviewed the defendant several hours after the shootings of November 27th.

In my opinion, one can get a more accurate diagnosis the closer one examines the suspect after a crime has been committed.

At that time, it appeared to me that Dan White had no remorse for the death of George Moscone.

It appeared to me, he had no remorse for the death of Harvey Milk.

There was nothing in my interview which would suggest to me there was any mental disorder.

I had the feeling that there was some depression but it was not depression that I would consider as a diagnosis.

In fact, I found him to be less depressed than I would have expected him to be.

At that time I saw him, it seemed that he felt himself to be quite justified.
(Looks to notes)
I felt he had the capacity to form malice.
I felt he had the capacity to premeditate. And . . .
I felt he had the capacity to deliberate,
to arrive at a course of conduct weighing considerations.

NORMAN: Did you review the transcript of the proceeding wherein the testimonies of Drs. Jones, Blinder, Solomon, Delman and Lunde were given?

LEVY: Yes. *(Pause)* I found nothing in them that would cause me to revise my opinion.

NORMAN: Thank you, Dr. Levy. *(Sits)*

SCHMIDT *(Stands)*: Dr. Levy, are you a full professor at the University of California?

LEVY: No. I am an associate clinical professor.

SCHMIDT *smiles, looks to jury.*

SCHMIDT: May I inquire of your age, sir?

LEVY: I am 55.

SCHMIDT: Huh. *(Picking up papers)* Doctor, your report is dated November 27, 1978, is it not?

LEVY: Yes.

SCHMIDT: And yet the report was not written on November 27, 1978?

LEVY: No. It would have been within several days//of that time.

SCHMIDT: And then it was dated November 27, 1978?

LEVY: Yes.

SCHMIDT: Well, regardless of the backdating, or whatever, when did you come to your forensic conclusions?

LEVY: I'd say the conclusions would have been on November 27th.

SCHMIDT: And that was after a two-hour talk with Dan White?

LEVY: Yes.

SCHMIDT: Doctor, would it be fair to say that you made some snap decisions?

LEVY: I don't believe//I did.

SCHMIDT: Did you consult with any other doctors?

LEVY: No.

SCHMIDT: Did you review any of the witnesses' statements?

LEVY: No.

SCHMIDT: Did you consult any of the material that was available to you, save and except for the tape of Dan White on the same date?

LEVY: No. That was all that was made available to me//at that time.

SCHMIDT: Now I don't mean to be facetious, but this is a fairly important case, is that fair?

LEVY: I would certainly think so,//yes.

SCHMIDT: But you didn't talk further with Mr. White?

LEVY: No. I was not requested to.

SCHMIDT: And you didn't request to talk to him further?

LEVY: No. I was not going to do a complete assessment.

SCHMIDT: Well, in fact, you didn't do a complete assessment, is that fair?

LEVY: I was not asked to do a complete assessment.

COURT: Doctor, you are fading away.

LEVY: *I was not asked to do a complete assessment.*

SCHMIDT: Thank you. *(Blackout. Commotion in court)* She wants to tell the story so it's not responsive to the questions.

Lights up. Screen: "Supervisor Carol Ruth Silver, Witness for the Prosecution."

SILVER *(Very agitated, speaking fast, heated)*: He asked in what other case did a dispute between Dan White and Harvey Milk arise! And it was the Polk Street closing was another occasion when Harvey requested that Polk Street, which is a heavily gay area in San Francisco, I am sure everybody knows, and on Halloween had traditionally had a huge number of people in costumes and so forth down there and has//traditionally been recommended for closure by the Police Department and—

SCHMIDT: I am going to object to this, Your Honor.

SILVER: It was recommended—

COURT: Just ask the next question.

SILVER: I am sorry.

NORMAN: Did Mr. Milk and Mr. White take positions that were opposite to each other?

SILVER: Yes.

NORMAN: Was there anything that became, well, rather loud and perhaps hostile in connection or consisting between the two?

SILVER: Not loud but very hostile. You have to first understand that this street closure was recommended by the Police Chief and had been done customarily in the years past//and is, was—came up as an uncontested issue practically.

SCHMIDT: Your Honor, I again—

COURT: Please, just make your objection.

SCHMIDT: I'd like to.

COURT: Without going through contortions.

SCHMIDT: There is an objection.

COURT: All right. Sustained.

NORMAN: Miss Silver, did you know, or did you ever see Mr. White to appear to be depressed or to be withdrawn?

SILVER: No.

NORMAN: Thank you. *(Sits)*

SILVER *flabbergasted, upset.*

COURT: All right. Any questions, Mr. Schmidt?

SCHMIDT: Is it *Miss* Silver?

SILVER: Yes.

SCHMIDT *looks to jury, smiles. Lights up on* MOSCONE'S FRIEND.

SCHMIDT: Miss Silver, you never had lunch with Dan White, did you?

SILVER: Did I ever have lunch?

MOSCONE'S FRIEND: George was socially brilliant in that he could find the injustice.

SCHMIDT: I mean the two of you?

SILVER: I don't recall having done so//but I—

MOSCONE'S FRIEND: His mind went immediately to what can we do?

SCHMIDT: Did you socialize frequently?

MOSCONE'S FRIEND: What can we practically do?

SILVER: No, when his son was born//I went to a party at his house and that kind of thing.

SCHMIDT: Did Mr. Norman contact you last week, or did you contact him?

MOSCONE'S FRIEND: Rather like the image of Robert Kennedy in Mississippi in 1964.

SILVER: On Friday morning I called his office to—

MOSCONE'S FRIEND: Y'know, he'd never seen that kind of despair before

SILVER: because I was reading the newspaper—

SCHMIDT: Yes.

MOSCONE'S FRIEND: but when he saw it//he said,

SILVER: And it appeared to me that—

COURT: Don't tell us!

MOSCONE'S FRIEND: "This is *intolerable*."

SILVER: I am sorry.

MOSCONE'S FRIEND: And then he did something about it.

Beat.

COURT: The jurors are told not to read the newspaper, and I am hoping that they haven't//read the newspapers.

SILVER: I apologize.

COURT: Okay.

SCHMIDT: Miss Silver—

COURT: I am sorry, I didn't want to cut her off—

SILVER: No, I understand.

COURT: from any other answer.

SCHMIDT: I think she did complete the answer, Judge. In any event, you contacted Mr. Norman, did you not?

SILVER: Yes, I did.

SCHMIDT: And at that time, you offered to Mr. Norman to round up people who could say that Dan White never looked depressed at City Hall, is that fair?

SILVER: That's right. Well, I offered to testify to that effect and I suggested that there were other people//who could similarly testify to that fact.

SCHMIDT: In fact, you expressed it though you haven't sat here and listened to the testimony in this courtroom?

SILVER: No, I have never been here before Friday when I was subpoenaed//and spent some time in the jury room.

SCHMIDT: But to use your words, after having read what was in the paper, you said that the defense sounded like *(As if* HE *were spitting on his mother's grave)* "bullshit" to you?

SILVER: That's correct.

Subliminal music.

DENMAN: I thought I would be a chief witness for the prosecution.

SCHMIDT: Would that suggest then that perhaps you have a bias in this case?

DENMAN: What was left unsaid was what the trial should have been about.

SILVER: I certainly have a bias.

SCHMIDT: You are a political enemy of Dan White's, is that fair?

SILVER: No, that's not true.

DENMAN: Before, y'know, there was a lot of talk about assassinating the Mayor among thuggish elements of the//Police Officers Association.

SCHMIDT: Did you have any training in psychology or psychiatry?

DENMAN: And those were the cops Dan White was closest to.

SILVER: No more than some of the kind of C.E.B. courses lawyer's psychology for lawyers//kind of training.

DENMAN: I think he knew a lot of guys would think he did the right thing and yeah they would make him a hero.

SCHMIDT: I mean, would you be able to diagnose, say, *manic depression depressed type,* or could you distinguish that from *unipolar depression?*

SILVER: No.

Pause.

DENMAN: I was Dan White's jailer for 72 hours after the assassinations.

SCHMIDT: Did you ever talk to him about his dietary habits or anything like that?

DENMAN: There were no tears.

SILVER: I remember a conversation about nutrition or something like that, but I can't remember//the substance of it.

SCHMIDT: I don't have anything further.

DENMAN: There was no shame.

COURT: Any redirect, Mr. Norman?

NORMAN: Yes.

DENMAN: You got the feeling that he knew exactly what he was doing and there was no remorse.

Pause.

NORMAN: Miss Silver, you were asked if you had a bias in this case. You knew Harvey Milk very well and you liked him, didn't you?

SILVER: I did; and also George Moscone.

NORMAN: Miss Silver, speaking of a bias, had you ever heard the defendant say anything about getting people of whom Harvey Milk numbered himself?

Lights up on MILK'S FRIEND.

SILVER: In the Polk Street debate—
MILK'S FRIEND: The night Harvey was elected,
    I went to bed early
    because it was more happiness than I had been taught
    to deal with.
SILVER: Dan White got up and gave—
    a long diatribe—
MILK'S FRIEND: Next morning we put up signs saying "Thank You."
SILVER: Just a—a very unexpected and very uncharacteristic of Dan,
    long hostile speech about how gays and their lifestyles
    had to be contained and we can't//
    encourage this kind of thing and—
SCHMIDT: I am going to object to this, Your Honor.
COURT: Sustained, okay.
MILK'S FRIEND: During that, Harvey came over and told me
    that he had made a political will
    because he expected he'd be killed.
    And then in the same breath, he said (I'll never forget it):
    "It works, it works . . . "
NORMAN: All right . . . that's all.
MILK'S FRIEND: The system works// . . .
NORMAN: Thank you.

Pause.

DENMAN: When White was being booked, it all seemed fraternal.
    One officer gave Dan a pat on the behind when he was booked,
    sort of a "Hey, catch you later, Dan" pat.
COURT: Any recross?
DENMAN: Some of the officers and deputies were standing around with half-
    smirks on their faces. Some were actually laughing.
SCHMIDT: Just a couple.
DENMAN: The joke they kept telling was,
    "Dan White's mother says to him when he comes home,
    'No, dummy, I said milk and baloney, not Moscone!' "

Pause.

SCHMIDT: Miss Silver, you are a part of the gay community also, are you?
SILVER: Myself?
SCHMIDT: Yes.
SILVER: You mean, am I gay?
SCHMIDT: Yes.

SILVER: No, I'm not.

SCHMIDT: I have nothing further.

MOSCONE'S FRIEND: George would have said, "This is intolerable," and he'd have done something about it.

COURT: All right. . . . You may leave as soon as the bailiff takes the microphone off.

SILVER *sits for awhile, shaken.*

COURT: Next witness, please.

DENMAN: I don't know . . .
All I can say is, if Dan White was as depressed
as the defense psychiatrists said he was before he went to City Hall,
then shooting these people sure seemed to clear up his mind . . .

SILVER *exits towards door.* LU *with TV lights.*

LU *(On camera)*: Miss Silver, Supervisor Silver, would you like to elaborate on
Mr. White's anti-gay feelings or hostility to Harvey Milk or George Moscone?

SILVER: No comment, right now.

SILVER *distraught, pushes through crowd, rushes past.*

LU *(On camera)*: Did you feel you were baited, did you have your say?

SILVER *(Blows up)*: I said I have no comment at this time!!! *(Exits)*

COURT: Mr. Norman? Next witness?

NORMAN: Nothing further. Those are all the witnesses we have to present.

COURT: The People rest?

NORMAN: Yes.

COURT: Does the Defense have any witnesses?

SCHMIDT *(Surprised)*: Well, we can discuss it, Your Honor. I am not sure there is anything to rebut.

Lights. Commotion in court. Screen: "The People Rest." Lights up on SCHMIDT *at a lectern, a parish priest at a pulpit. Screen: "Summations."*

(In a sweat, going for the home stretch):
I'm nervous. I'm very nervous.
I sure hope I say all the right things.
I can't marshall words the way Mr. Norman can—
But—I believe strongly in things.

Lord God! I don't say to you to forgive Dan White.
I don't say to you to just

let Dan White walk out of here a free man.
He is guilty.
But the degree of responsibility is the issue here.
The state of mind is the issue here.
It's not who was killed; it's why.
It's not who killed them; but why.
The state of mind is the issue here.

Lord God! The pressures.
Nobody can say that the things that happened to him
days or weeks preceding
wouldn't make a reasonable and ordinary man
at least mad,
angry in some way.

Surely—surely, that had to have arisen, not to kill,
not to kill, just to be mad, to act irrationally,
because if you kill, when you are angry, or under the heat of passion,
if you kill, then the law will punish you,
and you will be punished by God—
God will punish you,
but the law will also punish you.

Heat of passion fogs judgment, makes one act irrationally,
in the very least,
and my God,
that is what happened at the very least.

Forget about the mental illness,
forget about all the rest of the factors that came into play
at the same time:
Surely he acted irrationally, impulsively—out of some passion.

Now . . . you will recall at the close of the prosecution's case,
it was suggested to you this was a calm, cool, deliberating,
terrible terrible person
that had committed two crimes like these,
and these are terrible crimes,
and that he was emotionally stable at that time
and there wasn't anything wrong with him.

He didn't have any diminished capacity.
Then we played these tapes he made directly after
he turned himself in at Northern Station.

My God,
that was not a person that was calm and collected and cool
and able to weigh things out.
It just wasn't.

The tape just totally fogged me up the first time I heard it.
It was a man that was, as Frank Falzon said, broken.
Shattered.
This was not the Dan White that everybody had known.

Something happened to him and he snapped.
That's the word I used in my opening statement.
Something snapped here.

The pot had boiled over here,
and people that boil over in that fashion,
they tell the truth.

Have the tape played again, if you can't remember what was said.
He said in no uncertain terms,

"My God,
why did I do these things?
What made me do this?
How on earth could I have done this?
I didn't intend to do this.
I didn't intend to hurt anybody.
My God,
what happened to me?
Why?"

Play the tape.
If everybody says that tape is truthful, play the tape.
I'd agree it's truthful.

With regard to the reloading and some of these little
discrepancies that appeared to come up.
I am not even sure of the discrepancies, but if there were
discrepancies,
listen to it in context.
(Picks up transcript, reads)
"Where did you reload?"
"I reloaded in my office, I think."
"And then did you leave the Mayor's office?"
"Yes, then I left the Mayor's office."

That doesn't mean anything to me at all.
It doesn't mean anything to me at all.
And I don't care where the reloading took place!

But listen to the tape.
It says in no uncertain terms,
"I didn't intend to hurt anybody.
I didn't intend to do this.
Why do we do things?"
I don't know.
It was a man desperately trying to grab at something . . .

"What happened to me?
How could I have done this?"

If the District Attorney concedes
that what is on that tape is truthful,
and I believe that's the insinuation we have here,
then, by golly,
there is voluntary manslaughter,
nothing more and nothing less.

Now, I don't know what more I can say.
He's got to be punished
and he will be punished.
He's going to have to live with this for the rest of his life.
His child will live with it
and his family will live with it,
and God will punish him,
and the law will punish him,
and they will punish him severely.

But please, please.
Just justice.
That's all.
Just justice here.
(HE *appears to break for a moment*)
Now I am going to sit down and very soon,
and that's it for me.

And this is the type of case where, I suppose,
I don't think Mr. Norman is going to do it,
but you can make up a picture of a dead man,
or two of them for that matter,
and you can wave them around and say

somebody is going to pay for this
and somebody *is* going to pay for this.

Dan White is going to pay for this.
But it's not an emotional type thing.
I get emotional about it, but
you can't because you have to be objective about the facts . . .

I get one argument.
I have made it.
And if I could get up and argue again,
God,
we'd go on all night.

I just hope that—
I just hope that you'll come to the same conclusion
that I have come to.
And thank you for listening to me.

SCHMIDT *holds the lectern, then sits.*

NORMAN: Ladies and gentlemen of the jury, having the burden of proof,
I am given an opportunity a second time to address you.

I listened very carefully to the summation just given you.
It appears to me, members of the jury,
to be a very facile explanation and rationalization
as to premeditation and deliberation.
The evidence that has been laid before you
screams for murder in the first degree.

What counsel for the defense has done is suggest to you
to *excuse* this kind of conduct and call it something that it isn't,
to call it voluntary manslaughter.

Members of the jury, you are the triers of fact here.
You have been asked to hear this tape recording again.
The tape recording has been aptly described
as something very moving. We all feel a sense of sympathy,
a sense of empathy for our fellow man, but you are not to let
sympathy influence you in your judgment.

To reduce the charge of murder to something less—
to reduce it to voluntary manslaughter—

means you are saying that this was not murder.
That this was an intentional killing of a human being
upon a quarrel, or heat of passion.
But ladies and gentlemen,
that quarrel must have been so extreme
at the time
that the defendant could not—
was incapable of forming
those qualities of thought which are
malice, premeditation and deliberation.
But the evidence in this case doesn't suggest that at all.
Not at all.

If the defendant had picked up a vase or something
that happened to be in the Mayor's office
and hit the Mayor over the head and killed him
you know,
you know that argument for voluntary manslaughter
might be one which you could say the evidence admits
a reasonable doubt. But—

Ladies and gentlemen:
The facts are:
It was *he*—Dan White—who brought the gun to City Hall.
The gun was not there.
It was *he* who brought the extra cartridges for the gun;
they were not found there.

He went to City Hall and when he got there
he went to the Polk Street door.

There was a metal detector there.
He knew he was carrying a gun.
He knew that he had extra cartridges for it.

Instead of going through the metal detector,
he *decided* to go around the corner.
He was capable at that time of expressing anger.
He was capable of, according to the doctor—
well, parenthetically, members of the jury,
I don't know how they can look in your head and tell you
what you are able to do. But—
They even said that he was capable of knowing at that time
that if you pointed a gun at somebody and you fired that gun
that you would surely kill a person.

He went around the corner,
and climbed through a window into City Hall.

He went up to the Mayor's office.
He appeared, according to witnesses,
to act calmly in his approach, in his speech.

He chatted with Cyr Copertini;
he was capable of carrying on a conversation
to the extent that he was able to ask her how she was,
after having asked to see the Mayor.
(Looks to audience)
He stepped into the Mayor's office.
After some conversation,
he shot the Mayor twice in the body.
Then he shot the Mayor in the head twice
while the Mayor was disabled on the floor.
The evidence suggests that in order to shoot the Mayor
twice in the head
he had to *lean down* to do it.
(HE *demonstrates, looks to jury)*
Deliberation is premeditation.
It has malice.
I feel stultified to even bring this up.
This is the *definition* of murder.

He reloaded the gun.
Wherever he reloaded the gun,
it was *he* who reloaded it!

He did see Supervisor Milk
whom he knew was acting against his appointment
and he was capable of expressing anger in that regard.

He entered the Supervisors' area
(a block from the Mayor's office across City Hall)
and was told, "Dianne wants to see you."
He said, "That is going to have to wait a moment,
I have something to do first."

Then he walked to Harvey Milk's office,
put his head in the door and said,
"Can I see you a moment, Harv?"
The reply was, "Yes."

He went across the hall and put three bullets
into Harvey Milk's body,
one of which hit Harvey directly in the back.
When he fell to the floor disabled,
two more were delivered to the back of his head.

Now what do you call that but premeditation and deliberation?
What do you call that realistically
but a cold-blooded killing?
Two *cold-blooded executions.*
It occurs to me that if you don't call them that,
then you are ignoring the objective evidence
and the objective facts here.

Members of the jury, there are circumstances here
which no doubt bring about anger,
maybe even rage, I don't know,
but the manner in which that anger was felt
and was handled
is *socially something that cannot be approved.*

Ladies and gentlemen,
the quality of your service is reflected in your verdict.

NORMAN *sits.* JOANNA LU, *at door, stops* SCHMIDT.
TV lights.

LU *(On camera)*: Mr. Schmidt, do you—
SCHMIDT: Yes.
LU *(On camera)*: Do you feel society would feel justice is served if the jury returns
two manslaughter verdicts?
SCHMIDT *(Wry smile)*: Society doesn't have anything to do with it. Only those
12 people in the jury box.
COURT: Ladies and gentlemen of the jury,
Now that you have heard the evidence,
we come to that part of the trial where you are instructed
on the applicable law.

In the crime of murder of the first degree
the necessary concurrent mental states are:
Malice aforethought, premeditation and deliberation.

In the crime of murder of the second degree,
the necessary concurrent mental state is:
Malice aforethought.

In the crime of voluntary manslaughter,
the necessary mental state is:
An intent to kill.

Involuntary manslaughter is an unlawful killing without malice aforethought
and without intent to kill.

The law does not undertake to limit or define the kinds of passion
which may cause a person to act rashly.
Such passions as desperation, humiliation, resentment,
anger, fear, or rage,
or any other high-wrought emotion . . .
can be sufficient to reduce the killings to manslaughter
so long as they are sufficient to obscure the reason
and render the average man likely to act rashly.
There is no malice aforethought
if the killing occurred upon a sudden quarrel
or heat of passion.

There is no malice aforethought
if the evidence shows that due to diminished capacity
caused by illness, mental defect, or intoxication,
the defendant did not have the capacity
to form the mental state constituting malice aforethought,
even though the killing was intentional,
voluntary, premeditated and unprovoked.

A siren begins. Screen: Images of the riot at City Hall—broken glass, cop cars burning, riot police, angry faces. Audio: Explosions.

GWENN *(On video)*: In order to understand the riots, I think you have to understand that the Dan White verdict did not occur in a vacuum—
COURT: Mr. Foreman, has the jury reached verdicts / /in this case?
GWENN: that there were and are other factors which contribute to a legitimate rage that was demonstrated dramatically at our symbol of Who's Responsible, City Hall.

Screen: Images of City Hall being stormed. Line of police in riot gear in front.

FOREMAN: Yes, it has, Your Honor.
GWENN: The verdict came down and the people rioted.
COURT: Please read the verdicts.
GWENN: The people stormed City Hall, burned police cars.

Screen: Image of City Hall. Line of police cars in flames.

FOREMAN (Reading): The jury finds the defendant Daniel James White guilty of violating Section 192.1 of the penal code.
GWENN: Then the police came into our neighborhood.
And the police rioted.
FOREMAN: Voluntary manslaughter, for the slaying of Mayor George Moscone.

MARY ANN WHITE *gasps*. DAN WHITE *puts head in hands. Explosion*. RIOT POLICE *enter*.

GWENN: The police came into the Castro and assaulted gays.
They stormed the Elephant Walk Bar.
One kid had an epileptic seizure and was almost killed for it.
A cop drove a motorcycle up against a phone booth
where a lesbian woman was on the phone,
blocked her exit
and began beating her up.
COURT: Is this a unanimous verdict of the jury?
FOREMAN: Yes, it is, Judge.
GWENN (*Off video*): I want to talk about when people are pushed to the wall.
COURT: Will each juror say "yea" //or "nay"?

Violence on stage.

YOUNG MOTHER: What about the children?
MOSCONE'S FRIEND: I know who George offended.
I know who Harvey offended.
JURORS (*On tape*): Yea, yea, yea //yea, yea, yea.
MOSCONE'S FRIEND: I understand the offense.
YOUNG MOTHER: What do I tell my kids?
GWENN: Were the ones who are responsible seeing these things?
YOUNG MOTHER: That in this country you serve more time for robbing a bank than for killing two people?
JURORS (*On tape*): Yea, yea, yea //yea, yea, yea.
GWENN: Hearing these things?
MILK'S FRIEND: I understand the offense.
GWENN: Do they understand about people being pushed to the wall?
YOUNG MOTHER: Accountability?

Yea's end.

MILK'S FRIEND: Assassination.
I've grown up with it.
I forget it hasn't always been this way.
YOUNG MOTHER: What do I say?
That two lives are worth seven years and eight months //in jail?

MILK'S FRIEND: I remember coming home from school in sixth grade—
JFK was killed—
six years later, Martin Luther King.
It's a frame of reference.

Explosion.

COURT: Will the foreman please read the verdict for the second count?
DENMAN: It's a divided city.
MOSCONE'S FRIEND: The resentment of change is similar. I can understand that.
    It's my hometown. *(Irish accent)* They're changin' it, y'know?
DENMAN: The people were getting caught up in the change
    and didn't know.
MOSCONE'S FRIEND: You grew up in old Irish Catholic //San Francisco . . .
DENMAN: They didn't know why it was—
    like Armageddon.
MOSCONE'S FRIEND: and Bill Malone ran the town and "these guys"
    are disruptin' everything.
FOREMAN: The jury finds the defendant Daniel James White guilty of Section
    192.1 of the penal code, voluntary manslaughter, in the slaying of Super-
    visor Harvey Milk.

DAN WHITE *gasps.* MARY ANN WHITE *sobs.* NORMAN, *flushed, head in hands.*
Explosions. Violence ends. RIOT POLICE *control the crowd. TV lights.*

BRITT *(On camera):* No—I'm optimistic about San Francisco.
COURT: Is this a unanimous decision by the jury?
FOREMAN: Yes, Your Honor.
BRITT: I'm Harry Britt. I was Harvey Milk's successor.
CARLSON: If he'd just killed the Mayor, he'd be in jail today.
YOUNG MOTHER: To this jury, Dan White was their son.
MILK'S FRIEND: Harvey Milk lit up my universe.
YOUNG MOTHER: What are we teaching our sons?

WHITE *raises his hands to his eyes, cries.* MARY ANN WHITE, SEVERAL JURORS *sob.*

BRITT: Now, this is an example I don't use often because
    people will misunderstand it.
    But when a prophet is killed . . .
    It's up to those who are left
    to build the community or the church.
MOSCONE'S FRIEND: Dan White believed in the death penalty;
    he should have gotten the death penalty.
YOUNG MOTHER: How do you explain //the difference?

BRITT: But I have hope and as Harvey said,
   "You can't live without hope."
MOSCONE'S FRIEND: I mean, that son of a bitch //killed somebody I loved.
MILK'S FRIEND: It was an effective //assassination.
MOSCONE'S FRIEND: I loved the guy.

   Pause.

MILK'S FRIEND: They always are.
GWENN *(Quiet)*: Do they know about Stonewall?
BRITT: Our revenge is never to forget.

   The FOREMAN *walks to the defense table, gives* SCHMIDT *a handshake.* NORMAN
   turns away.

LU *(On camera)*: Dan White was examined by the psychiatrist at the state prison.
   They decided against therapy. Dan White had no apparent signs of mental
   disorder. . . . Dan White's parole date was January 6, 1984. When Dan
   White left Soledad prison on January 6, 1984, it was five years, one month,
   and eight days since he turned himself in at Northern Station after the
   assassinations of Mayor George Moscone and Supervisor Harvey Milk.
   Mayor Dianne Feinstein, the current Mayor of San Francisco, has tried to
   keep Dan White out of San Francisco during his parole for fear he will be
   killed.

   The COP *enters.* SISTER BOOM BOOM *enters.*

BOOM BOOM: Dan White! It's 1984 and Big Sister is watching you.
LU *(On camera)*: Dan White reportedly plans to move to Ireland after his release.
MOSCONE'S FRIEND: What do you do with your feelings of revenge?
   With your need for retribution?
BRITT: We will never forget.

   Screen: Riot images freeze. A shaft of light from church window.

BOOM BOOM: I would like to close with a reading from the Book of Dan. *(Opens
   book)* Take of this and eat, for this is my defense. *(Raises a Twinkie. Eats it. Exits)*
LU *(On camera)*: Dan White was found dead of carbon monoxide poisoning on
   October 21, 1985 at his wife's home in San Francisco, California.

   Lights change. DAN WHITE *faces* THE COURT.

COURT: Mr. White, you are sentenced to seven years and eight months, the maximum sentence for these two counts of voluntary manslaughter. The Court

feels that these sentences for the taking of life is completely inappropriate but that was the decision of the legislature.

Again, let me repeat for the record:
Seven years and eight months is the maximum sentence
for voluntary manslaughter, and this is the law.

Gavel. Long pause. WHITE *turns to the audience/jury.*

WHITE: I was always just a lonely vote on the Board.
I was just trying to do a good job for the city.

Long pause. Audio: Hyperreal sounds of high heels on marble. Mumbled Hail Marys. Rustle of an embrace. SISTER BOOM BOOM *enters. Taunts* POLICE. POLICE *raise riot shields. Blackout. Screen: "Execution of Justice." Gavel echoes.*

END OF PLAY

The Incredibly Famous Willy Rivers

Stephen Metcalfe

About Stephen Metcalfe

Born in New Haven in 1953, Stephen Metcalfe is a graduate of Westminster College in Pennsylvania. His one-act plays *Jacknife* and *Baseball Play* were first staged at New York's Quaigh Theatre in 1980; his full-length play *Vikings* was produced by Manhattan Theatre Club that same year. *Vikings* was later seen at the Edinburgh Festival and heard on *Earplay*. *Strange Snow*, commissioned by MTC and given its premiere there in 1982, was selected for TCG's *Plays in Process* series and recently included in TCG's 1985 anthology *Coming to Terms: American Plays & the Vietnam War*. *White Linen*, a cowboy play with songs, was staged by Michigan's BoarsHead Theater in 1982; Cincinnati Playhouse in the Park premiered *Loves and Hours* in 1984. *Half a Lifetime*, seen at Manhattan Theatre Club in 1983, has been filmed by Home Box Office and will be aired this spring. *Megs* (formerly *Jacknife*) was staged by the author as part of the 1985 Shorts Festival at Actors Theatre of Louisville. A new play, *Emily*, will premiere at San Diego's Old Globe Theatre this summer. Metcalfe has been the recipient of a CAPS grant and a National Endowment for the Arts playwriting fellowship.

About the Play

The Incredibly Famous Willy Rivers opened on December 12, 1984 at WPA Theatre in New York, under the direction of Stephen Zuckerman, with music by Denny McCormick. The play has been optioned and a commercial production in 1986 is anticipated. *Willy Rivers* was originally published by TCG in the January 1986 issue of *American Theatre* magazine.

Characters

Actor 1   WILLY RIVERS
Actor 2   SUIT/DAD
Actor 3   SUBWAY GIRL/PUNK
Actor 4   FRIEND'S WIFE/BLONDE
Actor 5   DARLENE
Actor 6   FRIEND/GYPSEY DAVEY/BLONDE'S HUSBAND
Actor 7   ANCHORMAN/ACTOR
Actor 8   GOATMAN JANGO/ORDERLY
Actor 9   BEGGAR/HOST/PRISONER

Time

The present.

Place

The stage.

The Play

The Incredibly Famous Willy Rivers

ACT ONE

Scene 1

*The faint sound of whistling, of cheering, of stamping feet—applause that suggests anticipation and expectation. The sound is distant, muted; as if coming through yards and yards of concrete, as if creeping through from some distant place. The sound turns into a more intense—what? Static? Applause? Feedback? All three? Silence. And then a voice out of the blackness—*WILLY'S VOICE.

WILLY: Ladies and gentlepeople, boys and those of the female persuasion, if there are any dogs and cats in the audience, they're invited to howl. . . . I think we can safely say—no, I don't think, I know—that he is a legend in his own time. There is a lovely black-and-white portrait of him on page 17 of your complimentary souvenir program. A full color 24 by 36-inch poster of him is on sale at convenient locations throughout the arena and say, while you're there, people, how 'bout a big beer and a chili dog! Ladies and gentlemen, there ought to be music and don't worry, there will be; ladies and gentlemen, the incredibly famous Willy Rivers!

The sound again: static, feedback, distorted applause. Lights have been slowly coming up. A MAN *is sitting center. The sound fades away. The* MAN—WILLY—*speaks.*

That was horrible. Let's get down! Let's get funky! Let's all get incredibly moist and sticky wet! Let's have a hometown welcome for your fave rave and mine, the incredibly famous Willy Rivers!

The sound again. It is coming from a large cassette deck that WILLY *is holding.* HE *turns the sound to high and applause on the verge of distortion reverberates throughout the theatre.* HE *turns it off. Silence.*

The incredible Willy Rivers! *(Sound. Off)* The famous Willy Rivers. *(Again. Off)* Willy Rivers. *(Silence, then softly)* Oh, boy . . . *(*HE *rolls onto his back and stares at the ceiling)* Hold on to your seats, I have a feeling it's going to be a long one.

A MAN IN A THREE-PIECE SUIT *enters.*

SUIT: Willy.

WILLY: Oh, oh. Devil with a blue suit on.

SUIT: It's time.

WILLY: No. Can't be time. No can be. I'm not ready. *(*HE *leaps to his feet)* All right, let's get organized! I want rabid fans on my left! I want screaming hordes on my right! Any girls ain't been under me, line up along the wall, I'll go as long as I can!

SUIT: Willy, we're waiting.

WILLY: O.K., where the hell is my lucky jacket? That jacket's my trademark, Jack! How in hell am I supposed to convince anybody that a middle-class kid from the heartland of America is misfitted, maladjusted and James Dean mean if I don't have my lucky jacket? That jacket has got wings on it, man!

SUIT: You're wasting time.

WILLY: I hope nobody went into their life savings for this nickel-and-dime extravaganza! I have never! Been treated! In first class! Like this! In my life!

SUIT: Willy.

WILLY: Sir?

SUIT: Cut the shit.

WILLY *seems to sag.* HE *is terrified of something.*

WILLY: I can't. Nothing feels right.

SUIT: No one has come to hear your excuses.

WILLY: It's like there's too much blood pumping through my body.

SUIT: That's nerves. Nerves are to be expected.

WILLY: My back hurts. My throat and hands.

SUIT: That's all in your mind.

WILLY *(Snapping)*: It is not in my mind. My body, man, predicts the weather and it is tellin' me that the weather, man, bites the big one.

SUIT: And so?

WILLY: And so . . . (HE *rushes to his tape deck and puts on the headphones*) You ever seen one a these? This is a superdeluxe, class A, top of the line, get down and boogie Walkman. And that's what I'm gonna do. Walk, man.

SUIT: Willy, we don't have all night.

WILLY: Can't hear you! You wanna talk to me you're gonna have to put it on a cassette and plug it in. Panasonic Willy Rivers! I bet God wears headphones.

SUIT: We have a contract.

WILLY: What? I can see your lips move but I can't hear a thing. Speak no evil, see no evil and I can't hear no evil at all, man.

SUIT: Everyone is ready except you.

WILLY: Hey, I was born ready, buddy.

SUIT: Ahh, you can hear me. You know your cue. (*Exiting*) Ladies and gentlemen, the incredibly famous Willy Rivers.

WILLY: No! Hey! You tell'm if they clap their hands I'll piss in their pockets! I don't take charity, not me, not this kid. (*Psyching himself now*) O.K., man. A river flows through here and it's wild and fast and in places the whitewater leaps to fifty feet high. And the name of that river . . . is Willy! Where's my guitar? Hey! How the hell am I supposed to rock and roll without a guitar!? (*Pause.* HE *sags, the false bravado gone*) Lord, lord . . . where am I gonna find the strength to do this? (*Softly, to himself*) Oh, it is absolutely amazing the things that flash across a man's mind when he feels like he's going down and under for the third time. It is amazing the things that flash across your mind.

Light change. Music. Faces. Images. Sounds. FIGURES *move and call out in the chaos.*

Scene 2

The flashing lights and the roar of a moving subway train. Lights up on WILLY *and a* YOUNG WOMAN *in heavy makeup and tight clothing.* SHE *is reading a newspaper.* SHE *glances up at* WILLY, *looks him over; decides* SHE *likes what* SHE *sees. The* YOUNG WOMAN *speaks with a heavy Queens accent.*

GIRL: Hey. (*Pause*) Hey. (*Pause*) Hey. (*Pause*) Hey. (*Pause*) Hey, bozo! Don't ya see I'm talkin' at ya, cheese!

WILLY: Sorry, what?

GIRL: Ya hear?

WILLY: Hear what?

GIRL: He! Is makin' a comeback!

WILLY: Who?

GIRL: Ya so unread.

WILLY: Yeah, uh . . . lately I don't seem to have much time to read the papers.

GIRL: Tsk. Willy.

WILLY: Willy. Uh-huh. Yeah. I knew that. *(Pause)* Willy who?

GIRL: Ya so ignorant! Willy Rivers!

WILLY: Yeah. How exciting. Willy Rivers. He's makin' a . . . a what?

GIRL: Tsk. A comeback? From the *shootin'*?

WILLY: Oh. Yeah. That Willy.

GIRL: Ya obviously so incredibly ill-informed. I myself personally cried when he got shot. Ya wanna know the truth, I died when he got shot. I bled fahr'm.

WILLY: Willy Rivers. He sure is very famous.

GIRL: And rich.

WILLY: Oh, yeah.

GIRL: And cute. He's got one a them faces.

WILLY: The rich, famous and cute. *(HE and the GIRL sigh as one)* They live the life, don't they?

GIRL: Celestial.

WILLY: Where'd we go wrong.

GIRL: Speak fah ya'self I'm sure. *(Pause)* Y'know, I sawr him once.

WILLY: I touched him.

GIRL: No! Well . . . I made it with him.

WILLY: You too?

GIRL *(A shocked gasp; then annoyed)*: Ooh, incredibly famous people of immense importance, they're always swingin' both ways a somethin'. Anyway, y'know, I bet he remembers me.

WILLY: I bet you gave him something to remember.

GIRL: Oh, speak fah ya'self, I'm sure!

WILLY: Hey. Hey. Hey. Are you going to get tickets?

GIRL: One can only hope.

WILLY: What is it he does again?

GIRL: Well . . . I ain't sure. But from what I understand, it tears ya heart out.

WILLY: He's good, huh?

GIRL: Tsk. Good-shmood! When there's the possibility that some psycho's gon-na be packin' a piece and blastin' away, know what you are at? A multimedia event!

WILLY: The things *some* people charge admission to, huh?

GIRL: Ain't it the truth. Charge a guy and you's a whore. Add a gun an' a few seats and you's a spectacular entertainment.

Pause.

WILLY: I knew that.

Pause.

GIRL: Hey. Hey. HEY! Let's say the two of us stop off somewheres. I'll let you buy me a Lite beer from Miller.

Light change. Chaos. An electric guitar screams out of the black—Hendrix or maybe Clapton when he played for Cream.

Scene 3

The sound of the guitar breaks down; feedback; and now the sound is rough and clumsy and halting. Lights up on WILLY *trying to shape his left hand onto the neck of the guitar, trying to play.* HE *groans in frustration.* SUIT *enters.*

SUIT: Practicing?

WILLY: I started off playing to records. Man, I'd turn the stereo up to a thousand and I'd dance with that first guitar of mine like it was my baby. Mom had a headache from the mid-sixties on. Why do you play the stereo so loud, Willy!? You're gonna ruin your eardrums! She never understood that loud is the only way rock and roll sounds good. She was also convinced I woulda turned out normal if the Beatles hadn't been on Ed Sullivan. She didn't think I did teenage things. Go out with a girl, Willy! Get her pregnant. Go total the car! Go protest something like all your other friends! Go protest traffic lights, Doberman pinschers. Go protest bell-bottom pants! My mom prayed for a moment's peace. Now my dad, my dad sorta knew how much it all meant to me. Course he didn't have to listen to it all day long. But he'd come home and let Mom blow off steam for awhile and then he'd come down to the basement and he'd look at the posters I'd taped to the walls, black-light crazy shit, and he'd turn to me and he'd say, go for it, Willy. For your mom's sake, go for it quietly but go for it. My dad . . . he was a fan. *(HE strikes a chord. It sounds rough and tinny)* That was an A chord, man. The perfect A chord. I learned a chord a day. Perfect chords. I practiced till my fingers bled. All that practice. . . . And man? I can't play worth a shit anymore. *(Flexing his hand, putting down the guitar)* Nerve damage.

SUIT: You're a headliner now, Willy, you don't have to play. Others will play for you. All you have to do is stand there and look good.

WILLY: Hey . . . maybe I should mouth the words too?

SUIT: We can arrange that if you like.

WILLY: You're never gonna understand. When you play the sound right, it's like stepping into another plane of existence, man. Your body is pistons, tubes, valves. You're aware of rods flowing into cylinders, of liquid seeping from chamber into chamber, of billows as they fill and empty, of life, man! You're aware of the tiny delicate bones in the inner room of your ear, of filaments dancing to the pulse of a beat. You hear with your heart when you play, man. The music speaks words, man. You are, man. Man!

SUIT: Willy, that's a crock of shit and you know it. I've been thinking, Willy. This is your show. Your comeback. You should be surrounded by people who care about you, by people who supported you when you were nothing special.

WILLY: Yeah?

SUIT: I was thinking it would be nice if you invited some. People who care about you, I mean. Unless, of course, you want me to go out and hire some professionals?

WILLY: No . . . I mean, hey. I got people who care about me. I got good people.

SUIT: That's fine. The mark of a man is the people who care about him, am I right? On us, Willy, this is the big leagues, spare no expense. Invite anyone you want.

WILLY: Who . . .

SUIT: Who should you invite? I thought I made that clear. Your friends.

SUIT *exits. Light change. Music. Chaos.*

Scene 4

Lights up on WILLY *and a* MAN *in tennis whites. The* MAN *is holding a tennis racket and bag.* WILLY *and the* MAN *are sitting, laughing uproariously. The laughter fades to nervous silence. The* MAN *keeps glancing at his wristwatch.*

FRIEND: So. Huh?

WILLY: Yeah.

FRIEND: Unbelievable.

WILLY: Yeah.

FRIEND: Such a long time.

WILLY: Too long.

FRIEND: Yeah. Hey, you get that card I sent you?

WILLY: Card?

FRIEND: Yeah. A Christmas card. Me, the wife, the kid, y'know, the dog, the cat, the tree. Everybody smiling. You didn't get that card?

WILLY: No.

FRIEND: It was a nice card.

WILLY: Sounds like it.

FRIEND: It wasn't cheap.

WILLY: They aren't.

FRIEND: Living color. Years from now, people will look at that card and say, will you look at that?

WILLY: So lifelike.

FRIEND: So real.

WILLY: Everybody's old or dead now.

Pause. THEY *nod at each other, silent. The* FRIEND *glances at his watch.*

FRIEND: My ride's due at any time.
WILLY: We can talk till he gets here.
FRIEND: He'll beep. I'll have to go right out.
WILLY: Fine. You drop by, you take your chances. I just wanted to say hello.
FRIEND: I appreciate it. A guy like you. When he beeps though, I'll have to run.
WILLY: Don't want to keep a person waiting.
FRIEND: Specially a doubles partner. Specially a doubles partner with a good overhead. Hey, my wife'll be home soon. I bet she'd love to chat. You know something? She couldn't believe it when I told her that we were best friends in high school. Boy, will she be surprised! She's crazy about success. Especially overnight success.

Pause. THEY *nod at each other in silence. The* FRIEND *glances at his watch and smiles.*

WILLY: How's your game?
FRIEND: Fine.
WILLY: Good. *(A beat)* Play a lot?
FRIEND: Yeah, I do.
WILLY: Great.
FRIEND: About eight or ten hours a day.
WILLY: That's a lot.
FRIEND: Except Tuesdays.
WILLY: Sorry?
FRIEND: Unemployment on Tuesdays. Yeah, for awhile I was looking for a job but then I decided, what the hell, 150 a week, tax-free, doing nothing.
WILLY: You'd be hard pressed to do better than that working hard at something you hated.
FRIEND: Exactly. So I don't. I play tennis.
WILLY: You must be getting good.
FRIEND: I am. Topspin.
WILLY: Sorry?
FRIEND: Topspin. Topspin is the key to good ground strokes. Gives you room to clear the net, keeps the ball safely within the baselines. Topspin. Topspin is the key to control. You might even say that topspin is the key to life. So!! You gettin' any!!?
WILLY: Uh . . .
FRIEND: You are, aren't you. God, times have changed. Double dates, remember? A little nookie at the drive-in movies.
WILLY: Me in the back seat, you in the front.
FRIEND: Second base, bare tit, huh? Third base, a little sticky finger. Huh? Huh!?
WILLY: Christ, old friends.
FRIEND: Yeah.

WILLY: Old friends are the best friends.

FRIEND: Shared experiences. That's what old friends have.

WILLY: They don't have to explain things, they know.

FRIEND: Hey, when you got shot? It was like I got shot. I wanted to get in touch.

WILLY: You didn't.

FRIEND *(With vast good humor)*: Who the hell would have ever thought anybody'd want to shoot you, huh?

WILLY: Not me.

FRIEND: You certainly were on the outskirts in high school.

WILLY: Off in my own little world, yeah.

FRIEND: You want to know the truth, people thought you were stuck up. They thought your head was in the clouds. If you want to know the truth—

WILLY: I don't.

FRIEND: Everybody thought you were a twerp!

WILLY: Huh.

FRIEND: Guys always asked me why I let you hang with me. I mean, you remember who was voted most likely to succeed, don't you.

WILLY: You.

FRIEND: Me. I mean, you?

WILLY: Willy Rivers is weird, they'd say.

FRIEND: And they were right!

WILLY: I was.

FRIEND: You were! But hey, we were friends!

WILLY: Are.

FRIEND: And look at you now, huh? Hey! What are you worth?

WILLY: I, uh . . . don't know.

FRIEND: That much, huh? Well, you deserve it. Getting shot. How do you put a dollar value on entertainment like that? It's mindless entertainment. Mindless entertainment is priceless. It keeps you from thinking. I play tennis? I have a litany. Only the ball, only the ball, only the ball. It keeps me from thinking of other things. A kid could get hit by a truck in the parking lot, I wouldn't notice, that's how good my concentration is. Go ahead, say something to me, say something. (HE *scoops up his racket and takes a stance as if* HE'S *returning serve. It's as if* HE *goes into a trance, recites a mantra)* Only the ball. Only the ball. Only the ball.

WILLY: I feel so alone.

FRIEND: Only the ball. *(Snapping out of it)* Did you say something?

WILLY: Yes.

FRIEND: I didn't hear you! Concentration! What'd you say?

WILLY: I feel so alone.

FRIEND: You should. Life! It's a game of singles. *(Pause)* Hey. Do you want to know something? My wife. She'd like to go to bed with you. Yeah. She said so. When I tell her we were friends once?

WILLY: We still are.

FRIEND: She says, boy, I'd crawl on my belly for a chance to fuck him. He was a twerp, I say. He could twerp me anytime, she says.

WILLY: People say funny things.

FRIEND: I don't laugh.

WILLY: People say things they don't really mean. Your wife, she doesn't even know me.

FRIEND: That's what she likes about you. All of a sudden, you're anything she wants you to be. (A beep) There he is! My ride! Been great to see you. Stay as long as you want and come again, O.K.? But call first. Bye! (HE exits)

WIFE (Off): I'm home!

FRIEND (Off): It's not my ride, it's only my wife! Honey, we have a guest! Do I have a surprise for you!

HE and his WIFE enter. HE has his hands over her eyes. SHE is wearing coveralls and a hard hat.

This! Is the incredibly famous Willy Rivers, honey! (HE pulls his hands away)

WILLY: Hi. It's very nice to meet you.

WIFE: Oh, my god.

WILLY: I've heard so much about you.

WIFE: I'm going to faint.

FRIEND: Here's my little breadwinner. How are things down at the Ford plant, dear?

WIFE: I'm going to die.

FRIEND: Sit down, old friend. Maybe the little woman will whip us up some frozen egg rolls and jalepeño bean dip. Reminiscing is hard work.

WIFE: Ohhh . . . (SHE falls to her knees)

FRIEND: Hard day on the assembly line, dear? She's exhausted. Dear? She's a little hard of hearing. That Ford plant's noisy.

The WIFE begins crawling on her belly toward WILLY.

WILLY: They're planning this big comeback for me and I wonder if you'd like to attend?

The WIFE flips over on her back and begins doing the backstroke.

You and your wife. Seats and hotel rooms will be taken care of. You could meet some nice people.

FRIEND: I'd love to, buddy of mine. Unfortunately I have league, old buddy. Tennis. Tennis league.

WILLY: I see.

The WIFE is on her knees in front of WILLY, touching him to see if HE's real.

FRIEND: If she's bothering you, Willy, just give her a solid smack on the snout with a rolled-up newspaper. *(A horn beeps)* There he is! Great to see you, Willy. Be in touch, O.K.? And leave the little woman your mailing address, won'tcha? We're gonna be sure you get that Christmas card this year and god knows it'd be nice to get in touch if somebody tries to shoot you again! *(HE kisses his WIFE on the top of the head)* Don't wait up, dear, I'll be late. Bye! *(HE exits)*

WIFE: Take me now before I die.

Light change. Music. Chaos.

Scene 5

REPORTERS converge on WILLY from all directions. WILLY tries to get away but THEY keep heading him off. THEY thrust cassette recorders at him, wave notebooks and pencils. A BEGGAR in rags and torn sneakers enters and silently panhandles the REPORTERS. THEY push him away. SUIT enters and watches.

REPORTERS *(Adlibbing)*: Willy! Willy! Question, Willy, question! Here, Willy! Question! Question!

REPORTER: You've come from nowhere, Willy!

WILLY: Please, I—

REPORTER: What was nowhere like?

WILLY: No questions, I—

REPORTER: Tell us about vague obscurity!

REPORTER: Is it true you're afraid to go out in public?

WILLY: Let me pass, please, I—

REPORTERS *(Adlibbing)*: Your scars! Show us your scars! We want to see scars!

REPORTER: You workin', guy?

REPORTER: Tell us about the hinterlands, kemosabe.

REPORTER: Is it true you've turned against everyone who supported you for years?

WILLY: Will you please let me through!

REPORTERS *(Adlibbing)*: Question, Willy! Scars, Willy! Question! Scars!

REPORTER: What's your favorite, Willy?

REPORTER: What's your preference, if any?

WILLY: Filipinos under the age of consent. And now if you'll—

REPORTER: What do you think of vertical smiles, Willy?

WILLY: Love'm to pieces. Excuse me!

REPORTER: Come back!

REPORTER: Is there any sexual significance to that term?

REPORTER: Seen any sights?

WILLY: No.

REPORTER: Heard any sounds?

WILLY: No.

REPORTER: Felt anything worth feeling!?

WILLY: No! No! No!

Sudden silence.

REPORTER: Have a little pity.

REPORTER: We're all just doin' our jobs.

REPORTER: Just this one time and we'll all be your friends for life.

WILLY: One at a time.

REPORTER: Is music a metaphor for life, Willy?

REPORTER: Is life a metaphor for life, Willy?

REPORTER: What is music, Willy?

REPORTER: What is life, Willy?

REPORTER: Are there alternatives?

REPORTER: What are the alternatives?

REPORTER: Are they fun?

REPORTER: What is fun?

REPORTERS *(Adlibbing)*: Your scars! We want scars! Show us your scars!

REPORTER: We've heard some disturbing rumors, Willy!

WILLY: They're true, undoubtedly. Please, I—

REPORTERS *(Adlibbing)*: Question, Willy! Willy, question!

WILLY: Please.

REPORTER: One word, Willy. Poignant!

REPORTERS *(Adlibbing)*: Questions, Willy, questions!

WILLY: Please!

REPORTER: Carry a grudge, Willy?

REPORTER: Are you bitter?

REPORTER: Or don't you care?

WILLY: I've really got to go.

REPORTER: Fave drugs!?

REPORTER: Ill feelings!?

REPORTER: Regrets!?

REPORTER: Sense of loss!?

REPORTER: Loss of appetite!?

REPORTERS *(Adlibbing)*: Out of my way! Me next! Willy! Willy! Stop pushing! Willy, Willy! Questions! Scars!

The REPORTERS are screaming and cursing and grabbing at WILLY. The BEGGAR is caught in the melee, unable to escape. HE and WILLY cover their heads and cower. The REPORTERS surround them like hungry wolves.

WILLY: Argghhh!

BEGGAR: Savages! All a ya's, savages!

Sound! The lead-in to a news program. The REPORTERS *step back, growing silent. A* MAN *steps from the wings.* HE *is in a brightly colored blazer and tie.* HE *holds a mike.* HE *straightens his tie and cues someone that* HE'S *ready. The bright lights of a television camera hit him.*

ANCHORMAN *(In a huge, orotund voice):* Hi! Channel Five News and we're here with that man with the bulletproof heart and—I gotta say it—in all modesty, a close personal friend of mine, the incredibly famous Willy Rivers. *(HE thrusts his mike at the still cowering* WILLY*)* Willy, you are looking some kind of good!

WILLY *(Rising):* I feel good, I feel fast, I feel relaxed.

ANCHORMAN: You heard it, ladies and gentlemen, and you heard it here.

BEGGAR: Alms, alms?

ANCHORMAN: How's it feel to be making a comeback, Willy?

WILLY: Like I never left.

ANCHORMAN: That's the hombre we all know and love. Will, you are just looking so good!

WILLY: I feel good.

BEGGAR: Spare change, guv?

WILLY: I feel fast.

BEGGAR: Subway tokens?

WILLY: I feel relaxed.

BEGGAR: He ain't no better'n me.

ANCHORMAN: Ladies and gentlemen, this guy is a sweetheart and a real man besides. I wouldn't take you seriously, Will-o, if you weren't.

BEGGAR: He just happens to be famous.

ANCHORMAN: How about a couple for the photographers?

WILLY: Why not?

BEGGAR: And then dinner!

Flashbulbs pop. Cameras click away.

ANCHORMAN: Is this a classy crew of paparazzi or what?

BEGGAR: Dubloons, macaroons, quadroons, octoroons?

ANCHORMAN: Wait a sec, lads, wait a sec. Any love interest, Willy? No? Good. We'll take care of that.

HE *whistles. A breathtaking* BLONDE *in a tight dress hurries on.*

Isn't she lovely? Grab a thigh, dear! *(SHE immediately grabs his thigh)* Whoa. No, wrong thigh, dear. Isn't she beautiful? *(SHE grabs* WILLY'S *thigh)* There we go. Isn't she sweet? Little more cleavage, dear, most of these lads work for family magazines. Great. Love it. When did you realize it was true love, Will-o?

The BLONDE *puts her hand on* WILLY'S *crotch.*

WILLY: Just now.
ANCHORMAN: Is it serious, dear?
BLONDE *(Looking at* WILLY'S *crotch)*: It's getting serious very quickly.
ANCHORMAN: Isn't she delightful? Kiss her, lad!

But before WILLY *can move, the* BEGGAR *sweeps the* BLONDE *into his arms, bends her back and kisses her passionately.*

Beautiful, we love it, let's go. This is Channel Five News. Good night.

Television lights dim. EVERYONE *begins exiting in a different direction.*

REPORTERS: Page One. Where's a phone? That's a wrap, I got what I came for! Let's pack it in, today's news is tomorrow's headlines.
ANCHORMAN: Good luck, Willy. And stay away from people's gunsights, you mad muchacho, you.
BLONDE *(Handing* WILLY *a slip of paper)*: Call me sometime.

The ANCHORMAN *and the* BLONDE *exit. The* BEGGAR *exits through the audience.*

BEGGAR: Tuppence? Krugerrands? Pounds, crowns, peek at the family jewels? Shillings, kopu, yen? What ya say, Ronrico, just till I start sellin' my sperm again. Sovereigns, marks, rubles, pieces of eight? Stocks, greenbacks, government bonds? Be a sport, sir, I'll let you sodomize my shoe. Gold futures? Tradable commodities? Tax-free municipals? Savages, all a ya's. Savages!!
WILLY: Savages. Alms? Alms?

Light change. The sound of cheering, of distant music. GOATMAN JANGO *enters.* HE *is a Rastafarian with huge, long, matted dreadlocks.*

Ladies and gentlemen, the incredibly incredible Goatman Jango!

GOATMAN *turns, surprised. A moment and then* HE *laughs; soundless, hysterical laughter.*

GOATMAN: Ah, Jah. Ah, Jah. We need a little sanity, man, am I right. Goddam fuckin' right. Willy! *(THEY embrace)* Hey! Willy, man, hey, I hear you be havin' this comeback.
WILLY: You heard right.
GOATMAN: Hey, man, maybe you some kinda crazy or somethin', right? Shoot me once, shame on you, man. Shoot me twice, goddam stupid shame on me.
WILLY: How'd your set go?

GOATMAN: Ah, Jah. We be talkin' whitebread here tonight, man. I be in dese states united now, man, six months, man. Lousy, man. Cold. De sun, man it be peerin' through de haze all de time and it hardly be warmin' de blood, man, right? Food be lousy with blandness, de beer be warm and de ganja don't take you no place you ain't been before on a bad day.

WILLY: Good houses?

GOATMAN: Whitebread college kids. On scholarship. Or else sloppy little punks, man, in torn clothes for effect only and dey think dey an' me be on de same wavelength 'cause we don't have a use for authority. Deir authority is flannel blanket with satin trim, man. My authority be pointed boot in de ass. I ain't complainin', man. But dis one goddam crazy universe where punk kids can pay thirty dollars to see Goatman or maybe de incredibly famous Willy, and still have the balls to be wearin' a torn T-shirt. Right?

WILLY: You know what de hell kinda bloody right!

GOATMAN: Ha-ha-ha! De famous Willy! Ah, you be a good soul, Jah. True, true.

WILLY: I play my songs and I take my pay and I never bitch about the bad breaks. Right? *(A moment)* My comeback, man, I'd like you to be there.

Pause.

GOATMAN: I be playin', man.

Pause.

WILLY: I find myself thinking of a time when the Goatman was in one mean-ass whitebread joint . . . wantin' bad to score some rum at the bar. This was in the land of Mississippi, land of pickup trucks and unbelievers.

GOATMAN *(Laughing)*: Land where de cowboys wear their hats three sizes too small me think.

WILLY: And who was sittin' next to you?

GOATMAN: De beautifully famous Willy! I remember! De cowboy with de neck de color of cherry tomatoes, he be lookin' at me, checkin' out de locks an' the gold an' how fine my teeth gleam in de light a de cafe that be dim and seemingly lit by moonlight, man. An' he say in this loud voice—huh?

GOATMAN *snaps his fingers, expectantly.* WILLY *answers for him.*

WILLY: I ain't sure I can sit in a joint that serves goddam, crazy-looking niggers.

GOATMAN *laughs.*

GOATMAN: You see a course dat he be talkin' about de beautifully famous Goatman, de brainless honky schmuckface.

WILLY: But de Goatman plays smooth and dumb, by Jah!

GOATMAN: Oh, yah! And he smiles so pretty and his teeth gleam like so much

shark teeth on sand under Jamaican stars and Goatman say—Sumbitch, pardner, hey! You some kinda crazy fuckin' right and if dey serve me any crazy-
looking niggers I will not eat them!

WILLY: You pissin' on me, nigger?

There is such menace in WILLY's *voice that* GOATMAN *tenses in surprise and then
anger.*

GOATMAN: No, pardner, but maybe I'd like to.

WILLY *(Softly)*: That cowboy stood and there was trouble in the air, man.

GOATMAN: Hey, I know. De Goatman smelled trouble before. Knives, Willy.
Razors. And a man wantin' to see what color de Goatman's blood be and,
man . . . I don't buy it. *(As if by magic, a switchblade appears in his hand.
Pause. Suddenly* HE *laughs)* But you, Willy. Oh, you famous, lovely Willy!
I see you look up from your tequila-margarita-old fashioned martini or
whatever de hell it is de whitebread drinks, and you say—huh? *(HE snaps
his fingers)*

WILLY: Sit down, piss ant. Are you so stupid and thick that you don't recognize
the incredibly famous Goatman Jango? You touch one strand of his
disgustingly matted and putrid hair and they'll be riding your ass out of
town on a rail. Right?

GOATMAN: You know what kind of bloody right! He knew! He knew! Dere
was money on the line! Huh?

WILLY: When it comes to the color green, the whole world is bleedin²-heart
liberal, man.

GOATMAN: Ten minutes later, dat cowboy be askin' for de Goatman's autograph,
yes. De Goatman bein' so famous and all an' fame like money bein' a universal commodity in short supply all right. Ten minutes later dat cowboy be
buyin' the drinks! *(HE laughs)*

WILLY: I saved your black ass.

Silence.

GOATMAN: An' I thanked you for it. I can't be makin' your comeback, Willy.
(Pause) Willy, when I hear about you bein' shot to pieces in front of a live
audience and cable cameras, know what I figure? I figure you come against
one who needed de renown more den de money, needed de screams more
den de love. I figure it was a cowboy so stupid and thick, he think he be
shootin' at something incarnate and not something made up by de press
releases.

WILLY: You figured right.

GOATMAN: A course. I'm smart. I know dat de world is but a dream, man.
Swirlin' smoke dat ya take deep and exhale, right? Oh, so right. *(HE takes
out his knife.* HE *looks at it a moment.* HE *places it in* WILLY's *palm and gently*

closes WILLY's *hand around it.* HE *kisses* WILLY's *hand)* Be kind, man. For your soul's sake. An' man . . . *(HE reaches up and removes his dreadlocks. Beneath the wig his hair is close-cropped)* Laugh lots!

GOATMAN *laughs. And* WILLY *joins in. But then the laughter seems to stick in* WILLY's *throat. Light change. Chaos.*

Scene 6

The sudden sound of machine-gun fire, explosions, the whistle of missiles. A SOLDIER *dressed in bloody combat fatigues and carrying a machine gun comes running on.* HE *"fires," making machine-gun sounds the way a child would playing make-believe.*

ACTOR: Rats! Rats! Commie Rats! *(Explosions!* HE *rolls and comes up firing from the hip)* You killed my brother! You killed my brother! *(HE yanks a grenade from his belt and, panting with exhaustion, pulls the pin and throws it)* Eat shrapnel, scum! *(Explosion.* HE *leaps for cover and comes up shooting)* Butchers! Murderers! You're against everything freedom-loving men hold true. *(Explosions!* HE *rolls and scrambles for cover. Shooting. Whistling missiles. Explosions.* HE *pulls out binoculars and peers into the distance)* Jesus, Mary and Joseph! Wiped out! What is a solitary yankee doodle dandy to do. *(Explosion)* Assholes!

The ACTOR *runs like hell for cover and begins returning fire.* WILLY *has been watching with delighted amusement.* HE *approaches.*

WILLY: Hey, man.
ACTOR: Hey! The recently internationally famous Willy. Qué pasa, amigo? *(Shooting)* What's up?
WILLY: Not much. Listen, they're planning this big comeback for me and I was hoping you could be there?
ACTOR: A comeback, huh? When's it gonna be?
WILLY: Any moment now.

Explosion. The ACTOR *furiously returns fire.* WILLY *doesn't blink.*

ACTOR: You killed my brother! You killed my brother!
WILLY: So what do you think? I mean, I know you're in the middle of this television movie and you're just a little bit busy.

The ACTOR *takes a grenade from his belt and hands it to* WILLY.

ACTOR: Drop this for me, huh? *(WILLY does)* Grenade! Leap on it, Willy, leap on it! *(WILLY does.* HE *immediately leaps on top of* WILLY*)* Boom! Willy. Oh, God, Willy. You shouldn'ta done it, Willy, sacrificing yerself for a bunch of ne'er-do-wells like me an' the boys. What do I tell your wife Connie and your snot-nosed bambinos Homer and Roscoe? Speak to me, Willy, speak to me. *(A beat)* Hey, not bad, man. You seen a tank anywhere, Willy? That's my cue.

WILLY: Gee, I passed a tank back that way.

ACTOR: What? Aw, man. I musta missed it. Where's my bazooka? Aw, man, aw.

WILLY: Tough luck.

ACTOR: Exactly. How am I supposed to wipe out a helpless village without the proper hardware? You don't happen to have a flamethrower on you, do you, man?

WILLY: Hey, I must of left it in my other pants. Can't you use your machine gun?

ACTOR: I guess. God. It's gonna take forever. *(HE shoots from the hip)* Not bad, huh? Behind the back. Between the legs—you gotta be careful with this one. Eat lead, you godforsaken religious fanatics! We'll hold onto these oil fields or die trying!

WILLY: Whoo! Some fun.

ACTOR *(Peering through binoculars)*: I just knocked out a squadron of Shiite Moslems, opium-crazed and screaming for blood.

WILLY: I want you to come to my comeback 'cause you're brave, man, I can see how brave you are.

ACTOR: Brave's my middle name, kid. When they need a good man for an impossible mission that no one can return from, I raise my hand. *(An air-raid siren goes off)* That's my cue. Excuse me a mo'. *(HE fires and fires. A shot!* HE *is hit.* HE *sprawls to the ground.* HE *crawls towards* WILLY, *gasping in pain)* I'm hit. God, I'm hit. I don't wanna die. I don't wanna die. *(Clasping* WILLY's *ankles)* Am I gonna make it, Sarge? Am I gonna make it? Medic! My large intestine is wrapped around my ankle like a wreath! *(HE dies. A moment.* HE *suddenly sits up and studies his nails)* God, this red stuff is such a pain the way it gets in your cuticles. So! What'ja think of my death scene? Pretty good?

WILLY: Very realistic.

ACTOR: That's a compliment coming from you, amigo, 'cause, hey, you've been there.

WILLY: Listen, my comeback, can you make it? Maybe you could come armed.

There is a droning sound. The ACTOR *looks skyward.*

ACTOR: 'Bout time! It's the bombers. I been expecting'm.

WILLY: So listen, I can count on you?

ACTOR: For you, amigo, this Buster Brown'll be there. We incredibly famous have got to stick together, am I right? (*Explosion. Light change*) What the— What's that?

WILLY: Looks like a mushroom cloud.

ACTOR: What? Who wrote that into the script? Nobody tells me a damn thing.

WILLY: That must of cost your guys in special effects a bundle.

ACTOR: Who cares. Time to call it a day.

A shot. The ACTOR *falls and is motionless.* WILLY *laughs.*

WILLY: You guys, you kill me. You're always on. Television movies, man. Jesus. Nobody gets hurt, everybody gets up and goes home. Hey, if this was real, I bet they couldn't get you up off your belly with a backhoe, huh? Hey. My comeback. I can count on you, right? (*And then with growing panic*) They shot you. Oh, no. They shot him. The star. Somebody shot the star! Somebody is shooting the stars! Somebody is shooting all the stars! Help me! Help me!

The ACTOR *suddenly springs to his feet, laughing.*

ACTOR: Fooled ya. Come on, kid. Willy, what's the matter? Come on, dinner's on me.

The ACTOR *exits, whistling.* WILLY *stands there looking lost and terrified. Light change. Music. Chaos.*

Scene 7

The sound of keys turning in a lock. The sound of a door opening and closing. Light as a wall switch is hit. WILLY, *who has been asleep on the floor, sits up with a frightened shout.* DARLENE *gasps and drops her bags of groceries.*

WILLY: Hi, darlin'. Fell asleep. Didn't mean to startle you. Forget I still have a key? Guess I should have called. You look . . . so good. Like always. Know something? I'm always thinking I see you at a distance. Walking a beach. Across a street, waiting for the red. In passing cars. I'll go, like—hey! That's Darlene. Can't be. It is. No. Yes! And I go tearing off in pursuit.

DARLENE: It's not me, is it.

WILLY: Hasn't been yet. And so I make a fool out of myself in front of a strange woman.

DARLENE: I'm sure they don't mind, Willy, when they see it's you.

WILLY: Darlene? You ever think you see me?

DARLENE: No.

WILLY: Oh. Would you run for a better look if you did?

DARLENE (*Picking up her bags*): Have you eaten, Willy?

WILLY: Not for days and days.

DARLENE: Are you hungry?

WILLY: There are pangs.

DARLENE: I'll get dinner off the floor and into a pan.

WILLY: Where's the kid.

DARLENE: She has a name.

WILLY: Where's Patty?

DARLENE: At my mother's.

WILLY: Oh. How come?

DARLENE: I'm going away for a week.

WILLY: Oh. Where.

DARLENE: I'm just going away.

WILLY: Heard I was in town, huh? Where you going?

DARLENE: The Bahamas.

WILLY: Only people I know who go to the Bahamas are dope dealers. You getting into dope?

DARLENE: I've had my share of dopes.

WILLY: Goin' by yourself?

DARLENE: Would you like a beer or a glass of wine?

WILLY: Jesus, Darlene, you still have this bad habit of never lying.

DARLENE: We're not married anymore. I don't have to tell you.

WILLY: If the truth's gonna hurt you either change the subject or you don't say a thing.

DARLENE: I'm not going by myself. That shouldn't hurt you.

WILLY: Did I say it did?

DARLENE: You looked like it did.

WILLY: It serious?

DARLENE: Yes.

WILLY: All right, don't lie but couldn't you learn to fudge a little bit?

DARLENE: You shouldn't care.

WILLY: Did I say I did?

DARLENE: You look like you do.

WILLY: Maybe the kid could stay with me while you're gone.

DARLENE: She has a name.

WILLY: I'm around for awhile.

DARLENE: Willy, she has a name.

WILLY: They have me making this comeback. Too bad you're going to miss it.

DARLENE: She has a name.

WILLY: Patty. O.K.? Patty. Her name is Patty. Can Patty come stay with me while you're off fucking someone in the Bahamas?

DARLENE: No.

Pause.

WILLY: Sorry. Sorry, Darlene. I don't know . . . every time I see you, no matter how long it's been, I realize . . .

DARLENE: What.

WILLY: I realize how much I . . . you know . . .

DARLENE: What.

WILLY: You know.

DARLENE: I've never doubted all the times you've loved me, Willy. I've just never been able to handle all the times you haven't. Did you know I thought you were dead?

WILLY: Hey.

DARLENE: I was watching the news. They showed a film clip. The women screaming. The men struggling with that guy. You. On your back, your arms and legs at funny angles and your eyes were open and even on. . . . Even on television I could tell you weren't seeing anything. I was sure you were dead.

WILLY: What'd you do?

DARLENE: I turned off the set. I took the phone off the hook. I didn't answer the door when people knocked.

WILLY: What'd you do with the—Patty.

DARLENE: I brought her into bed with me that night and I held her.

WILLY: It help?

DARLENE: It helped me.

WILLY: Darlene? You want to see my back?

DARLENE: Is it horrible?

WILLY: No, it's beautiful.

DARLENE: No.

WILLY: Listen, can I . . . ? You mind if I sorta . . . ? (HE *takes her arms and puts them around him.* HE *holds her close.* SHE *doesn't resist*) Squeeze a little, will ya? *(With a sigh,* SHE *does.* THEY *kiss)* Can we go in the bedroom?

DARLENE *(A moment)*: All right. You can't spend the night.

WILLY: Please.

DARLENE: No.

WILLY: Will you still make me dinner?

DARLENE: Come on.

SHE *leads him away by the hand. Light change. Music: an acoustic guitar.*

Scene 8

Shadows up on WILLY. HE *is sitting, shirtless.* HE *strums an acoustic guitar, shaping the chords with effort. The feeling is that* HE's *sitting by a window looking down into the street. The lights of passing automobiles play off him. A* WOMAN'S VOICE *calls out of the dark.*

BLONDE: Willy? Willy? (SHE *enters.* SHE *wears a long sheer nightgown*) Hi. I woke up and you weren't there and then I heard you out here. Whatcha doin'? Couldn't sleep? Sometimes I, like, can't sleep. It's no fun. You wanna, like, try again?

WILLY: I wouldn't be any better than last time.

BLONDE: Oh, it was O.K. It was very good. Really. I mean, I've had worse. You just weren't in the mood I don't think. I sometimes am not in the mood. But it doesn't matter if I'm not 'cause, like, you can't tell and I can just pretend that I am. Oh, but I didn't. Not with you. Oh, no never. You really turn me on and I like you a lot.

WILLY: You hardly know me.

BLONDE: Oh, but I feel like I do. I feel like I've known you forever. I was very excited when you called.

WILLY: I didn't want to be alone. I was with someone and they were leaving town and . . . well, I called. I wake you?

BLONDE: I didn't mind. Play me something? (HE *shakes his head no*) Teach me to play something?

WILLY: Would you like to learn the perfect E chord?

BLONDE: You think I could?

WILLY: It won't be easy. (HE *hands her the guitar and forms a chord with her left hand*) And your hand goes like this.

BLONDE: Wow. I'm getting a cramp.

WILLY: Shake it out, Momma.

BLONDE: You're funny.

WILLY: Strum.

SHE *does. It sounds horrible.*

BLONDE: I think I need an amplifier.

WILLY: Press hard.

SHE *strums.*

BLONDE: I did it.

WILLY: An E chord.

BLONDE: Wow! Are there any songs in the chord of E?

WILLY: Raise that finger.

BLONDE (*Strumming*): Oh!

WILLY: E minor.

BLONDE: It sounds like . . .

WILLY: It sounds like a man has lost something and can't find it.

BLONDE: Oh. Well, yeah, it sorta does. . . . No. It sounds like flamenco dancers. It sounds like gypsies. Wow, I'm playing the guitar. I've never been able to play anything before. I mean, my boobs have a tendency to get in the way of most normal human activities. You play.

WILLY: I can't. My fingers don't . . .

BLONDE: Oh. From the . . . ? It's a beautiful scar. Does it hurt?

WILLY: There are pangs.

BLONDE: I'm glad it didn't happen to me. I do my best work on my back. You smiled. I saw. Good.

Lights from a passing car play off them.

WILLY: You ever wonder who drives cars at night? Maybe nobody. Maybe the cars drive themselves. Maybe they wait till their owners are all in bed and then they go off and meet somewhere and have a big party. Get bombed on high-test. Snort motor oil. Caress each other's exhaust pipes. Nine months later the unlucky ones give birth to compacts.

BLONDE: You're not like I thought you'd be.

WILLY: How'd you think I'd be?

BLONDE: Well, adventurous.

WILLY: Like on my album covers? *(Pause)* Have you ever bought one of my albums?

BLONDE: See, I heard they were making a movie of your life story and all, and I thought you must be sorta adventurous for them to do that. And sorta dangerous. And sorta comical in all the witty things you must all the time sorta say. And like, if you have any influence and could set up an audition . . . *(Pause)* Movies are great, you know? Sometimes in movies everybody is sad? Somebody has died and everybody is in mourning. Everybody is miserable and they still seem to be having a better time than I ever have. On my best days even. I thought you'd be like that. Having a better time.

WILLY: What do you think now?

BLONDE: I don't know. You're nice but you seem . . . sad. *Sad*-sad. Don't be sad. At least you'll always be able to say you were famous for a little while. I'd give anything to be like you. Noticed. Most of us never get noticed for anything. I want more than that. I want . . . I want men to threaten to throw themselves off tall buildings if I won't marry them. And when I won't? They do. I'd like to feign humility while all the time accepting important awards. Thank you, everyone, thank you. I'd like to thank . . . me. I want . . . I want. . . . I don't know what I want. It all.

WILLY: Look, I'm having this . . . you want to come to a . . . never mind.

BLONDE: Sometimes people like me but sometimes they seem embarrassed to have me around.

WILLY: No.

BLONDE: It's O.K. Thank you for teaching me the perfect E.

WILLY: Keep the guitar. Practice.

BLONDE: You wanna . . . uhm? It'll be better this time. I know you now and I won't expect anything. Come on, sweetheart. I'll do it all.

SHE *kisses him and then exits into the dark.* WILLY *rises and turns to watch her go. The lights of a passing car play off him. The scar is like an angry red road down his back.* WILLY *follows the* GIRL *into the dark.*

Scene 9

Light change. Music. A VOICE *out of the blackness.*

SUIT: Ladies and gentlemen, the incredibly notorious Gypsey Davey!

Lights up on WILLY *putting on his shirt. A* GIRL *enters as if pushed through an open doorway.* SHE *is small and pale and her hair is spiked and streaked violet.* SHE *wears tattered clothing and leather.* SHE *is more frightening than comic, is very attractive in a waif-like sort of way.* SHE *stares at* WILLY, *all challenge, as a* VOICE *sings from offstage.*

GYPSEY: It was late last night when the boss came home, askin' about his lady.

WILLY *joins in, harmonizing.*

WILLY & GYPSEY: An' the only answer he received, is she's gone with Gypsey Davey.

GYPSEY *enters.* HE *is a huge man in fringed buckskin and cowboy boots and hat.* HE *has been drinking. The* PUNK *sits on the floor and "watches television."*

GYPSEY: Be you the incredibly famous Willy Rivers?
WILLY: I be. An' who be you, handsome stranger?
GYPSEY: I be the notorious poontanger, Gypsey Davey. Is your dance card filled, you homo?
WILLY: Who leads, ye or me?
GYPSEY *(Embracing* WILLY*)*: You since you're havin' a comeback, Jack! Whoo-ee, Momma! Tell your daughters to pretend they're wheelbarrows, Willy Rivers gonna drive . . . them . . . home!
WILLY: How's life, Gypsey?
GYPSEY: Sweet-potato sweet, boss. You really gonna let'm take a second shot?
WILLY: What am I if I ain't a star?
GYPSEY: True enough. What are we without our public? *(*HE *grabs a half-full bottle of bourbon from the jacket pocket of the* PUNK*)* You hear my latest? Jewel-encrusted solid plutonium.
WILLY: Any good?
GYPSEY: Jesus, faithless women, drunks, pickups, shotguns, freight trains and your basic halfwit virgin cousin.
WILLY: An' the flipside?

GYPSEY: Same thing recorded slower. It be selling, famous Willy, how it sells. Hold it. Wait! Check this out, pardner. Come here, darlin'. *(HE lifts the PUNK up off the floor and sets her on her feet)*

PUNK: How come we don't have this room? I like this room better than our room.

GYPSEY: It's the same room, darlin'.

PUNK: The furniture faces in a different direction.

GYPSEY: Haw! Ain't she somethin'? Don't she make your gonads come to attention? Are we a couple or what? I love her, honest. I can't get enough of her. She's fourteen-carat gold, matie. Watch this. *(Grabbing her roughly)* Ramones, darlin'. Rock and roll as decadence. Thousand-watt Marshall amps in feedback land with the lead guitarist, an acid freak in a Mohican and a tutu, playin' a Stratocaster with his teeth.

PUNK: Tsk. Take it into traffic.

GYPSEY: Haw! Join in, Willy. You and me been there. South a Houston!

WILLY: East a Sheridan Square!

GYPSEY: Mudd Club!

WILLY: CBGB's!

GYPSEY: A band named after somebody barfin'!

WILLY: Sid Vicious scarfin' hisself and his old lady in some fleabag in Chelsea!

GYPSEY: Violence!

WILLY: Hate!

GYPSEY: Shaved heads!

WILLY: Razorbladed retinas!

GYPSEY: Unrest and discontent seethin' in the urban cauldron of a youthful wasteland.

WILLY: The bomb!

GYPSEY: Boom!

WILLY: Nothing!

GYPSEY: Nuclear winter!

WILLY: Radioactive babies!

GYPSEY: God is dead!

WILLY: Or wearing headphones and the music's turned to ten!

WILLY *and* GYPSEY *collapse to the floor, exhausted and panting. The* GIRL *stands there, unmoved.*

GYPSEY: She's gold, Willy, solid gold. She's dyed her bush that color too.

PUNK: Die. Just die.

GYPSEY: I ain't complainin', darlin'! Took a little gettin' used to first time I went carpet-munchin' but I'm gettin' so's I like it.

PUNK: Roll over and die twice.

GYPSEY: No. We understand. Don't we, Willy? Way back when he and me joined hands.

WILLY: Grew our hair.

THE INCREDIBLY FAMOUS WILLY RIVERS • 139

GYPSEY: Chanted mantras.

WILLY: Sang protest songs.

WILLY & GYPSEY *(Singing)*: Kum-bai-ya, my lord, kum-bai-ya.

GYPSEY: Passé, darlin'.

WILLY: Useless.

GYPSEY: Wouldn't make the inside pages a *Newsweek* let alone the cover.

WILLY: You do what you do.

GYPSEY: I hear ya. Couple a years from now though, honey, you're gonna hope that shit washes out.

> GYPSEY *scoops up the bottle of bourbon. A look passes between the* GIRL *and* GYPSEY *and* SHE *approaches.* HE *takes a gulp of bourbon and then, through clenched teeth, spits it in a hard stream into the* GIRL'S *open mouth.* BOTH *of them laugh.*

You wanna blowjob, Willy? This little darlin' gargles spermatozoa.

> *The* PUNK *approaches* WILLY, *sinks to her knees in front of him.*

WILLY *(Gently)*: No.

GYPSEY: Here's the key to our room, darlin'. Go on back and stick something up your nose.

PUNK *(To* WILLY*)*: I like this room better.

> SHE *exits.* GYPSEY *now speaks in a normal voice, with no trace of country accent.*

GYPSEY: Do you think I'm a degenerate?

WILLY: Yup.

GYPSEY: Me too. (HE *takes a big belt of booze.* HE *offers the bottle to* WILLY, *who refuses it)* How are you, Willy?

WILLY: I'd say terrified sums it up. And yourself, Gene?

GYPSEY *(Taking a drink)*: Surviving nicely, thanks. Gene. When's the last time anyone called me Gene.

WILLY: When's the last time you spoke like a normal human being?

GYPSEY: Long time, boss.

WILLY: Anybody ever wonder how a boy from Marblehead, Massachusetts picked up a Southern accent?

GYPSEY: Nope. Neither has anyone asked how a graduate of the Juilliard School of Music seems only able to play three chords.

WILLY: Nobody wonders, nobody cares.

GYPSEY: Course not. They just figure the territory comes with the cowboy hat. (HE *begins carefully laying out lines of cocaine)* Chill out, son. It'd be a real mistake to think people take us at any more than face value. When it gets down to basics, celebrity comes in second to the price of milk, bread and ground beef.

WILLY: Why me.

GYPSEY: Breakdown in security, I guess. I tell you, there's coming a time when the rich are gonna live in fortresses. Locked doors, armed guards, tanks instead of station wagons. Haves versus the have nots, Willy. That's what's coming. You lived in a gilded fishbowl for too long. New York, L.A. and TWA. It's a jungle out there, son. Most people don't read the newspaper, they *are* the newspaper. You got a man who works fifty hours a week in a steel mill to feed his kids, he's got no savin's, his car is rusting to pieces, his house is falling apart, his son is getting into drugs, his wife is pushing a size eighteen and every time he turns on the tube, he sees people who have what he thinks he oughta have and knows he never will. That can make for some anger, son. That can make for a little despair. That can make you want to shoot somebody. Either that or dance to rock music. *(HE takes an enormous snort of cocaine)*

WILLY: Gypsey? I've been sleeping fourteen hours a day lately. More.

GYPSEY: Ah. *(HE takes another hit)*

WILLY: It's not the sleep I like. It's the moment before waking. You drift. I could drift forever.

When GYPSEY *speaks now, the accent is back full force. It's as if* HE's *shifted from first to fifth gear.*

GYPSEY: I'm givin' all this up soon and becomin' a surfer I think!! 'At's a fine obsession, lookin' for perfection in a curl a water! *(HE takes a belt of bourbon)*

WILLY: Why'd that guy shoot me, Gene? Why shoot a stranger?

GYPSEY: I'm also thinkin' strongly on becomin' a marathon runner! I'd look some kinda cute in a pair a sheer nylon shorts and I hear you get high from oxygen deficiency! *(HE takes another belt)*

WILLY: Will you stop with that and listen to me!?

GYPSEY: Aw, man! Anything you do, if you love it, shit, that's the only reason you need to do it. But ya gotta be careful. People get jealous. You got somethin' good, people want to take it.

WILLY: Unless you screw it up yourself.

GYPSEY: Hey. Listen, man, listen.

HE *sings. The melody is from the aria in* Gianni Schicchi *that the daughter sings to her father. The words are* GYPSEY's. HE's *countrified it.*

Oh, my love, I love you
You know how much I love you
You know I'll always love you
Love you with all my heart.

GYPSEY *stops. Pause.* WILLY *has turned away in disgust.* GYPSEY *sings again. But this time the melody is pure and clear and the voice is deep and sad and recognizable as a voice once classically trained.*

Oh, my love I need you
You know how much I need you
You know I'll always need you
Need you with all my . . .

Pause.

WILLY: Why'd you stop, Gene, that's pretty. You write that?

GYPSEY: My next big hit, son. Music by Puccini, lyrics by yours truly, the incredibly notorious Gypsey Davey. . . . Ah, christ, fuck me. (HE *chugs the
bourbon)*

WILLY: Aw, Gene, look at you, man.

GYPSEY: I was gonna be a singer, a real one.

WILLY: You don't have to worry about people shootin' at you, you're killing
yourself.

GYPSEY: I loved to fuckin' sing.

WILLY: You're no help at all, man!

WILLY *exits, leaving him.*

GYPSEY: Yeah, I don't blame ya! Go! My fault, right? Mine, mine, mine. (HE
wets his fingers and wipes up the rest of the cocaine. HE *licks it off his fingers)* Too
late. Don't you do it. *(Exiting)* Gimme a call, son. I'm aroun'. I got lights.

GYPSEY *hits a switch. Lights to black. The sudden sound of a restless crowd; cheers,
voices, stamping feet. A* VOICE *speaks out of the black.*

SUIT: Ladies and gentlemen, the incredibly famous Willy Rivers!

*The screaming and applause of the crowd is deafening. It's like an arena is being
shaken to its roots by the sound of cheers. Lights crisscross the stage like laser beams.
Music as* WILLY *hits the stage.*

WILLY *(Screaming to be heard)*: Thank you! Thank you very much!

The music changes gears; hard-driving, expectant. WILLY *reaches for the mike and
sings.*

The stage dims
The noise stops
I look out on ten thousand faces
The drums start
It's only a heartbeat away
I grab the light

The words take flight
Fulfill all the expectations
They surge like a tide
They careen and glide into space
Rock and roll
Fills a young man's soul
Fills him with a kind of freedom
He escapes for awhile
The work and the trial of his day
He looks at me
And he likes what he sees
Likes the light and the beat and the badness
The leather and lace
Doesn't seem out of place to a kid

The boy with the backbeat fills them with expectation
The boy with the backbeat they take as the truth
The boy with the backbeat they take as a kind of rapture
The boy with the backbeat cries on

The boy wails
The boy flails
Possessed by some inner rhythm
The boy sings
The mike like a wand in his hand
The joint rocks
People stand in their seats
Clap hands in a shared communion
The boy never stops
He moves like he generates heat

The boy with the backbeat fills them with anticipation
The boy with the backbeat they take as their own.
The boy with the backbeat fills them with a holy madness
The boy with the backbeat cries on.

He cries on. And on. He cries on and on and on and on and on . . .

A MAN *runs out of the audience onto the stage.* HE *dances with the music, his arms above his head in ecstasy. Suddenly* HE *draws a pistol from under his shirt, raises it and fires.* WILLY *is hit, goes sprawling. The* ASSASSIN *fires again and* WILLY *jerks as the bullet hits him in the back. Chaos.* MEN *run from the wings and drag the* GUNMAN *away. Feedback.* WILLY *is lying in a pool of blood. Screams. Fade to silence. The lights on* WILLY *dim to black. The sound of an ambulance grows and then fades away. Lights up.* WILLY *is center, the horror of the memory still with him.* SUIT *is standing next to him but* WILLY *is oblivious.*

SUIT: Willy. Willy. It's time.

Lights fade to black.

END OF ACT ONE

ACT TWO

Scene 1

An electric guitar screams out of the black, the notes one on top of another, clear yet unbelievably fast. Lights up on WILLY. HE *stands, holding the guitar, staring at his hands, unable to play, the solo now nothing more than a memory. Light change. A glitzy curtain drops down in front of* WILLY. *Music—the big-band sound. It's a late-night talk show. From behind the curtain comes the* HOST. HE *cavorts around the stage, all smiles.* HE *cuts the music. Riotous applause.* HE *cuts it to sudden silence with a gesture.*

HOST: Oooh! What a wonderful crowd. Ah! So exciting. How many people took the bus? Oooh! *(To an audience member)* How ya doin'? Been here before? Hey! You're somebody now! Come on, everybody, repeat after me! I'm somebody now! *(A beat)* Perfect. Ladies and gentlemen, I just can't wait. You are not going to believe who's here. We are talking about a media myth, ladies and gentlemen. This man was shot and almost killed on national television. You don't get much more vital than that and god, I wish I had the courage to do it, I bet all of you out there do too.

WILLY *suddenly comes out from behind the curtain.*

Wha. . . . Well, here he is! Getting impatient, are we, big guy? Boo-boo-boo-ha-ha-ha! Come on out here! Ladies and gentlemen, let's have a big, warm round of welcome for the incredibly famous Willy Rivers!

WILLY *comes forward to thunderous applause.* HE *is higher than a kite.*

Tack on over, Willy! Come on down to our stage, Topo Gejo! Careful! Boo-ha-ha!
WILLY: Bang! Bang! Gotcha!
HOST: Whoa!
WILLY: Ha-ha-ha! Just a little tasteless humor!
HOST: It certainly is! But don't worry, we thrive on it! Boo-ha-ha! *(Kissing* WIL-LY's *cheek, missing by a mile)* Willy, Willy, moi, moi, how ya doin', Willy?
WILLY: I feel good, I feel fast, I feel relaxed.
HOST: I hear you're making a comeback, Willy.
WILLY: What a ya think brings me here, man?
HOST: You've come to tell us about it?
WILLY: Gosh, oh, blinky, I sure have! But first! Hey. You gonna ask me about my sex life?
HOST: Oh, he's such a kidder!
WILLY: Come on! Why ya think you stay so high in the ratings, man? Ask me when's the last time I got laid. Ask me! Ask me if I suffer from impotence

or premature ejaculation. Ask me if I've slept with a woman of every race.

HOST: Boo-boo-boo-boohaha-boohahaha-hahahaha-boohahaboo! Have all of you out there noticed how the incredibly famous are also incredibly witty?

WILLY: It's almost like—whoa!—our lines were written for us!

HOST: Is that a hard concept to handle or what!

WILLY: Enough chitchat! What else we got on this show tonight?

HOST: Well, I think we have a maaaaaaaarvelous show for our viewing audience tonight.

WILLY: All to ease the boredom of their paltry, dreary, uneventful lives!

HOST: Do we have a—Cosmo Harrington, ladies and gentlemen, our stage manager, and just knowing him makes me feel like somebody!

WILLY: We have a show for'm, Cos!? We don't!? All right, everybody go on home! Cos says we don't have any kind of show for you at all. Somebody made a mistake. They're somebody now!

HOST: This beautiful guy is such a comedian! *(Half-whisper)* Cool your jets or you're out of here.

WILLY: Hey! How awful to be nobody, huh? No better than a frog. Drowning. Hey. In a small-time, small-town bog.

HOST *(Applauding)*: Oooh. I think Willy would like to thank Emily Dickinson for inspiring that little verse. Emmie. *(Blowing kisses towards heaven)* Moi! Moi!

WILLY: Yeah, I'd also like to thank your staff writers for taking it and bastardizing it completely, all for the viewing audience's amusement. Keep up the good work, guys, you're cheese weenies! *(There is the sound of boos from the audience)* Fuck you.

HOST: We'll bleep that.

WILLY *(Raising a middle finger)*: Bleep this.

HOST: Ahem. Our other guests tonight include that beautiful Hungarian blonde we all love so much.

WILLY: You mean the one in her mid-sixties who'd have us believe she's in her thirties?

HOST: She speaks English with the cutest little accent.

WILLY: Has a well-publicized dislike of the mentally handicapped and, you guessed it, she's had a lot of husbands.

HOST: Boo-ha-ha-ha-boo! *(Half-whisper)* You're being an asshole.

WILLY: Brontosaurus matrimonius! *(More boos from audience)* Thank you. The feeling's mutual.

HOST: Ladies and gentlemen, we'll bring out a *real* singer for you in a minute.

WILLY: What's he gonna do for us, Cos? I put a bar in the back of my car and I'm driving myself to drink? Should be a trip!

HOST: O.K., that does it, go on, get out of here, leave!

WILLY: Hey, hey, the singer, man. Let's catch him by surprise. He's a homosexual, ladies and gentlemen! *(More boos)* Uh-huh, yeah, he is and if we catch him off guard, make him giggle or something, you'll pick up on it right away! *(To the HOST)* Shall we ruin his career? Why don't we?

HOST: Why not? You're already ruining yours.

WILLY: Aw . . . have I offended anyone tonight. Well, hey! I guess I'm—come on, everybody!—somebody now! Bring on the Hungarian blonde, Cos! Come on, ladies and gentlemen, let's have a nice warm round of applause for plastic surgery!

HOST: Will somebody give this guy the hook?

WILLY: She's going to tell us about her hysterectomy and I just know we're going to laugh until we're sick.

HOST: I want this guy out of here right now.

WILLY: The singer, Cos! He's such a savage!

MEN *rush on and grab* WILLY. HE *struggles as* THEY *try to pull him offstage.*

Hey! This is great! A wish come true! Once again people are trying to kill me on national television and I just can't thank them enough!

HOST: We're going to take a short break.

WILLY *breaks free. The* MEN *are quickly after him.*

WILLY: But before we go, remember, anybody can be somebody in this great country of ours!

HOST: Can we give this bum some traveling music?

Music! The big-band sound.

WILLY: Oh, it's been so great being on the show! Lately the craziest things seem to happen when I'm around! You've all made me feel like such a star! Thank you! Thank you! (*The* MEN *drag him away*) Hey! I guess I'm . . . somebody now! I'm somebody now! I'm somebody now! I'm somebody now! (HE *is pulled offstage*)

HOST (*As if nothing has happened*): We'll be right back after this word from our sponsor.

The big-band music turns to distortion as the HOST *runs to the curtains, drags them down and runs offstage. Chaos.*

Scene 2

SUIT *enters to find* WILLY *huddled and lost in thought.*

SUIT: Willy, Willy, enough, Willy.

WILLY: Oh, oh, devil with a blue suit on.

SUIT: How much longer? People don't like to wait. I've had enough. From here on things run like a clock.

WILLY: I can't do it.

SUIT: Look, maybe all you need is a little something to give you courage. A little something to ease the stage fright.

WILLY: Like what, a bulletproof vest?

SUIT: What's the matter with you? When did you start thinking the worst thing they could throw at you were tomatoes?

WILLY: Sacrifice somebody else to'm! Give'm gladiators, man! Give'm two guys in loincloths going at each other with razor-edged knives! They'll love that! Be sorta like boxing or football but to the death! Yeah! That'll get'm off the streets and into stadiums where people like you can keep an eye on'm! Talk to the Marines, man! Order up some volunteers! 'Cause, man, I am not goin' on!

SUIT: Willy . . . they're waiting for you. If you only knew the love they're waiting for you with.

WILLY: They want me dead.

SUIT: They want to pay homage.

WILLY: To my memory, not to me.

SUIT: Willy, you're bigger than ever. You're more famous than ever—

WILLY: Jesus, sometimes it's like getting shot to pieces was the best stroke of P.R. anybody could have come up with for me!

SUIT: Kid, you don't get press for good deeds. No one buys tickets to see you because you're an upstanding member of the community. Survivors grab the spotlight. Hostages. Victims of circumstance.

WILLY: What about my music?

SUIT: May I be honest?

WILLY: Oh, shit, I'd prefer not.

SUIT: Tastes and opinions change. In ten years people might think your music— anybody's music—is a bore.

WILLY: Lies! I want lies!

SUIT: In a hundred years they'll think this "music" was never any good to begin with. But you, Willy. You!

WILLY: A stranger tried to kill me.

SUIT: It was a stroke of luck. A career-breaker. Willy, it's time. You're going on and you're going to show them miracles. We are going to ascend heights you never imagined. We are going to stand at the top of mountains and look down and the world is going to be at our feet.

WILLY: Screaming for me to jump.

SUIT: They'll catch you.

WILLY: No.

SUIT: The only thing more disgusting than some punk who is on the verge of having it all is to hear him cry about it! Poor me, poor me. You're going on. You're facing the music. After that, you're on your own. You can sink as deep into oblivion as you want. *(HE starts to exit. HE stops and turns)* Unless you're good.

SUIT exits. Light change. The echoing sound of cell doors slamming shut. A MAN skips on like a small unassuming child. HE is followed by an ORDERLY.

ORDERLY: Five minutes. No more.

The PRISONER approaches WILLY. HE smiles, shyly.

PRISONER: Hi.

WILLY: Thank you for seeing me.

PRISONER: It's a pleasure. I didn't think you'd be able to swing it. You did. I'm glad. Did they frisk him? *(The ORDERLY nods)* I wondered. Not that I think you'd try anything. Yes, it's a pleasure and an honor and I've been looking forward to it. *(HE holds out his hand for WILLY to shake. A moment. WILLY shakes it)* Now we're friends. I have watched you play so many times.

WILLY: You have?

PRISONER: Oh, yes. In my opinion, you're an artist. You always have been. Like me.

WILLY: You?

PRISONER: An artist changes one's perception of reality. I changed yours a lot.

WILLY: You did.

PRISONER: Don't thank me. At the time, changing your perception of reality wasn't my intention.

WILLY: What was your intention?

PRISONER: I was trying to kill you. *(Pause)* However, since death might be considered a drastic change in perception, I guess you could say my intentions have been consistent from the beginning. Artistically speaking.

WILLY: Why.

PRISONER: Why what, Willy? *(HE giggles)* That sounds funny. All those *W* sounds. WhywhatWilly. Why. Because why, that's why.

WILLY: That's not an answer.

PRISONER: I think he's getting violent.

ORDERLY *(To WILLY)*: Don't.

PRISONER: You ever killed anybody?

WILLY: No.

PRISONER: Ever want to? He has. I bet you have. It's great. You're so in control. Of course I'm talking premeditated. You're so . . . powerful. You walk down the street and no one knows how powerful you are. You're like God. All you have to do is act and everything changes. You've taken a color out of a painting and substituted one of your own. You've given somebody else's melody different notes. You're a pebble that's been dropped in a pond.

Concentric circles get wider and wider. He's getting violent. He's going
to hurt me.

ORDERLY: He hasn't twitched.

PRISONER: You watching him?

ORDERLY *(Sighing)*: Like a hawk.

PRISONER: When you're capable of killing, you're not afraid of anyone! You
laugh inside 'cause you know that hardly anybody is capable of striking
out the way you are. For keeps.

WILLY: But why me?

PRISONER: You look good. People like you. Girls, I bet, like you. I bet they
want to fuck you. I bet you have fun. I don't have fun. I never did. Why
you. Why not me. Why not me!?

ORDERLY: Cool out.

PRISONER: I was contemplating the President but it didn't look like he'd be passing through town for quite some time. You were elected. *(HE giggles)* I made
a pun. I did, I made a pun, huh!?

ORDERLY: I'm ecstatic.

PRISONER: If you must know, it was nothing personal. When I pulled the trigger I wasn't even thinking of you. No. I was thinking of me. I was thinking of me and what everybody else was gonna be thinking of me.

WILLY: What were they going to think of you.

PRISONER: I dunno but they were gonna and that's something. I'm a pretty
far-out dude, you know.

WILLY: I'm sure.

PRISONER: Better believe it.

WILLY: I do.

PRISONER: Yup. And so does everybody out there. I have gotten over a hundred death threats! And at least twenty-five proposals of marriage. That's
something.

WILLY: It is.

PRISONER: There's a campaign started to free me.

WILLY: I'm sure.

PRISONER: Oh! And I've found Jesus.

WILLY: Where?

PRISONER: Have you always been so cynical?

WILLY: What were you before . . . ?

PRISONER: Before we met? I was a custodial engineer. I worked at a hotel. I
picked up after people like you. Televisions thrown from the fourteenth
floor in an attempt to hit the swimming pool. Parties. Groupies. I heard
of this one girl, she was casting molds of you people? Of your . . . things.
For posterity's sake? That happen to you? She entice you into a little . . .
you know . . . and then whip out the Playdough? Famous people sure do
lead the life of Sodom and Gomorrah, huh? Lucky we don't turn to salt.
You know, even before I made my initial artistic statement of trying to shoot

your lights out, I was interested in the creative process. I mean, right this minute, here and now, are you creating? Is it thunderbolts? Is that how the muse strikes you? I'd really like to know.

WILLY: At this moment, it's like I'm sitting here sifting through garbage, and kerplew, a dove is shitting in my hat.

PRISONER (*Giggling happily*): Kerplew!

WILLY: This nonsense would make a song I say to myself.

PRISONER: Kerplew!

WILLY: Add some violins and some congas and somewhere some drug-addled kid'll dance to it.

PRISONER: Kerplew!

WILLY: Top ten.

PRISONER: Kerplew!

WILLY: Platinum.

PRISONER: Kerplew!

WILLY: Rich as Croesus and for what. It's enough to make you mad. I want to thank you.

PRISONER: Really?

WILLY: Oh, yeah! You coulda gone after a really big, big name but did you? No! You chose me! You are the straw that has stirred my drink! And talk about personal enlightenment! The things I was concerned with, man! I wasn't concerned with the things that most people are concerned with. Breakfast, lunch, dinner. No, not me. I was in search of meaningful existence. Thanks to you, now I'm into barely surviving. It makes living risky. It makes it intriguing on a daily basis. Nothing like facing death to make existence meaningful, right? Aw, christ . . .

PRISONER: Is it time for me to go yet?

WILLY: No! I don't blame you, really, it was my mistake. I spent all my time trying to be famous. I might as well have painted a bull's-eye on my back. A low profile, that's the ticket. Keep your head down and out of the line of fire. Those who know, buddy, those who really control, those who play the pieces, the chessmasters, buddy, the suits, they're faceless. They're smart. I wasn't smart at all. My priorities got all fucked up. Creative, special, famous. Bullshit! When a person can become famous for something as senseless as pulling a trigger, why try to be famous at all. (*As if accepting an award*) Thank you, yes, thank you, Mom and Dad. It takes a certain sort of imagination to carry off this personal form of creative expression that I am justifiably famous for, don'tcha know. (HE *aims his finger at the* PRISONER, *like a gun*) Kerplew.

PRISONER (*"Shooting" back*): Kerplew!

WILLY: Yes, it takes a certain sort of nom de plume . . .

PRISONER: Kerplew!

WILLY: A little bit of c'est la guerre, right?

PRISONER: Kerplew!

THE INCREDIBLY FAMOUS WILLY RIVERS • 151

WILLY: A little bit of je ne sais quoi.
PRISONER: Kerplew, kerplew, kerplew!
WILLY: Sheep. All of us.

The PRISONER bleats—Baaa-aa! WILLY throws himself at the PRISONER and begins strangling him. The PRISONER shrieks like a helpless child. The ORDERLY leaps between them, struggling to pull WILLY away. HE succeeds, throwing WILLY bodily.

Run for the fucking hills! Sex and death, death and sex, that's all anyone's concerned with around here. Get out of the line of fire. Get away from the battle zone. In ten years it'll all mean nothing and in a hundred years it'll all be forgotten. Flatulence to flatulence, muck to muck, may we rest in peace. Kerplew! Nothing means nothing. Kerplew! Nothing adds up to nothing. Kerplew, kerplew! Sex and death. Death and sex! Get fucked and die. Get fucked and die! Get fucked and die!!
ORDERLY: Time.
PRISONER: I gotta go. Listen, I want to mention that I'll be coming up for parole? If you could put in a good word for me, maybe publicly forgive me, it'd be a help. Maybe our fan clubs could organize something that would be to our mutual benefit. (HE *sticks out his hand.* HE *takes* WILLY's *lifeless hand and inserts it into his own outstretched hand.* HE *shakes*) Good. We really are friends. It's been very nice meeting you. Formally, I mean. Don't forget, a word from you would help. (HE *skips offstage like a small child*)
ORDERLY: Looney tunes. This fruitcake costs the state several hundred dollars a day. You ask me, we should dig a ditch, bury bozos like him in the dirt up to their necks with only their heads above ground. Then we run over their heads with tractors. Till the ground is as level as a Kansas field. Then we plant wheat. Mental cases like that, it's a sickness, know what I mean? It's catching. Well, off to the wars. It's all gonna get worse before it gets better. That's my motto. (HE *stops just before* HE *exits.* HE *aims a finger at* WIL-LY) Kerplew!

The ORDERLY exits. Pause.

WILLY: Only the ball, only the ball, only the ball. . . . Friends! I need friends for my comeback! Darlene!?

Light change. Music. WILLY'S VOICE *calling out of chaotic light and sound.*

Scene 3

Night. WILLY *runs on, breathless.*

WILLY: Darlene? Darlene!? Darlene, where are you?

DARLENE *(Off)*: Willy? *(A hall light is turned on.* SHE *enters, pulling a robe on)* Willy, what's the mat—

HE *grabs her and hugs her desperately.*

WILLY: Oh, thank christ, I thought you might have left already.
DARLENE: Do you know what time it is?
WILLY: O.K., listen. You can't go.
DARLENE: What are you talking about?
WILLY: I want us together again.
DARLENE: What?
WILLY: I'm gonna do this one last gig, the very first and last one and you'll come and you'll be there with me and then that'll be it. I'll come back here with you and we'll live here, you, me and Patty—
DARLENE: What's the matter with you?
WILLY: No! We'll go away, the three of us. To the mountains or someplace, way the hell out there where nobody can get us. What.
DARLENE: Have you lost your mind?
WILLY: Yes. No! Everything is fine now. Darlene, I want us together again.
DARLENE: Do we draw up a contract? One that says when you're finished with me I'm not entitled to your money, your property or your life?
WILLY: No . . . hey. . . . O.K., we'll get married again.
DARLENE: Oh, Willy.
WILLY: Oh, Willy what? Ahh, *W* sounds, I'm starting to sound like him.
DARLENE: It must be bad luck to have an imagination. It must make a person unrealistic.
WILLY: Darlene, what are you saying? Are you saying no?
DARLENE: Willy—
WILLY: Darlene! I need you!

Again, HE *grabs her and holds her. Pause.*

DARLENE: Willy?
WILLY: Mmm?
DARLENE: I remember you saying to me once that if you had to choose between your career and your personal life, you'd want a happy personal life.
WILLY: I said that? Of course I said that.
DARLENE: But you never did it. All the choices you made took you away from me.
WILLY: I was making us a living.
DARLENE: I'm not talking about the work. Do you know what it's like to answer the phone and have some two-bit reporter tell you that your husband was seen arm in arm with so-and-so and do you have a comment? Do you?

Silence.

WILLY: Darlene, I. . . . I'd get lonely.

DARLENE: I don't think you know what lonely is compared to what I felt.

WILLY: It was always you, is you I . . .

DARLENE: Love. You never say it. You use it so easily in songs but you never say it. It's pretty faces you love.

WILLY: You're pretty.

DARLENE: I'm not bad. But I'll grow old.

WILLY: Gracefully.

DARLENE: Steadily. You'll get bored. You'll want others. And because of what you are, they'll be there for you. And Willy, you'll take them. Like always.

WILLY: No.

DARLENE: Yes.

WILLY: Darlene . . . believe me when I say I'm through with all that.

DARLENE: I can't. You know, I used to envy you, Willy.

WILLY: Why.

DARLENE: 'Cause I'm a human being. I'd like people to pay attention and call my name. But I don't envy you anymore. I pity you.

WILLY: Gimme a break.

DARLENE: I do. The attention goads you and pushes you and you're never satisfied with anything you ever achieve. Turn your back on it, Willy, right now. No thinking you're gonna run away after this bullshit comeback is over.

WILLY: Darlene, if you can help me this one time, I can do it.

DARLENE: See? You want it. You always will. I think you ought to leave, it's getting late.

WILLY *(Embracing her desperately)*: Darlene, after!

DARLENE: Don't.

WILLY: Darlene, marry me!

DARLENE: Willy! You use me. You use how I feel about you. You care about me but then you leave me and I can't take it anymore. You feel bad, I know. But then you write a song about it and you feel better.

WILLY: I never did that to hurt you.

DARLENE: Well, it did.

WILLY: Why can't you ever leave that alone?

DARLENE: You use the people who love you.

WILLY: You were never just something for me to write songs about, Darlene, and you know it!

DARLENE: I know it? All I know is that when you left and it just about killed me, you and one of your friends turned it into some pop-40 hit.

WILLY: You got my royalties! I set it up that way!

DARLENE: I didn't want royalties. I wanted you. Goodbye, Willy. And Willy? I'm changing the lock. (SHE *exits)*

WILLY: Darlene, I wrote it for you. I wrote it for you!

Light change. A VOICE *calls out of the dark.*

SUIT: Ladies and gentlemen, the incredibly incredible Goatman Jango!

Music! Lights. The sounds of whistles and cheers as GOATMAN *enters and takes the mike.*

GOATMAN: Hold onto your torn T-shirts, whitebread, 'cause de Goatman be singin' you a song written for him by his friend, close and personal, de incredible Willy. Now de Willy, man, he be havin' this comeback and I hope he knows I'd be dere if I could. Dis song is taken from Willy's very own famous life, hey, and his experiences of a famous nature. Right? You know what de hell kinda bloody right! Hit it! *(And* HE *sings)*

Da day we broke apart
My heart went icy numb
Dere was not any pain, no, no
Just a shot a Novocain
Like de ocean I was calm, baby
Like de calm before a wind
Coulda been a hurricane, oh, yeah
Or a shot a Novocain
But de daylight, she quickly ran
And de nighttime, she climbed on in
And I called for you in vain
And for a shot a Novocain
For a shot of Novocain
Just a shot of Novocain
To ease de pain
I will never have a home
And I'll always be alone.
It will always be de same
Just a shot of Novocain
Yes, a shot of Novocain
A shot of Novocain to ease de pain

(HE speaks now as the music plays on) Willy! I hope you be gettin' back together with that pretty wife a yours, man! But if not, just remember! Breakin' up, it be tough on de heart but it be easy on de bank account! Right! You know what kinda goddam bloody hell right! *(Cheers. Applause)* Thank you! Thank you very much!

Lights fade on GOATMAN. *Music fades.* WILLY *groans.*

WILLY: No more pain.

Black. The sound and flashing light of an ambulance.

Scene 4

Lights up on SEVERAL PEOPLE *milling, all of them engaged in hushed conversation.* WILLY *enters.*

WILLY: What's going on?
MAN: Friend or relative?
WILLY: What?
MAN: Are you a friend or relative?
WILLY: A friend. What's going on? Who's hurt?
MAN: We've had a little accident but it's under control.
WILLY: Accident. What do you mean, a little accident?
MAN: Shush. Getting excited isn't going to help anyone.

MEDICAL AIDES *wheel the* BLONDE *in on a stretcher.* SHE *is unconscious, covered to the neck with a sheet.*

WILLY: Oh, god, no . . .
MAN: I'm afraid she took one too many sleeping pills.
WILLY: How many too many?
MAN: About thirty or forty too many.
WILLY: Aw, no . . . (HE *gently caresses the* BLONDE'S *hair)* Hey, come on . . . you've got to come to my comeback. Front row center seats.
MAN: She can't hear you.
WILLY: I can see that. Is she going to be all right?
MAN: Yes. We got to her in time.
WILLY: Who found her?
MAN: No one.
WILLY: What?
MAN: She called herself. She had second thoughts. She always does. And she called for help before it was too late and she'd passed out.
WILLY: She's done it before?
MAN: Has a history of it. They've got to get her into the ambulance now.
WILLY: You're going to be O.K.
MAN: She can't hear you.
WILLY: I know she can't hear me!
MAN: Sorry.
WILLY: Why would she do this.
MAN: She left a note. (HE *takes a note from his pocket and hands it to* WILLY)

WILLY *(Reading)*: I can no longer bear the disappointment.

MAN: I think that sums it up.

WILLY: She's such a beautiful woman.

MAN: Breathtaking, yes.

WILLY: Other women would kill to be so beautiful.

MAN: I'd imagine so, yes.

WILLY: It makes you feel good just to look at her.

MAN: Obviously she tried to kill herself when no one was.

WILLY: Who the fuck are you?

MAN: I'm her husband.

WILLY: I'm, uh . . .

MAN: You're Willy Rivers, yes.

WILLY: I'm a . . .

MAN: A friend of my wife's, yes, I'm sure. It's kind of you to stop by.

WILLY: I wanted to make sure she came to, uh . . .

MAN: Your comeback, yes, you said. When is it?

WILLY: Any minute.

MAN: I don't think she'll be up to it by then. Well . . . I'll tell her you stopped
by. It will cheer her up to no end, believe me.

WILLY: Good-bye.

MAN: If you pass any reporters on the way out, be sure they recognize you.
My wife would want them to know you're involved.

WILLY: Do you want to come to my comeback?

MAN: You're very kind but there are other things on my mind just now.

Light change. Music! Chaos!

Scene 5

WILLY *watches the* ACTOR, *wearing slacks, sports jacket and shirt open to reveal
gold chains, leap out of an open doorway.* HE *is holding a huge pistol.* HE *goes into
a marksman's stance, aiming out at the audience.*

ACTOR: Awright, police, freeze! *(The sound of three deafening shots; the pistol kicks
in his hands)* Three in the ten ring. Who loves ya, baby? *(HE suddenly spins,
crouches and aims right)* Grab a piece of the sky, scumbag! The bomb's due
to go off in ten minutes. Where's the mayor stashed? *(HE spins, crouches,
aims left)* Twitch and you got a new navel, sweetheart. It's not the law I
love, it's a simple thing called justice. *(HE straightens, puts the pistol in his
shoulder holster and salutes the audience with one finger)* Aloha.

WILLY: Hey, man, I've been thinking about you a lot.

ACTOR: The incredibly famous Willy Rivers! Qué tal, amigo?

WILLY: Listen, my comeback, you're coming, right?

ACTOR: What's this?

WILLY: My comeback. You said you'd be there.

ACTOR: Not me, man.

WILLY: Of course it was you!

ACTOR: Mighta been some hunk who looked like me. A lot of us he-men look alike.

WILLY: For christ sake, please, I need some of my friends there.

ACTOR: We're not friends. We're just sort of famous together.

WILLY: But we've met, we've shaken hands, we've shared talk!

ACTOR: We have? You're right, we have. Hell, by industry standards we are friends. We're dear friends. We're brothers for chrissake! What is it you want, man, name it, I'll do it.

WILLY: Please . . . come to my comeback.

ACTOR: Love to, baby. But I'm in the middle of this television pilot. Crime is a nefarious thing, compadre. You have to nip it in the bud. And I do. Thank god that on TV it grows fast. Aloha!

There is the sudden sound of screaming tires and then an explosion from offstage.

WILLY: What the—. What was that? Oh, my god, that car is on fire!

ACTOR: I don't have my glasses. Is it a Mercedes?

WILLY: No, it's a Cadillac.

ACTOR: Ah, it's just rehearsal then. Probably the culmination of a high-speed chase.

Music that suggests melodrama and on-screen tension.

WILLY: The driver is burning! He's burning!

The ACTOR grabs WILLY by the shirt collar and shakes him.

ACTOR: For chrissake, pull yourself together. I know you've seen the underbelly of life but be a man, by christ, be a man! *(The music stops.* HE *relaxes and claps* WILLY *on the shoulder)* That was beautiful, Willy. You're justifiably famous. You'll get your residual check in the mail. Excuse me while I polish my gun.

WILLY: Was that fun? Did you enjoy it? Do you enjoy this? Something exciting happens every minute. You do more in an hour than most people do in a lifetime. All the times you've barely escaped death, I'd think you'd be a traumatized, paranoid psychopath. But are you? No. You're a hell of a guy. *(The* ACTOR *grins and nods)* You never go to the bathroom and you have perfect teeth. Are you coming to my comeback or not, you son of a bitch!

ACTOR: Afraid you're on your own, kid. This is reality we're talking about. *(HE suddenly spins, crouches and aims)* You! Dog breath! What's it gonna be, me or the swat team!? *(HE grins and reholsters his gun)*

WILLY: It's your fault.

ACTOR: Huh?

WILLY: You and this mindless bullshit pretend. You violate violence. You make it this charade that has no meaning or consequence. When a man dies, somewhere people cry for him. *(HE suddenly pulls a switchblade and holds it on the ACTOR)*

ACTOR: Hey, come on, man.

WILLY: When you cut a man, he bleeds.

ACTOR: Please, Willy, kid. I'll come to your comeback.

WILLY: Too late.

WILLY plunges the knife into the ACTOR's stomach. The ACTOR falls to the floor and dies.

ACTOR: Why . . . why would you want to go and hurt me . . .

WILLY: Good to see you man. *(HE spits on the corpse. There is the sudden sound of another car crash)* Hey. Look both ways before you cross the freeway.

WILLY moves away, walking as if in a daze. The ACTOR suddenly giggles and rises. HE looks at the audience.

ACTOR: What. You thought that was for real? Come on! *(HE whistles the theme from* The Twilight Zone. *HE draws his gun, crouches and aims at the audience)* That's *Mister* Law Enforcement Officer to you people. Wipe those smiles off your faces. We have ways of making you toe the line, fuck the fifth amendment. *(HE fires and fires until the gun is empty.* WILLY *flinches at every shot as if they were blasting into his body)* I can't say fuck on prime time. I gotta remember that. Aloha! *(HE exits)*

WILLY: Gypsey . . . Gypsey Davey . . .!

Light change. Music. Chaos! WILLY'S VOICE *calling out for* GYPSEY.

Scene 6

Lights up on the PUNK. SHE *sits on the floor, drinking bourbon, the blue light of the television bathing her.*

WILLY *(Off)*: Gypsey? Gypsey, you there?

PUNK: It's open.

WILLY (*Enters*): Where's Gypsey?

PUNK: Around.

WILLY: Around where.

PUNK: Somewhere around.

WILLY: When's he coming back?

PUNK: Here?

WILLY: Yeah, here.

PUNK: In due time. Wait.

Pause.

WILLY: How old are you?

PUNK: Ageless.

WILLY: Why don't you turn up the sound?

PUNK: I like it off.

WILLY: How come you hang around with Gypsey. Why don't you hang around someone your own age?

PUNK: Money.

WILLY: You're into money.

PUNK: Everyone and everything is into money. I'm young but I'm not stupid.

WILLY: There's more to life than money.

PUNK: Hah. You have money, you have it all. If money can't buy it, it's not worth having. Money can't buy you love? Somebody poor made that up. Yes, I'm into money. I'm into people who spend their money. On me.

WILLY: That's all you want, huh?

PUNK: No, that's not all I want. I want to party all day and rock and roll all night. You'll excuse me. I'm watching television.

WILLY: What are you watching?

PUNK: A game show. I love watching what greed does to people.

WILLY: Where's Gypsey.

PUNK: Around.

WILLY: How'd you meet him.

PUNK: I hung around. I like the music scene; the booze, the drugs, the hotel suites, the restaurants, the limos. I like that. The music sucks but I put up with it. It's amazing how stupid you so-called creative artists really are. The egos. Unbelievable. How can product have ego? Does Kellogg's corn flakes have an ego? No. It'll be around longer too. What you are is making someone money. That's why they keep you around, kissing your ass. Money. Art? Art is worth fart. Unless you can sell it. Then it's a commodity.

WILLY: Where's Gypsey.

PUNK: He's in the bathroom.

WILLY: Here?

PUNK: He's taking a bath.

WILLY: Gypsey! Yo, Gypsey Davey, it's Willy!

PUNK: He can't hear you.

WILLY: Why not.

PUNK: He's dead.

WILLY: What?

PUNK: He's dead. He has been for about three hours. He got fucked up, passed out and suffocated on his own vomit. (WILLY *runs off*) Stupid. He had everything to live for. He was rich.

WILLY (*Off*): Aw, Jesus!

PUNK: Door number three, you stupid cunt. Door number three and you're set for life. No. There's nothing but a small bag of dogshit behind door number two. What'd I tell you. Dogshit. Well, don't worry about it. Everybody's laughing at you.

WILLY (*On a phone, off*): Hello? Yeah, uh . . . wait. What room is this?

PUNK: Who knows.

WILLY: What room is this. Well, somebody's dead. In the bathtub. I don't know why.

PUNK: He got sick of it.

WILLY: Hey, shut up!

PUNK: Cool out.

WILLY: Yeah, O.K., send somebody up. I'll wait.

WILLY *enters. Silence.* HE *sits. The* GIRL *moves behind and begins to kiss his neck.*

Don't.

PUNK: You don't like it? (SHE *continues*) Look, I need someone. And I'm good. I'll do whatever you want. For whoever you want. But I don't come cheap. What ya say? (*Suddenly* SHE *bites hard on his ear.* SHE *grabs his hair and pulls his head up and back.* WILLY *screams*) What a ya say? Cat got your tongue? O.K., repeat after me. (*Singing*) I want to party all day and rock and roll all night! Come on, sing. (SHE *pulls his hair hard*)

WILLY (*Mumbling*): I want to party all day and rock and roll all night.

PUNK: That stinks. Do it again.

WILLY (*Singing*): I want to party all day and rock and roll all night!

PUNK: That's good. That's very good. You'll do. (SHE *sits on* WILLY's *lap, straddling him*) You're mine now. Mine.

SHE *kisses him. A moment. And then* WILLY *kisses her back. His arms go around her and* HE *stands, lifting her. Her legs go around his waist. But suddenly* WILLY *breaks the kiss and throws the* PUNK *away from him.*

WILLY: No. Not yet. Not today.

Black. Silence.

Scene 7

WILLY'S VOICE *out of the black. Soft. Gentle.*

WILLY: Dad? Dad?

Lights up on WILLY *and an* OLD MAN *in pajamas, bathrobe, shawl and slippers. The* OLD MAN *clenches a* Baseball Digest *magazine in his hand.* HE *stares at* WILLY, *delighted but uncomprehending.*

Hi, Dad, it's me. How you doin', huh? I came to visit. It's Willy, Dad.

DAD: If ya must know, I root for the Tig's.

WILLY: Huh?

DAD: Detroit. Baseball. You better believe it, Larry!

WILLY: Not Larry, Dad, no. It's me, Willy.

DAD: You gotta love it. You just do.

WILLY: Dad, has the stroke made you senile or are you just crazy like me?

DAD: I myself could of been a ballplayer.

WILLY: That's news to me.

DAD: It was a matter of balance. There's something wrong with my inner ear. When I look up, I get dizzy. I fall.

WILLY: No, you don't.

DAD: I do.

WILLY: No.

DAD: I . . . I root for the Tig's.

WILLY: Dad? I would have visited sooner but I've been kind of laid up. Maybe you heard?

DAD: Hold on to your seat and I will tell you of fan dancing.

WILLY: Aw, Dad . . .

DAD: There's a group of us, dear friends all. There's Stink Wilson from down towards the Chrysler plant. We call him Stink because he makes farting noises with his cupped hands. *(HE demonstrates and then giggles happily)* There's Funker the Dude and there's Vin Early who owns the Sunoco station and his retarded brother, Bus, who makes noises that no one can understand and there's Phil and Benny and Dowker. We root for the Tig's.

WILLY: That's news to me too.

DAD: You gotta love it. A gift. You just do.

WILLY: Funny, isn't it. Kids always expect parents to be strong. Parents, good parents, always pretend to be strong. Nothing you don't know, Dad, not a problem you can't solve. When you're a kid you don't appreciate how well grownups put on an act. Like they put on a tie. Like they put on a wedding band.

DAD: Once a year we meet. We pile into Benny's Chevy van. We drive and we drink and we're young and we're carefree.

WILLY: You never did that, Dad.

DAD: We drive Interstate 80.

WILLY: You were an executive, Dad.

DAD: We're bound for New York City, home of the hated Yankees. We're so young. So carefree.

WILLY: You were a vice-president. You never hung out with guys from the Sunoco station.

DAD: I root for the Tig's!

WILLY: You voted straight Republican your whole life.

DAD: We drive through Queens which is an up-and-coming ghetto on the outskirts of New York City. We stop at the only White Castle hamburger stand in the entire metropolitan area. We buy beef cookies! *(HE laughs, delighted with himself)*

WILLY: Whatever you say, Dad.

DAD: I myself have been known to eat 188 of them in one sitting. We order to go.

WILLY: Dad, sometimes you just want someone, someone who cares about you, to tell you what to do.

DAD: We drive to Yankee Stadium. We're young. We buy right field general admission tickets. Carefree! We sit there, alone in a sea of pinstripe tattoos and crazed Long Island accents. We wear our Tiger colors with pride.

WILLY: They want me to make this appearance, Dad. I don't know if I can.

DAD: I will tell you of fan dancing!

WILLY: Yeah. O.K., tell me.

DAD: High, high in the stands we sit. We drink Yankee Budweiser but we scream for Stroh's. Benny chews tobacco and Phil eats peanuts the shell and all. Funker the Dude plucks his fake pewter flask from the inside pocket of his imitation mohair blazer and we drink gulps of Fleishman's. Young. Stink Wilson is farting trumpet-loud and Dowker starts throwing beef cookies at the right fielder. Carefree. Vin Early is doing an a cappella version of "Take Me Out to the Ball Game" and his retarded brother, Bus, starts bawling along, starts bawling something totally unintelligible and incredibly loud and contagiously retarded, starts moaning and gurgling as if in tongues, and suddenly he leaps to his feet and wails like a wolf calling to the moon, urging on, urging on and we join in, all of us. We do it 'cause we love it, ya got to, ya just do! And then . . . and then . . . *(HE seems suddenly lost and confused)*

WILLY: Dad, what then?

DAD: I . . . I . . . *(His mouth works soundlessly. HE stares at WILLY in confusion)*

WILLY: It's time, Dad. It's your turn.

DAD: But what do I do?

WILLY: Dad . . . you climb to the top of general admission, higher and higher to where the air is thin and clear. You grab hold and you pull yourself up and over the top to the stadium's edge. You stand.

DAD (*Standing*): Yes.

WILLY: So proud.

DAD: So tall.

WILLY: Down below you the cars and buses are like children's toys.

DAD: I look back. Oh.

WILLY: The stadium lights surround you like small suns.

DAD: Thin it is, my path, like the crease on a mountain top. But I'm young. I'm young. I dance.

WILLY: Dance.

The OLD MAN *begins to shuffle to some silent, inner music.*

I am a fan dancer.

DAD: Yes.

WILLY: For the fans do I dance.

DAD: How glorious a gift.

WILLY: Security is screaming and police are charging. There are sirens and screams and bright-edged beams cut the night sky. I am the focus. I am the fulcrum.

DAD: The fan dancer.

WILLY: I dance for the fans. The game has stopped. The world has stopped. All eyes are on me and for a brief precious moment, I make the fans forget. I dance.

DAD: Oh.

WILLY: I dance. And the fans cheer me. They cheer hard and long and loud and true. They cheer as if cheering for themselves for once. Don't look down, they cry! Don't look down, they call! Don't look down or back or behind or you will fall!

The OLD MAN *spreads his arms as if in ecstasy.*

DAD: I will not look down, say I!

WILLY: I will not look down, I call!

DAD: I will look nowhere but up . . . at the madly swirling stars . . .

WILLY & DAD: Tonight!

The OLD MAN *throws a triumphant fist in the air, rears back and looks straight up. There is the echo of a crowd cheering and lights seem to dance off him and stars seem to come out overhead, surrounding him like a halo.* HE *grows dizzy.* HE *sways.* HE *staggers and falls.* WILLY *catches him.*

WILLY: Dad!

The lights return to normal. Silence. WILLY *and the* OLD MAN *seem equally confused.*

DAD: I root for . . . (HE *caresses* WILLY's *face tenderly*) I root for the fans.
WILLY: I do too, Dad.
DAD: I root for ordinary people.
WILLY: I do too, Dad. I do too.

WILLY *helps the* OLD MAN *to his feet.* THEY *hug.* DAD *walks slowly off into the dark. Light change.*

Hold onto your seats and I will tell you of fan dancing. The moment before you grab the light is an age long. Your heart is engine-loud in your ears and your gut is like a logjam. You can aim your thoughts anywhere. You can take your eyes and toss them out into the night and they turn and look down on you. You seem to hear a voice pleading. I can't, I can't, I can't. You can and you will, a voice answers. Forgotten, a voice cries, not this time. Can't, can't, crazy, crazy, run, run, run, now, hide, yes, no, yes, why!? Because . . . you love it. And anything you do, if you love it, shit, that's the only reason you need to do it at all. Go. And suddenly your feet are moving and the light breaks over you and you're aware of a presence. Watching. Waiting. There to be transported with you. And so . . . you dance. (*Pause. Softly*) Don't shoot me. Oh, dear god, please don't let them shoot me.

Lights to black. The sound of cheering. Out of the darkness, a VOICE.

SUIT: Ladies and gentlemen, it is our very great pleasure to introduce to you . . . please, let's all let him know how glad we are to have him back . . . a real welcome for. . . . Ladies and gentlemen, the incredible . . . Willy Rivers!

Music! Lights up on WILLY, *his back to the audience.* HE *turns, mike in his hand, and sings.*

WILLY: There's a girl and her hair's painted purple and green
There's a man in a chair with an old magazine
There's a guy in a tub and his blood's turning cold
There's a woman on a stretcher who's afraid of growing old
There's a boy in the big house and
He thinks his life's just fine
Ain't afraid a God almighty, ain't afraid a doin' time
Put a weapon in his hand and he's a man among men
He'll take you through the valley
And he'll walk you back again.

Yeah, they all want to take you
They want to grab you by the heart

They want to wring you out dry
They want to never let go
Till your cheers and your tears and your hands
Tear this place apart
Till your cheers and your tears and your hands
Tear this place apart

There's a boy with a guitar
And his head is filled with dreams
He doesn't need a spotlight
He's got a pair of old blue jeans
Some say the boy is gifted
Some say that he's deranged
The kid pays no attention
All that matters is the stage

Where he can take you
He wants to grab you by the heart
He wants to swing you up high
He wants to never let go
Till your cheers and your tears and your hands
Tear this place apart
Till your cheers and your tears and your hands
Tear this place apart

And some day he will.

(*Speaking*) Thank you very much.

Lights to black.

END OF PLAY

Between East and West
Richard Nelson

About Richard Nelson

Born in Chicago in 1950, Richard Nelson is a graduate of Hamilton College. Nelson's plays, which include *An American Comedy, The Return of Pinocchio, Rip Van Winkle or 'The Works', Bal, The Vienna Notes, Jungle Coup, Conjuring an Event,* and *The Killing of Yablonski,* have been produced by such theatres as the Mark Taper Forum, The Empty Space, Yale Repertory Theatre, Goodman Theatre, Playwrights Horizons and The American Place, as well as by theatres in Europe. He has translated and adapted Moliere's *Don Juan,* Goldoni's *Il Campiello,* Beaumarchais's *The Marriage of Figaro,* Chekhov's *Three Sisters,* Brecht's *Jungle of Cities* and *The Wedding,* Erdman's *The Suicide* and Fo's *Accidental Death of an Anarchist.* Nelson's most recent play *Principia Scriptoriae,* winner of the ABC Playwright Award, is scheduled to premiere in March 1986 at Manhattan Theatre Club, and to be staged by the Royal Shakespeare Company later the same year.

A volume of Nelson's original works, *An American Comedy and Other Plays,* was recently published by PAJ Publications, and he is editor of *Strictly Dishonorable and Other Lost American Plays,* to be brought out by TCG this spring. Nelson has received two Obie awards, a Guggenheim Fellowship, a Rockefeller Playwriting Grant, and two National Endowment for the Arts playwriting fellowships, the most recent being one of the NEA's first two-year grants.

About the Play

An early version of *Between East and West* was given a workshop production by Seattle Repertory Theatre in 1984. The play premiered at Yale Repertory Theatre, under the direction of John Madden, as part of Winterfest 1985, and was circulated by TCG as a *Plays in Process* script later that year.

Playwright's Note

When Gregor and Erna are speaking "English," they speak with strong accents and in a somewhat unconfident way. When they speak "Czech," they have no accents. In the text, the "English" lines are underlined.

The play consists of 18 scenes with the following titles:

1:	The Culmination	10:	The Free World
2:	Eight Months Earlier	11:	Siberia
3:	The Context	12:	His Memory
4:	Before	13:	Her Memory
5:	And After	14:	Siberia Continued
6:	Dustin Hoffman	15:	A Few Days Before
7:	Land of Opportunity	16:	Erna Recalls Another Scene
8:	By the Bootstraps	17:	Going Places
9:	Shadows	18:	Remainders

Each title should be projected all the time the scene is played and should remain in view for a few moments after the scene is over.

The play should be performed without intermission.

I wish to thank the John Simon Guggenheim Memorial Foundation for its support during the writing of this play.

Characters

GREGOR HASEK, a Czech emigre in his fifties, a stage and film director.
ERNA HASEK, his wife, also a Czech emigre in her fifties, an actress.

Time

1983.

Place

A one-room apartment on the Upper East Side, New York City.

The Play

Between East and West

For Ms. Ritter
and Her Husband

Scene 1
The Culmination

A one-room apartment, sparsely furnished. ERNA *sits watching television.* SHE *smokes.*

TELEVISION: "Shouting over the catcalls of backbenchers, Mrs. Thatcher today restated her support for the deployment of American Pershing missiles on British soil. While she spoke to Parliament, an estimated crowd of 100,000 Britons staged what is being described as the largest political demonstration since the war. . . ."

The door to the hallway opens and GREGOR *enters.* HE *wears a winter hat and coat.* ERNA *turns to him.*

"Mrs. Thatcher never referred to the Grenada invasion which has greatly strained relations with the Reagan White House. Instead she . . ."

ERNA *has gotten up and turns off the television. Pause.*

GREGOR: Do you want to tell me what you meant last night on the phone?

ERNA *doesn't respond.* GREGOR *takes off his hat and coat.*

ERNA: You didn't have to come, Gregor. . . .

GREGOR: I came.

ERNA: What about rehearsals?

GREGOR: They changed the schedule. We'll rehearse tonight. *(Pause)* I have to catch the next train back.

ERNA: When is the next train back?

GREGOR: One hour.

ERNA: You came back for one hour? How much does the train cost?

GREGOR: Erna, I came. *(Pause)* Erna, last night—

ERNA: I'll bet your American actors love you. Actors always love you. I loved you.

GREGOR: Erna, last night you scared me.

ERNA: I'm scared myself.

GREGOR: What about? *(No response)* I will be back in two weeks.

ERNA: You won't come back.

GREGOR: That's a stupid thing to say and you know it.

ERNA: I know it's stupid. Yes.

Short pause.

GREGOR: You don't have the heat on in here, do you? You must be freezing, I'll get you a sweater. *(Moves to the closet)*

ERNA: You can't just let things slip away, Gregor.

GREGOR: What's slipping away? *(HE gets the sweater)*

ERNA: Gregor . . . *(HE stops)* They will take and they won't stop. The moment you give, they take. That's how it is in a country like this.

GREGOR: What do you have against this country anyway?

ERNA: I don't have anything against it. And I don't have anything for it. That's only the way you think, not me. But you won't understand that.

GREGOR *(Pause)*: You've been alone too long.

ERNA: Just three weeks.

GREGOR: Why don't you come to Hartford with me.

ERNA: And sit in a hotel room? I'm sitting in this room.

GREGOR: You can watch rehearsals. You'll be treated very well. They'll adore you.

ERNA: Like they adore you.

GREGOR: Erna—what I'm doing is a job! Try to understand that—it's nothing more!

ERNA: I don't want to see you give up.

GREGOR: What have I given up?! What the hell do I have to give up?!!!

ERNA: You don't know.

GREGOR: Erna—would you like to talk to a doctor?

ERNA: A doctor? Oh that's right. In the West that's what you do, isn't it? Talk to a doctor. *(Pause)* I'd better pack.

GREGOR: You'll come to Hartford? *(Pause)* When?

ERNA: I'd better pack.

GREGOR: Come tomorrow. There's a train at ten. I'll make sure someone meets you. I'll talk to the stage manager. Erna . . . *(SHE has turned away)* It'll make us both feel better, I'm sure of it.

HE *puts his coat on, goes to kiss her.* SHE *doesn't respond.*

ERNA: I'm glad—you're sure of it.

GREGOR *(At the door)*: We'll go out to eat. What kind of food would you like? There's a very good Japanese restaurant near the theatre . . .

ERNA: Japanese? Yes. That would make sense for two Czechs in America.

HE *goes.* SHE *turns the television back on.*

TELEVISION: "The opposition Social Democratic Party, ignoring an appeal by former Chancellor Helmut Schmidt, said today that it could not accept the deployment of American medium-range missiles in West Germany. The decision, taken at a special party congress in Cologne, was the culmination of . . ."

Scene 2
Eight Months Earlier

The apartment eight months earlier. The day after GREGOR *and* ERNA's *arrival in America. The apartment has fewer things; there is no television.* GREGOR *has just entered and is taking off his jacket.* ERNA *fusses in the kitchen.*

GREGOR: It's not at all what I expected. I expected it to be different of course, but not this different.

ERNA: How different?

GREGOR: How different did I expect it? Or how different is it?

ERNA: Whichever makes you happy, Gregor.

GREGOR: You're really not interested, are you? You know, I can't understand that, Erna.

ERNA: Who said I'm not interested?

GREGOR: It's obvious.

ERNA: Gregor, I'm interested.

GREGOR: No you're not.

ERNA: I'm listening, aren't I? You were saying New York is so different.

Pause.

GREGOR: It's nothing like Prague, Erna.

ERNA: There's only one Prague.

GREGOR: You really should have come with me. It's hard to put into words. The second I walked out onto the sidewalk I could feel it. You want to know where I went?

ERNA: Where did you go, Gregor?

GREGOR: I went into the subway. I bought a token—they don't have tickets—tokens. And I waited for a train—you can travel as far as you want on one token.

ERNA: Really?

GREGOR: And a train pulled in. In fact, two. One going in each direction.

ERNA: Did you know where you were going?

GREGOR: No. I didn't understand the map.

ERNA: But you got on the train?

GREGOR: I wanted to, Erna. I wanted to go to the end of the line. To get out where the blacks live. I wanted to see that. You don't see that in Prague.

ERNA: You don't see what?

GREGOR: A whole section of blacks. You see pictures.

ERNA: You see pictures of blacks in New York City.

GREGOR: Yes. So I wanted to see for myself what it was like.

ERNA: And what was it like?

GREGOR: Erna, is that a strange thing to want to see on your first day in New York?

ERNA: Strange? Why? It's what I would want to do. We've heard so much about those places, Gregor.

GREGOR: That's true.

ERNA: So what was it like?

GREGOR: The black sections?

ERNA: Yes.

GREGOR: I never got there. I never actually got on the train.

ERNA: You never got on the train?

GREGOR: No. I wanted to. But I didn't. I let the train leave. I stayed on the platform.

ERNA: I see.

GREGOR: I didn't know where they were going.

ERNA: Oh.

GREGOR: I tried to ask a black man who was standing on the platform, but my English I guess is not so good as I thought.

ERNA: Your English is very good, Gregor. My English isn't very good.

GREGOR: In any case, he didn't seem to understand.

ERNA: I see, so you stayed on the platform all this time?

GREGOR: No. I went back onto the street and walked up Fifth Avenue. And I bought some cigarettes. (HE *takes out two packs*)

ERNA: Kents? You bought Kents?

GREGOR: For one dollar each.

ERNA: Each cigarette?

GREGOR: Each of these packages, Erna. For one dollar each.

ERNA: Only one dollar for American cigarettes. For Kents?

GREGOR: This is America, Erna. . . . I bought the cigarettes and I bought an umbrella. (HE *shows her a black umbrella*)

ERNA: It was raining? From up here it didn't look like it was raining.

GREGOR: I bought it from a boy on the street. I could have also bought a watch. But I just bought the umbrella. See here—it has a button. (*Presses the button and the umbrella opens*) And I went into the Plaza Hotel carrying the umbrella.

ERNA: You just walked in? Gregor, are you sure you can do that?

GREGOR: The doorman opened the door for me so I went in.

ERNA: What did you do in the hotel?

GREGOR: I went out again. Though I went out before he could open the door for me. He was busy opening the car door for a millionaire.

ERNA: For who?

GREGOR: A millionaire.

ERNA: How did you find out this man was a millionaire?

GREGOR: If you'd seen him, you'd know. I told you you should have come with me.

ERNA: I know. I will.

GREGOR: And Erna, across the street is the park and at the corner of this park were bums. Don't ask me how I knew they were bums, it was obvious. One had a plastic bag over his foot.

ERNA: Really?

GREGOR: So here was this millionaire and here was this bum. Both right there together. I guess that's democracy.

ERNA: A bum and a millionaire are democracy?

GREGOR: You know what I mean. I wanted to talk to the bum so I went up to him.

ERNA: What did you say?

GREGOR: Nothing. I never actually talked to him.

ERNA: Maybe the next time.

GREGOR: Yes.

ERNA: When you're more comfortable with English.

GREGOR: Yes. Then we can ask anybody anything.

ERNA: Not anything, Gregor.

GREGOR: What can't we ask, Erna?

ERNA: I don't know yet.

GREGOR: Then we can ask anybody anything.

ERNA: I guess so. But still be careful.

GREGOR: I'm always careful.

ERNA: That's not true.

GREGOR: Erna, can't we go one day without bringing that up, please?

Pause.

ERNA: So what did you do after you didn't speak to the bum?

GREGOR: What would you have done?

ERNA: What *would* I have done? I think I would have bought another package of Kents.

HE *takes out another pack of Kents.* THEY *look at each other and break out laughing.*

(Through the laughter) Next time—I'll go too.

Scene 3
The Context

ERNA *alone at the table, reading* The New York Times. *At her side are three large dictionaries—a Czech/English-English/Czech, a Czech and an English.* SHE *refers to these often.* SHE *smokes and drinks coffee as* SHE *reads. Even though it is morning,* SHE *has been up for quite awhile and is dressed.*

ERNA *(In a loud voice, reading)*: "Is Reagan's Foreign Policy Overheated or Warming Up?" *(SHE pronounces Reagan as Regan)* What is this "overheated or warming up"? Is it like a joke?

GREGOR *(Off, from the bathroom)*: Is what like a joke?

ERNA: "Is Reagan's foreign policy overheated or warming up?" I don't understand.

GREGOR *(Entering from the bathroom, unshaven and in his bathrobe)*: It's Reagan, not Regan. Regan's some other important official. The exchequer, I think. *(HE goes to stove, takes coffee mug)* What don't you understand?

ERNA: The joke. "Overheated or warming up."

GREGOR *(Putting hot water into his mug)*: Why is that a joke? *(Goes to refrigerator)*

ERNA: That's what I'm asking. Is it a joke—a play on words?

GREGOR *(With his head in the refrigerator)*: I wouldn't call American foreign policy just a play on words, Erna. *(HE takes an egg out of the refrigerator)*

ERNA: The headline, not the policy. I'll look it up myself.

SHE *begins to go through the dictionary.* HE *starts to cook his egg.*

GREGOR: Josef was telling me last night that outside of New York City nearly everyone thinks like Ronald Reagan.

ERNA (*Going through the dictionary*): Did he say why?

GREGOR: He said that in New York City they don't think like him at all. Because here everyone's a Democrat.

ERNA: Oh. (*Pause*) Is Josef a Democrat?

GREGOR: I didn't want to ask.

ERNA: Why didn't you want to ask?

GREGOR: I didn't know if I should, Erna. Outside of New York City are the farms. Though there are the steel mills in the west, too.

ERNA: Certainly the steelworkers are Democrats, Gregor.

GREGOR: Steelworkers are usually socialists, Erna. (*Pause*) It's like a car.

ERNA: What is?

GREGOR: "Overheated or warming up."

ERNA: Like a car?? Oh. I see. (SHE *puts away the dictionary*)

GREGOR: When a car runs too long it gets overheated, but when you start it up—

ERNA: I said—I understand now, Gregor.

HE *shrugs. His egg has boiled,* HE *starts to take it out.*

(*Without looking up*) That egg in the refrigerator is bad.

HE *looks at the egg.*

GREGOR: Then why was it in the refrigerator?

ERNA (*Looking at the paper*): I was waiting for you to go shopping with me.

GREGOR: Why do you need me to take you shopping? And that doesn't explain the egg.

ERNA: I don't need you to take me shopping.

GREGOR: If you don't need me to take you, why don't you go by yourself?

ERNA: I have. (*Short pause*) Twice.

GREGOR: So why was the bad egg in the refrigerator?

ERNA: Can't you just throw it away? (SHE *sets down the paper*) I'll throw it away.

GREGOR: I can throw the egg away. (HE *does*) There, I've done it.

ERNA: How sweet of you.

Pause.

GREGOR (*Looking into the refrigerator*): Is the cheese bad too? (SHE *shrugs without looking up*) It's bad.

ERNA: There's bread. It's hard but you can toast it. (SHE *gets up*) Here, I'll toast it for you.

GREGOR: I can toast it. (HE *takes out the bread, takes a large knife out of a drawer*)

ERNA: It's already sliced. It comes that way.

GREGOR: I can see that.

ERNA: Then why the knife?

GREGOR *(Puts down the knife)*: Habit.

Pause.

ERNA *(Reads)*: "Mr. Reagan tried to run over the opposition with a hard-line approach. . . ." What is this "run over"?

GREGOR *(Trying to mime it)*: You know—*run over.*

ERNA: Oh. Like with a car again.

GREGOR: Yes.

ERNA: Americans do love their cars, don't they? Least that's what everyone always says.

GREGOR: Who's everyone, Erna?

ERNA: Don't tell me you never heard that before?

GREGOR: Of course I've heard that.

ERNA: Then the person you heard it from is one of the everyone who's always saying it.

GREGOR: But they don't say it here.

ERNA: Everyone doesn't live here, Gregor. Or have you already forgotten that?

GREGOR: I haven't forgotten anything.

ERNA *(Turns to stare at him)*: No? *(Pause.* SHE *turns back)* Good. *(Pause)* You should read the paper too, Gregor, and find out what's happening in the world.

GREGOR: You mean at home? I don't need a newspaper to tell me what's happening at home.

ERNA: Oh, you're only interested in what's happening at home? Isn't what's happening here important to you too? I thought you were the one who had to live here.

GREGOR: I read the paper, dammit.

ERNA: You read a theatre paper. That's not a paper.

GREGOR: I read what I need to read. We need to know certain things.

ERNA: What do we need to know that's in a theatre paper?

GREGOR: Who's important—for instance.

ERNA: Oh. So who's important?

GREGOR: A million people.

ERNA: A million people can't be important—even here.

GREGOR *(Throws up his hands)*: For example—Dustin Hoffman's important!

ERNA: Is that what you've learned, that Dustin Hoffman's important? We could have stayed home to find that out.

GREGOR *(Moves to the bathroom)*: Besides, Erna, why should I bother to read the newspaper when you always read it to me?

ERNA: I don't read it to you—I ask you questions.

GREGOR: If I don't know what's happening—why ask me questions?

ERNA: Good question. Though I think that has something to do with what choices I have.

GREGOR: There are plenty of people who you could talk to.

ERNA: But they don't want to talk to me, Gregor.

GREGOR: Keep telling yourself that and it'll turn out being true.

ERNA: Come shopping with me and you'll find out it already is.

GREGOR: I see—now we're back to the subject of my taking you shopping.

ERNA: I didn't know we ever left it. I've just been waiting for you to finish breakfast.

GREGOR: I've finished! There's no food.

ERNA: That's my point about the shopping.

GREGOR: Fine. You want me to take you shopping. I'll take you shopping! Get your purse!

ERNA: Now? You aren't dressed!

GREGOR *(Goes to the bathroom door)*: Dammit, I'll get dressed! We'll go shopping. We'll come back to this apartment. We'll lock the door. You can continue reading me the newspaper.

ERNA: I don't read you the newspaper.

GREGOR *(Goes in, sticks his head out)*: What the hell, maybe I won't even shave today. After listening to you, you have to ask yourself, what is the goddam point!

GREGOR *closes the door. Pause. Telephone rings.*

ERNA: Telephone, Gregor.

GREGOR *(Off)*: Get it.

ERNA: Gregor!

GREGOR: Erna, pick up the phone! *(SHE lets it ring)* Erna!! *(HE hurries out with shaving cream on his face. Into phone)* Hello? Oh, yes. That is very nice. But. . . . Yes, but I do not think so. Very busy tonight. So thank you. Yes, I hug you. Goodbye. *(HE hangs up)*

ERNA: I thought you weren't going to shave.

GREGOR: That was Josef.

ERNA *(Shrugs)*: He doesn't want to talk to me. *(SHE takes a cigarette)*

GREGOR: What makes you think that?

ERNA: I don't think I'm American enough for him.

GREGOR: And I am?

ERNA: You've been trying hard enough, Gregor. *(Pause)* What did he want?

GREGOR: He invited us to watch the fireworks tonight on the Hudson River.

ERNA: Tonight?

GREGOR: It's American Independence Day.

ERNA: Today? *(SHE opens her paper)*

GREGOR: That's yesterday's paper. You won't find out anything in there.

ERNA: No. I bought it this morning.

GREGOR: This morning?

ERNA: Yes.

GREGOR: You can go out and buy the paper, but you can't buy food?

ERNA: You can't buy food from a machine, Gregor. *(HE moves back toward the bathroom)* You told Josef no?

GREGOR: Of course I told him no.

ERNA: You didn't ask me if I wanted to go.

GREGOR: Because I knew you wouldn't want to go.

ERNA: Who will be there? *(GREGOR shrugs)* I couldn't go.

GREGOR: I didn't ask you to go, Erna.

ERNA: That's just what I was saying.

GREGOR: You want me to call him back and see if we can still go and then I can ask you and you can tell me you don't want to go so I can tell him again we can't go?

Pause. SHE looks away. HE goes back into the bathroom, then suddenly comes out.

Just what is it that you want, Erna?!!!

Pause. HE stares at her. SHE gets up, gets another cigarette, lights it and goes by him into the bathroom, closing the door. GREGOR takes his toast and butters it. HE takes it to the table and sits down to eat, still with shaving cream on his face. ERNA comes out of the bathroom, her eyes red from crying. SHE still smokes. THEY look at each other.

ERNA: You don't have any meetings today?

GREGOR: It's a holiday. *(SHE nods)* So I can take you shopping.

SHE nods, and again takes the newspaper. Pause.

ERNA *(Reading)*: "That is a long haul with uncertain results." Gregor, what does this "long haul" mean?

GREGOR: "Long haul"? I don't know. Read me the whole sentence, maybe I can figure it out from the context.

Scene 4
Before

Early evening. ERNA and GREGOR sits on the couch waiting, dressed to go out.

ERNA: What time is it now? *(GREGOR shows her his watch)* Is he late? I haven't learned what's late here? *(HE shrugs. Pause)* Are you worried about showing the film?

GREGOR: No. *(Pause)* Just remembering what I went through to make it. That's all. They wouldn't understand here.

ERNA: Other people made it too, Gregor. *(Short pause)* I made it too. Or don't you remember?

GREGOR: You acted in it.

ERNA: Ah.

GREGOR: You were wonderful, Erna. It'll be nice to see you acting again.

ERNA: Who says I've ever stopped acting?

GREGOR *laughs to himself and nods. Pause.*

GREGOR: There were things I went through to make this film that even you never imagined.

ERNA: Like what?

GREGOR: Never mind. It's best to forget about all that now.

ERNA: Like what? You mean with the authorities? You think you were the only person to have problems with the authorities? Everyone had problems with the authorities.

GREGOR: Not everyone, Erna. Or have you already forgotten how they do things at home?

ERNA: Who didn't have problems with the authorities, Gregor?

GREGOR: Klima for instance. He never had a problem.

ERNA: Klima's in prison now, Gregor.

GREGOR: I don't mean now, I mean then. When we were all making films. They always approved Klima's scripts. With the rest of us, it was maybe one out of three, but with Klima. . . . And that's just how it was with my film, within a week of submitting it, Klima's script was approved. Just like that. Who knew why.

ERNA: So just like that they approved Klima's script—

GREGOR: They always did, Erna.

ERNA: Then what was the big problem?

Short pause. HE *smiles, turns to her.*

GREGOR *(Whispering)*: They approved *a* script, Erna, but that's not to say they approved *the* script.

ERNA: You mean there were two scripts for your film?

GREGOR: No, there was only Klima's script. You think I was crazy? But there was also a script in my head, one that hadn't—and maybe couldn't—be written down.

ERNA: I didn't know that.

GREGOR: No one knew about it—except the cameraman; his family too had been on the list after the war so we understood each other.

Pause.

ERNA: So there was a big difference between Klima's and your scripts?

GREGOR: A very big difference.

ERNA: And the script I was given on the set—then that was your script.

GREGOR: No, no, that was Klima's.

ERNA: Gregor—but that's the script I learned my lines from.

GREGOR: I know that. Klima was there all the time. I couldn't exactly change his script when he was there.

ERNA: But then you shot Klima's script.

GREGOR: I shot it, yes. But I shot it *as if* it were my script. I made it very different.

ERNA: Oh. *(Laughs to herself)*

GREGOR: What's funny? It was different, Erna. It wasn't the script Klima had in mind at all.

ERNA: But they were his words.

GREGOR: You can say a lot of different things with the same words! *(Pause)* Remember the house?

ERNA: The house in the film?

GREGOR: Yes, Erna.

ERNA: Of course I remember it. The big white farmhouse. The whole film was shot in that house.

GREGOR: I went through hell to shoot my film in that house! I could have shot Klima's script in any old farmhouse. But not mine. Oh they tried to make me. I spent six months looking for that house. See I had to have a house just like the one I grew up in. Like the house I was born in. Like the house they took away from us. *(Short pause)* Nothing else would do.

Pause.

ERNA: Gregor, I didn't know. . . .

GREGOR: In *my* script there had to be this house. *(Short pause)* I didn't dare just use my family's old house. *(Short pause)* That would have made them very suspicious. *(Short pause)* My house. *(Smiles to himself)* My film. *(Pause)* See— they won't understand here.

ERNA *(Taking his hand)*: Gregor . . .

Door buzzes.

GREGOR: That's Josef now.

Scene 5
And After

Later that evening. GREGOR *getting undressed.* ERNA *sits.*

ERNA: We don't belong. I hope that is clear to you now.
GREGOR: Actually I was just thinking the opposite, Erna.
ERNA: Yes?
GREGOR: Yes. (HE *is getting his pajamas out of a drawer*) Everyone liked the film, Erna.
ERNA: Everyone wasn't at the cinema, Gregor.
GREGOR: Everyone who was liked it, Erna.
ERNA: You talked to everyone then?
GREGOR: I talked to everyone who talked to me.
ERNA (*Snickers to herself*): That's just what I mean.
GREGOR: Erna, they liked it. My film was liked. You can't deny that.
ERNA: And therefore you think they like you.
GREGOR: I didn't say that.
ERNA: If they like your work, they like you. That's how you think.
GREGOR: That is not how I think, Erna.
ERNA: Or is it—since they said they liked your film, then you like them.
GREGOR: All I said was—they liked it. Dammit Erna, isn't that enough for now?
ERNA: I don't know—is it? (HE *ignores her and goes into the bathroom to change*) So maybe they liked it, but that doesn't mean they enjoyed it. I'm not sure they could ever enjoy it like it was meant to be enjoyed.
GREGOR (*Off*): How was it meant to be enjoyed?!

Pause.

ERNA: You know what I mean.

Pause.

GREGOR (*Off*): You talked to people. What did people tell you?
ERNA: I talked to no one.
GREGOR (*Entering in his pajamas*): I saw you talking to the manager of the cinema, Erna.
ERNA: Yes, I talked to him.
GREGOR: What did he say about the film?
ERNA: We didn't speak about your film. You think everyone was always speaking about your film? (*Pause*) We talked about other things.
GREGOR: Good.
ERNA: I asked him how much he paid his workers.

GREGOR *has gone into the kitchen and pours himself a vodka.*

GREGOR: Workers?

ERNA: Yes.

GREGOR *(Drinks the vodka)*: You asked him how much he paid his workers? What workers, Erna?

ERNA: That's what he asked. I said, the projectionist for example.

GREGOR: And what did the manager of the cinema say?

ERNA: He said the projectionist was a student.

GREGOR *washes the glass in the sink.*

GREGOR: When I was a student, I was a projectionist. Did you know that?

ERNA: We're not talking about you now, Gregor. *(HE shrugs, goes to get into bed)* So if the projectionist is a student, then he couldn't be considered a worker. He's an intellectual.

GREGOR: The manager of the cinema said the student was an intellectual?

ERNA: No, he just said he was a student—but isn't that what he meant?

GREGOR *(In bed now)*: I think he meant that he was a student, Erna. *(Pause.* SHE *takes another cigarette)* You know you get headaches when you smoke too much. *(SHE shrugs)* Do what you want.

ERNA: That's easy to say.

Pause. GREGOR *sits up.*

GREGOR: They said they liked it. Why would they lie, Erna?

ERNA: You're fifty-six years old and you ask why do people lie?

GREGOR: I mean in this case, Erna.

ERNA: Maybe it's not that they lied, maybe it's that you didn't understand.

GREGOR: What's not to understand? I don't understand.

ERNA: Maybe they liked it only as a foreign film, Gregor.

GREGOR: But it is a foreign film. I'm foreign. I made it. It's in Czech. There were subtitles.

ERNA: That's what I mean. They liked it because it was foreign. That doesn't mean they enjoyed it, Gregor. *(Pause)* You don't know Americans, Gregor.

GREGOR: And of course you do.

ERNA: I never claimed that. I never even claimed that Americans liked me.

GREGOR: They like you, Erna. Please.

ERNA: Because they like your film, they like you. And because they like you, they like me? Is that what I'm supposed to believe? *(HE rolls over, ignoring her)* Gregor? *(Short pause)* I don't want to lose you.

Pause. HE *sits up and looks at her.*

GREGOR: Really? You seem to be trying to.

Scene 6
Dustin Hoffman

ERNA *at the kitchen counter.* GREGOR *sits on the floor opening a large box. Pause.* HE *slowly pulls out styrofoam and then a smallish television set.*

GREGOR: Maybe I should have gotten a color set, what do you think? *(No response)* It's black and white.

Pause.

ERNA: How much did it cost?
GREGOR: The color set? *(SHE shakes her head)* There was a sale. We can afford it.
ERNA: Can we?
GREGOR: And Josef said I can take it off my taxes. He said, because I'll use it for business.
ERNA: A television?
GREGOR: Hand me a butter knife.

SHE *does.*

ERNA: What does it mean—take it off your taxes?
GREGOR: It seems, Erna, that the government will pay for part of the television.
ERNA: The American government buys its people televisions?
GREGOR: That's what Josef says.
ERNA: Does the government make the televisions?
GREGOR: Erna, this is America.
ERNA: How much did we pay and how much did the government pay?
GREGOR: The government hasn't paid anything yet—but they will.
ERNA: How much?
GREGOR: I don't know. Ask Josef. *(HE screws the antenna on with the knife)* Look in the newspaper, they say what's on in there.
ERNA: Then how do we know we can afford it, if we don't know how much we pay? *(Hands him the paper)* I went to the Consulate today.

Long pause.

GREGOR: A television will help you learn English, Erna.
ERNA: I said, I went—
GREGOR: I heard you. *(Short pause)* Our Consulate?

SHE *nods.*

ERNA: They had the Prague papers. Skreta's opened his *Macbeth*.
GREGOR: I knew that.

ERNA: They say it's spectacular.

GREGOR: Who's they, Erna? The Prague papers? Everything Skreta does they say is spectacular—since he came back.

ERNA: There were photographs—it looked spectacular. *(Pause)* So you bought a television so I would learn English.

GREGOR: I bought it because I wanted it, Erna.

ERNA: You sound like an American already, Gregor. *(Pause)* The attaché asked how you were.

GREGOR: He recognized you? Did they follow you? *(SHE turns away)* Erna, did they follow you?! *(SHE turns back, shakes her head)* How do you know?

ERNA: I went through Macy's department store. I don't think it's possible to follow anyone through Macy's department store.

GREGOR: Erna, please—be careful.

ERNA: I'm the one who always has been careful, Gregor.

GREGOR: Stop it!

Pause.

ERNA: Besides, they know where we live, Gregor. Don't fool yourself.

GREGOR: If they knew where we lived, they would have been harassing us by now. Where's the newspaper with the television programs?

ERNA: It's right there, Gregor. *(HE picks it up)* The attaché said we could come back. *(Looks at him, then away)* Skreta went back.

GREGOR: Skreta had an exit stamp in his passport, Erna. Skreta did not escape through Yugoslavia. Skreta went on an extended holiday. We left. They'll *say* anything, Erna. Don't you know that by now. We can't go back.

Pause.

ERNA: The attaché put an exit stamp in my passport, Gregor. *(SHE gets up and gets her passport to show him)*

GREGOR: What did you tell them, Erna?

ERNA: There was only the attaché. I only spoke to him.

GREGOR: What did you tell him, Erna?

ERNA: There wasn't anything to say. *(Short pause)* Gregor, I didn't plan it. I was on the bus and this man looks up at me, he offers me his seat—in Czech. Then he tells me how much he has admired my stage work. He'd seen almost everything, Gregor. I told him he wasn't old enough to have seen everything. He gave me his card—he was the attaché's driver.

GREGOR: His driver on a bus?

Pause.

ERNA: He said he understood, Gregor. He didn't pressure me.

GREGOR: But you went to the Consulate. Why?

SHE *looks at him, takes out a cigarette, lights it, turns away.*

ERNA: You never said how much the television cost.

Pause.

GREGOR: Eighty-three dollars. Plus tax.

ERNA: Plus tax? I thought you took it off your tax.

GREGOR: That's a different tax. *(HE turns the television on. Flips a channel. ERNA moves in front of the television)* Try a channel. *(SHE shakes her head. HE flips to another channel)* What are you smirking about?

ERNA: American television. *(SHE turns away)*

GREGOR: You've seen ten seconds!!

ERNA: I've heard about it.

SHE *goes back to the kitchen counter. Long pause.*

GREGOR: Erna, I bought the god damn television so you would learn how to talk to people!

ERNA: I know how to talk to people. I talked to people today!! *(SHE puts on sweater)*

GREGOR: Where are you going now?

ERNA: To buy a newspaper. *(SHE leaves. Television is on. SHE returns)* The mail came. There's a letter from Prague.

GREGOR: From your sister?

SHE *hurries and opens it.* GREGOR *has gotten up.*

ERNA: Here, you read these pages.

HE *takes them.* THEY *are devouring the letter.* SHE *happens to look up at the television.*

Gregor?

GREGOR *(Over the letter)*: What?

ERNA: Isn't that Dustin Hoffman?

GREGOR *(Looks up at the television)*: Yes.

THEY *go back to reading the letter.*

Scene 7
Land of Opportunity

GREGOR *at the table, writing in a small account book.* ERNA *sits with her feet up.*

GREGOR: Ninety-seven dollars in the shoes in the closet. One hundred and thirty-seven dollars taped under the bathroom rug. Four hundred and five dollars in the overhead light.

ERNA: If it hasn't burned up.

GREGOR: It hasn't. *(Pause.* HE *gets up, gets a chair, stands on the chair and checks in the overhead light, speaks as* HE *is getting down)* It hasn't. *(HE sits back at the table)* Sixty-five dollars under the mattress. Twelve dollars in the refrigerator. *(ERNA laughs)* What's funny?

ERNA: In Prague we hid our friends' plays, here we hide—*(SHE laughs)*

GREGOR: Why is that funny?

ERNA: Not funny, just ironic, that's all.

GREGOR: To you everything is ironic, isn't it?

ERNA: I wish that were true.

Pause.

GREGOR: We still have one thousand two hundred and fifty-three dollars left of what my cousin loaned us.

ERNA: Loaned *you.* Don't put me in your cousin's debt. He can hardly keep his hands off me as it is.

GREGOR: What an imagination. Everyone either hates you or is trying to paw you. You're not thirty anymore, Erna.

ERNA: I'm sorry?

GREGOR: Forget it.

ERNA: You said I wasn't thirty anymore.

GREGOR *(Without looking up)*: So?

ERNA: Why did you say that? *(HE shrugs)* I suppose you are thirty.

GREGOR: I enjoy being the age I am. I'm not ashamed.

ERNA: And I am?

GREGOR: You're an actress, Erna.

ERNA: What is that supposed to mean?

GREGOR: Look, isn't this a stupid thing to argue about?

ERNA: I didn't realize we were arguing.

GREGOR: We were just about to. Trust me. *(Pause.* SHE *moves away)* One thousand two hundred and fifty-three divided by. . . . I think we'll be fine for another four months.

ERNA: Three.

GREGOR: Three and a half.

ERNA: Three.

GREGOR: Three.

ERNA: Maybe two and a half.

GREGOR: Three, Erna.

Pause.

ERNA: And then what?

GREGOR: Something will happen. I'm having meetings.

ERNA: Everybody has meetings. I can have meetings.

GREGOR: So have them. *(Short pause)* They've seen my film. They liked it. They told me they liked it. We have three and a half months, Erna.

ERNA: Two.

Short pause.

GREGOR: Look, if nothing works out by then, I'll drive a taxi.

ERNA: You'll drive a taxi?

GREGOR: Yes.

ERNA: You don't know how to drive, Gregor.

GREGOR: I'll learn.

ERNA: You'll learn?

GREGOR: Yes.

ERNA: Of course. Why not? When we left you did say in America everything was possible. Unfortunately I did not understand everything to mean you learning to drive a car.

GREGOR: It can't be hard. It's something at least.

ERNA: Of course. *(Pause)* I can scrub floors.

GREGOR: You'd do that?

ERNA: Look what I've already done.

GREGOR: "Look what I've already done." I see. New tactic. The martyr. Don't worry, I'm not going to let you scrub floors. *(Short pause)* I'll scrub floors.

ERNA: But what else can an old former actress do?

GREGOR: Erna, you are not a former actress. . . .

ERNA: But a minute ago you said—

GREGOR: What I said had nothing to do with your acting. I'm sorry I said anything.

Pause.

ERNA: Maybe you can get the attaché's chauffeur to teach you how to drive. (HE *looks at her*) You could just ask.

Pause.

GREGOR: I'm not going to ask for an exit stamp, Erna. We've been through this. I'm on their list. Do you know what that means?

ERNA: But if you said the right things.

GREGOR: I've already said the right things, which is why we left.

ERNA: Which is why *you* left. *(Pause)* I left with you. *(Long pause)* Gregor, it is all coming apart.

GREGOR: Nothing is coming apart.

ERNA: Look up.

HE *doesn't.* HE *has been looking through a small datebook.*

GREGOR: I have three meetings today. *(Pause. Without looking up)* We have three months.

ERNA *(Looking away)*: Two and a half.

Scene 8
By the Bootstraps

Late evening. GREGOR *at the open window,* ERNA *at a distance, watching him.* HE *is drunk.*

GREGOR *(Shouting out the window)*: America I love you! Do you hear me, America?!

ERNA: I think America's heard enough for one night, Gregor, so you can close the window.

GREGOR *(Pointing)*: America, Erna.

ERNA: Now you tell me. I said close the window. You're drunk.

GREGOR: Yes. *(HE moves away from the window.* SHE *goes and closes it. To himself)* Yes. *(Turns to* ERNA*)* But Erna. . . .

ERNA: Yes, Gregor?

GREGOR: I think I have the right to be drunk.

ERNA: That's one person's opinion.

GREGOR: Besides the boy producer was paying. *(HE laughs to himself)* He didn't know shit. Erna, did I tell you he has his own theatre in this Hartford and he didn't know shit?

ERNA: Is that what you told the producer, Gregor, that he didn't know shit?

GREGOR: What? Erna, don't be stupid. Even in America you can't be stupid.

ERNA: You figured that out by yourself?

GREGOR: I told him I was grateful! I thanked him for considering me. I was charming. And I was grateful. We all should be. You too, Erna.

ERNA: Leave me out of this, please. Have your own fun. I want to go to bed.

GREGOR: Erna . . .

ERNA: What now, Gregor?

GREGOR: I told you about the play, didn't I? I might be directing this play.

ERNA: Tell me again tomorrow. Get undressed. *(Short pause)* Or maybe you need help?

GREGOR *(HE looks at his clothes, weaves a bit)*: I don't know.

SHE *goes to undress him.*

ERNA: Sit down. *(SHE pushes him down on the couch)* Pick up your feet.

HE *does.* SHE *starts to take off his shoes.*

GREGOR: Erna, we are going to get out of this goddam one room.

ERNA: Not tonight, Gregor. I'm not going anywhere with you tonight.

GREGOR: But I don't mean tonight.

ERNA: No? Lift your arms.

HE *does.* SHE *pulls the sweater over his head.*

GREGOR: Three months. We had only three months. This boy was really impressed with me. As well he should be.

ERNA: Impressed with how much you could drink?

GREGOR: Erna, it's about time we got something, do you understand?

ERNA: What something would you like to get? Another television set?

GREGOR *(Getting up)*: Erna . . .

ERNA: Stay still.

GREGOR *(Moving toward the window)*: I want you to look at this with me. . . .

ERNA: Gregor, leave that window closed. *(HE does)* And please keep your voice down.

GREGOR *(HE nods and begins to whisper)*: Look at all that. That is here, Erna. We are here. I mean . . .

Short pause.

ERNA: What *do* you mean? *(Pause. HE looks out the window)* Sit down and I'll take your pants off.

GREGOR *(Still at the window)*: Listen to me! Sh-sh. This is the world today. Like it or not, Erna, understand? *(SHE sits down)* This is . . . culture. Call it shit, Erna. Go ahead. But that's fine. Shit is fine. And we found it. It is ours. We're here. *(HE goes and sits next to her, lifts his legs)* Take my pants off. *(SHE begins to)* I just want to see your attaché friend's face, when he hears. I was choked, but I didn't strangle.

ERNA: He's not my friend, Gregor. And besides I doubt if he'll even hear.

GREGOR: Oh they hear. They're probably in the next room hearing right now.

ERNA: Gregor.

GREGOR: Figuratively. Figuratively, Erna.

ERNA: I'll get your pajamas. *(SHE goes to the bathroom)*

GREGOR: Wait! *(HE jumps up with his pants around his ankles)* I want you to understand one thing. One thing you don't understand, Erna.

ERNA: What is that?

GREGOR: Understand that if a man can achieve something in this world, Erna. Here! In America. Then—

ERNA: Then what?

GREGOR: Then, he achieves everywhere. Just by achieving here. That's what this is. It's the center.

ERNA: I don't understand.

GREGOR: Wait! If a man's a poet here, Erna. Listen to me! He is not a Czech poet here, Erna. He is a poet. Period. That's what I mean. That's what this is all about. That's why everyone wants to be here.

Short pause.

ERNA: Not everyone, Gregor.

GREGOR: Who? Who? No one we know, Erna.

Pause.

ERNA: Here, put your own pajamas on. *(Throws him his pajamas)*

GREGOR: I can. I can. *(HE tries. SHE picks up a blanket and moves toward the bathroom)* What are you doing?

ERNA: I'm going to sleep in the bathroom.

GREGOR: Oh.

SHE *goes into the bathroom, closes the door. HE tries to put his pajamas on and falls.* SHE *comes out and looks at him.*

I can do it myself!

SHE *goes back into the bathroom and slams the door.*

Scene 9
Shadows

Evening. GREGOR *at the table, looking through a photo album. Bread on the table.* ERNA *lights candles.*

ERNA: Where is this Hartford?

GREGOR *(Without looking up)*: In the north. I could take a train. Why didn't you tell me before that you'd brought these photographs?

ERNA: I didn't? (HE *looks up*) I must have been waiting for the right time. (HE *smiles, looks back down*) Here's a knife to cut the bread with. (*Gives him a knife*)

GREGOR (*Looking at a photo*): Vlasta in my *Lower Depths*. I haven't thought about Vlasta for years.

ERNA: Vlasta's been dead for years, Gregor.

GREGOR: For years?

SHE *nods.* HE *shakes his head. Pause.*

ERNA: The food last night with the producer, was it good?

GREGOR: The food?

ERNA: In the restaurant.

GREGOR: Yes, it was very good.

ERNA: Oh. (*Short pause*) Perhaps you're not very hungry then.

GREGOR (*Without looking up*): I'm hungry.

ERNA: Maybe you ate too much last night.

GREGOR: No, I'm . . . (HE *looks up at her*) I'm hungry, Erna.

ERNA: Good.

GREGOR *looks back over the album.*

GREGOR: Lukash, Erna.

ERNA: Lukash? (SHE *goes to him*) Where? (HE *points*) That's Lukash? In *The Lower Depths*? He wasn't in *The Lower Depths*.

GREGOR: This isn't *The Lower Depths*. I can't figure out what this is. It isn't one of mine. But that's Lukash.

ERNA: Yes. That's Lukash. I don't think I saw this play. (*Moves to go back to the kitchen*)

GREGOR: Wait. I remember. It's another Gorky. The one they closed.

ERNA: They closed a Gorky?

GREGOR: In rehearsal they closed it. They're in rehearsal clothes, see? Erna, where did you get these photographs?

ERNA: From friends, Gregor. (SHE *goes and gets a bottle of wine, shows it to him*)

GREGOR: What is this?

ERNA: Will you open it?

GREGOR: Czech wine? Erna, where did you find Czech wine?

ERNA: In the store. Just open it, please.

GREGOR: You asked for Czech wine?

ERNA: Why not? (SHE *goes and gets a cigarette.* GREGOR *smiles to himself, and shakes his head.* HE *looks back at the album as* ERNA *holds up a large book*) Gregor . . .?

GREGOR (*Looking up*): What is it?

ERNA: I borrowed it from the library.

GREGOR: You went to the library? When?

ERNA (*Reading the title*): "*Photographs of Prague*." I thought you might . . .

GREGOR *(Smiling)*: Yes. *(SHE sets the book back down)* Thank you. Why don't you sit down.

ERNA: In a minute. I want to put in the pie. *(SHE goes to the oven)*

GREGOR: You're making a pie? . . . Erna, I think you're trying to seduce me.

ERNA: Think whatever you want. I'm making a pie. *(Pause.* SHE *puts the pie into the oven)*

GREGOR: Erna, your *Three Sisters.*

ERNA: My Olga? *(Goes to look)*

GREGOR: No. Your Irina, I think.

ERNA: Yes. That's my Irina. Gregor, these are old.

GREGOR: Very old.

ERNA: Not that old. *(SHE moves back to the oven)*

GREGOR *(Over the album)*: Pavek as Sganarelle.

ERNA: Pavek? Really? *(SHE wipes her hands and goes to see)*

GREGOR: Why are you so interested in Pavek?

ERNA: I liked Pavek.

GREGOR: I didn't know that.

ERNA: You knew I liked Pavek.

GREGOR: No. I didn't know. When did you like him?

ERNA: Gregor, I only liked him. He was a great actor.

GREGOR: I see.

ERNA: Gregor—Pavek was a homosexual. We were friends.

GREGOR: Pavek? You know you shouldn't say that.

ERNA: Gregor, I can say it here.

GREGOR: I suppose so. *(Short pause)* Pavek a homosexual? I didn't know.

ERNA: That's why he killed himself.

GREGOR: I thought he killed himself because of gambling. That's what we all thought.

ERNA: I know that's what everyone thought. But he didn't gamble, Gregor. He was caught. He didn't want his daughter to know. He killed himself.

GREGOR: You knew this?

ERNA: We talked. If he killed himself there wouldn't be a trial. And his son-in-law could keep his job as a foreman. They made it all very clear to him.

GREGOR: He told you all this?

ERNA: Yes.

GREGOR: What did you say to him?

ERNA: What could I say?

GREGOR: Then you knew he was going to kill himself?

ERNA: I knew he was thinking about it. I told him to emigrate.

GREGOR: He wouldn't do that.

ERNA: No.

GREGOR: Not with his son-in-law being a foreman. He'd never be able to live with himself. He was too sensitive.

ERNA: He was very sensitive. *(Looks at the album)* That's not Pavek.

GREGOR: That's Marek as Don Juan. See that shadow—

ERNA: Yes.

GREGOR: That's Pavek.

ERNA: The shadow?

GREGOR: Can't you tell?

ERNA: Yes. That's Pavek. Of course.

GREGOR: He was a lovely man. Beautiful.

ERNA: His daughter was lovely too.

GREGOR: He lived for her. How was he caught?

ERNA: In the train station.

GREGOR: I didn't know that. They kept it all very quiet. Usually something like that everyone knows.

ERNA: Everyone didn't know. That's why he had to shoot himself.

Pause. GREGOR *looks at more photos.*

GREGOR: I can't figure out where you got all these. Half of them I've never seen before.

ERNA *(Going back into the kitchen)*: I had them.

GREGOR: With you? At home?

ERNA: I collected them from our friends.

GREGOR: Oh.

ERNA: Before we left.

GREGOR: Oh. Well it's nice to have something to remember Prague by.

ERNA: We have many things to remember Prague by, Gregor. *(Pause.* HE *laughs)* What?

GREGOR: Bruz in the Feydeau.

SHE *laughs.* HE *turns another page.*

ERNA: So you will be gone how long?

GREGOR: Five weeks. If I go.

ERNA: If? I thought . . .

GREGOR: I haven't been given a contract yet.

ERNA: Oh.

GREGOR: What does that mean?

ERNA: It means—oh.

Pause.

GREGOR: Look at Vanek's set for *The Cherry Orchard*, Erna.

SHE *goes and looks and moves back to the kitchen.*

ERNA: We could write Vanek. He's in Paris, isn't he?

GREGOR: No.

ERNA: He's not in Paris?

GREGOR: You know as well as I know that Vanek went back, Erna.

ERNA: I forgot.

GREGOR *(Without looking at her)*: No you didn't.

Pause.

ERNA: And in this Hartford, they have good sets?

GREGOR: I don't know.

ERNA: But you said you saw pictures.

GREGOR: I saw plans. For the stage. I didn't see pictures.

ERNA: They didn't show you pictures?

GREGOR: No.

ERNA: I just don't know how they put on plays in America in just five weeks.

GREGOR: I'd rather not talk about it. I don't want to get my hopes up.

ERNA: Okay.

GREGOR: Even if I don't get the job, we should at least be pleased that people are beginning to think of me.

ERNA: A lot of people think of you, Gregor. *(Pause.* SHE *goes back to the kitchen. Then noticing the expression on his face)* What's wrong?

GREGOR *(Looking at pictures)*: What is this?

ERNA: What?

GREGOR: These pictures.

ERNA *(Over his shoulder)*: I don't know.

GREGOR: Who gave these to you?

ERNA: Those? I don't remember.

GREGOR: Did Marek give them to you?

ERNA: Most of our friends gave me pictures, Gregor. What are they of?

GREGOR: Marek's party he gave for me.

ERNA: I wasn't there.

GREGOR: I know you weren't there. I remember everyone who was there. There were five of us. And no one was taking pictures. No one would at a party like that.

ERNA: Obviously someone took pictures. There they are.

GREGOR: This is a joke.

ERNA: What is?

GREGOR: Erna, what I said at that party is what I was denounced for.

ERNA: Gregor . . . ?

GREGOR: What I said to the officials later didn't help. But what I said at that party was the start.

ERNA: They are dark. Gregor, I didn't know.

GREGOR: This is someone's idea of a joke.

ERNA: It's a sick joke, Gregor.

GREGOR: When you asked our friends for pictures, did you say why?

ERNA: No. But I'm sure they knew.

GREGOR: Yes.

ERNA: They could see it in our faces.

GREGOR: Yes.

ERNA: We could always see it in someone's face before he left. *(Pause.* SHE *sits)* Marek gave me some. Also Bruz. Jaroslav. . . .

GREGOR: Jaroslav. I never did trust Jaroslav.

ERNA: He denounced you?

GREGOR: I don't know. *(Short pause)* I don't know. *(Short pause)* In any case, it doesn't matter now.

ERNA: No?

Pause.

GREGOR: Blow out the candles. I want to turn on some lights, it's dark in here.

SHE *blows out the candles.*

Scene 10
The Free World

GREGOR *sits.* ERNA *in the kitchen.* SHE *takes a kettle, fills it with water, places it on the stove.*

GREGOR: So you won't go? *(SHE shrugs)* It's ten to twelve. The producer said he'd see you at twelve.

ERNA: I never said I would, Gregor.

GREGOR: But I thought—

ERNA: Then maybe you thought wrong.

GREGOR: Yes. I'll call him later and apologize for you not showing up.

ERNA: I don't want you apologizing for me.

GREGOR: You don't leave me any choice, Erna.

ERNA: So now I'm hurting you.

GREGOR: You're not hurting me. I don't care what you do.

ERNA: Is that true?

GREGOR: It's a free world here, do what you want.

ERNA: You don't want that, Gregor.

GREGOR: I wouldn't bet on that, Erna. *(Pause.* THEY *look at each other)* It wasn't much of a part. And who knows if you'd even have gotten it. It was only an audition.

ERNA: I'd have gotten it.

GREGOR: How do you know? You don't know how things are done here.

ERNA: I know because my husband is directing the play.

GREGOR: Erna, is that the reason why—

ERNA: I don't know! . . . Please, just leave me alone for now. *(HE nods)* Where are you going?

GREGOR: You just said you wanted me to leave you alone.

ERNA: That doesn't mean I don't want to know where you're going.

GREGOR: I'm going to take a shower. *(HE moves to the bathroom)* Josef's coming by. Let him in when he buzzes.

ERNA: Josef's coming by?

GREGOR: I asked him over when I thought you'd be out.

ERNA: Josef can come when I'm here.

GREGOR: He doesn't speak Czech, Erna. You'd have to speak English. I didn't know if you were ready for that. *(HE goes into the bathroom)*

ERNA: Gregor . . . ?

HE closes the door. We hear the shower turned on. SHE *throws herself on the couch after turning on the television. After a moment,* SHE *sits up, looks at her watch, and gets up and puts her coat on.*

(Calling) Gregor, will you call the producer and tell him I'll be late.

GREGOR *(Off)*: I can't hear you, Erna!

ERNA: I said, call the . . . *(Buzzer sounds)* Gregor, I think it's . . .

GREGOR *(Off)*: Was that the buzzer?

ERNA: Gregor?!

GREGOR *(Off)*: Push the button, Erna! He's downstairs!

SHE *picks up the buzzer/phone.*

ERNA: Hello? Hello? *(SHE pushes buttons)* Gregor, no one is . . . *(The water boils, the kettle whistles. Into phone)* Just a . . . *(Telephone rings. In a bit of a panic)* Gregor!!

It rings.

GREGOR *(Off)*: Is that the phone?

SHE *hurries to the phone—the kettle whistling, television on. On her way* SHE *knocks over a glass.*

ERNA *(Into phone)*: Hello? I am sorry what?

GREGOR *(Off)*: Was that Josef?

ERNA *(Into phone)*: What? Please, I do not . . . *(Knock at the door)* Just a minute. One moment please. *(Into phone)* Can you speak to my husband? I am sorry, I was speaking Czech. I said, can you . . .

GREGOR *(Off)*: What are you doing out there?! Let him in, Erna!

ERNA *(Into phone)*: Hello? I do not understand, mister . . . *(Another knock. SHE calls back)* I do come! *(Into phone)* If I buy magazines I win free trip to this Miami Beach?

Television, whistle, knock. GREGOR *comes out in his robe.*

GREGOR *(Yells)*: Erna!!
ERNA *(Pleading)*: Gregor!

Scene 11
Siberia

ERNA *is ironing.* GREGOR *sits, writing down something on a small piece of paper.* HE *has a pile of books in front of him. Pause.* HE *gets up.*

GREGOR: Here's the phone numbers for the theatre and my hotel. *(HE holds out the paper.* SHE *nods, but doesn't look at him or take it)* I'll set it on the table. *(SHE nods. Pause)* You are going to be all right, aren't you?
ERNA: Of course. Why wouldn't I be all right? What time was your train?
GREGOR: I have an hour. *(HE goes back to sorting through the books, trying to decide what to take)*
ERNA: If you end up needing one of those, I can mail it to you.
GREGOR: Thank you. *(Short pause)* You're going to wear that shirt out—if you keep ironing it.
ERNA *(Shrugs)*: I want you to look nice. . . . I think Americans judge you by how you look.
GREGOR: Since when, Erna?
ERNA: It's not true?
GREGOR: If you'd seen the producer of the theatre—I doubt if he's worn an ironed shirt all his adult life.
ERNA: But he's still a boy. The boys can dress like that. You're not a boy anymore, Gregor.
GREGOR: If you're only worried about how I *look*, then why have you been up since five pressing my underwear?

Short pause.

ERNA: I just wanted to.

HE *smiles.* SHE *finishes ironing, folds the shirt and puts it in the suitcase.* HE *writes something.*

GREGOR: Here, you'll need the address of the theatre if you're going to send anything. *(SHE doesn't look at him)* I'll put it with the phone numbers. *(HE does. Pause)* I asked Josef to look in on you. *(SHE nods)* Maybe the two of you can go to a show.

Pause.

ERNA: Maybe.

Pause.

GREGOR: After all, it's only five weeks, Erna. And then you'll come to Hartford for the opening.
ERNA: I'll never understand how Americans can rehearse their plays in only five weeks.

Pause.

GREGOR: You will come up for the opening, won't you?
ERNA: I might be going to a show that night with Josef.

HE *smiles.* HE *packs some books in a bag. Long pause.* SHE *closes the suitcase.*

There's instant coffee in a bag. And I made you a lunch—cheese and salami. It's in the refrigerator. I'll get it. *(SHE does)* And there's toilet paper . . .
GREGOR: I think the hotel will have toilet paper.
ERNA *(Ignoring him)*: And I packed the clock . . .
GREGOR: What will you use?
ERNA: You can figure out the time by watching the television. There's two bars of soap with the toilet paper, and your coat brush.
GREGOR: I'll be sure to brush off the blonde hairs before I come home.

ERNA *looks up at him, then smiles.*

ERNA: And two cartons of cigarettes. The matches I stuffed in your slippers . . .

GREGOR: Erna, I'm not going to Siberia.

Long pause.

ERNA: Help me put the ironing board away.

HE *does.* THEY *set it in the kitchen area.* HE *takes her hand.* SHE *tries not to cry.*

GREGOR: Erna . . .

HE *hugs her,* SHE *hugs back. Pause. Lights fade.*

Scene 12
His Memory

This scene is GREGOR's *memory of their first moments in the apartment. Stage empty. Door opens,* GREGOR, *then* ERNA, *enter with suitcases.*

GREGOR: Hello? Is someone in here, please? *(To* ERNA*)* No one's here.

THEY *look around.*

ERNA *(Pointing to the door buzzer)*: What is this?
GREGOR: To let people in the front door. *(Noticing something on the table)* She left a note. *(*HE *reads)* "Dear Mr. and Mrs. Hasek. Sorry I couldn't welcome you myself, but business in L.A. calls."
ERNA: What is L.A.?
GREGOR: Los Angeles. *(Continues to read)* "Enjoy the sublet. Feel free to use anything here. And if you have any questions just call the super."
ERNA: What is this super?
GREGOR: It's nice, don't you think?
ERNA: Is that the bedroom?
GREGOR *(Opens a door)*: A closet. I don't think there is a bedroom. The couch folds out.
ERNA: I see. *(Opens her bag for a cigarette)* Gregor—the refrigerator!
GREGOR: My God.
ERNA: Why is it so big?
GREGOR: I don't know. *(*HE *opens it)* Erna, she left a bottle of vodka for us.
ERNA: It's not for us, Gregor.
GREGOR: Of course it's for us. Look in the cabinets for some glasses.
ERNA: I don't think we should, Gregor.
GREGOR: There are a couple here in the sink. *(*HE *opens the vodka)*
ERNA: Gregor, it's not ours.

HE *hands her a glass.*

GREGOR *(Toasts)*: To our new home.

Scene 13
Her Memory

This scene is ERNA's *memory of their first moments in the apartment. As in the previous scene,* ERNA *and* GREGOR *with suitcases.* GREGOR *has found the note.*

GREGOR *(Reading)*: "Dear Mr. and Mrs. Hasek. Sorry I couldn't welcome you myself but business in L.A. calls." *(To* ERNA*)* What is L.A.? *(*ERNA *shrugs.*

Reading) "I'm sure you will treat my home as if it were yours. Any problems just call the super."

ERNA: Call what?

GREGOR *(Shrugs)*: I don't know.

ERNA *(Pointing to the buzzer)*: What is this?

GREGOR *(Shrugs)*: To call the concierge? I don't think there's a bedroom.

ERNA: Maybe the couch folds out. Gregor—the refrigerator!

GREGOR: What do you need a refrigerator that big for? *(THEY look at each other. HE opens the refrigerator)* There's some vodka. *(Short pause)* Do you think we should . . . ?

ERNA: I don't know, Gregor.

GREGOR: She left it in the refrigerator.

ERNA: I wouldn't.

GREGOR: Maybe just a little, she'll never know.

HE *takes two glasses out of the sink. Pause.*

ERNA: What's wrong?

GREGOR: I'm just tired.

ERNA: Come here. *(SHE takes him by the hand)*

GREGOR *(Scared)*: Well, we made it. To us? *(SHE nods. THEY drink)* Don't you want to take off your coat?

ERNA: I'm not ready yet. Everything's still too new.

GREGOR: It's nice, isn't it? *(SHE holds him around the waist)* Isn't it? *(HE looks out the window)* Erna . . .

ERNA: What?

GREGOR: Look at those buildings. They're very tall aren't they?

ERNA *(Nods)*: Gregor, let's try not to be scared.

Pause.

GREGOR: We will try again here.

ERNA: We have each other, Gregor.

THEY *hug.*

Scene 14
Siberia Continued

The same as at the end of Scene 11. THEY *are hugging.* ERNA *slips something into* GREGOR's *hand.*

GREGOR: What's this?

ERNA: Don't look at it now. *(SHE moves away to get his coat)*

GREGOR: A picture? Yours?

ERNA: Look at it on the train. *(SHE helps him put on his coat)*

GREGOR: Thank you. *(Short pause)* Erna, what's left in the refrigerator for you?

ERNA: Plenty. Don't worry.

HE *nods.* HE *picks up his bags.*

GREGOR: I'll call when I get there. *(SHE nods)* You take care. Please.

SHE *nods.* HE *hesitates.*

ERNA: You're going to miss your train. *(HE kisses her on the cheek)* Will you go, I want to wash the dishes.

HE *smiles, nods, and slowly leaves.* SHE *closes the door behind him.* SHE *sighs, almost shaking now.* SHE *goes into the kitchen area, turns the water on, then suddenly hurries to the window, leaving the water running.* SHE *watches out the window and then sees him.*

Look up. Look up! Look . . .

SHE *waves—*HE *has looked up.* SHE *smiles, watches him walk down the street, turns back to the room, sits. Takes out a cigarette. Gets up and locks the chain lock on the door. Goes back and sits. The water runs.*

Scene 15
A Few Days Before

Rain on the window. GREGOR, *on the couch, in his robe; a thermometer in his mouth.* ERNA *over him. Pause.* GREGOR *takes the thermometer out of his mouth and looks at it.*

GREGOR: I'm fine. *(ERNA takes the thermometer and looks at it)* I'm fine. *(Short pause)* I'll be fine.

ERNA *(Moving to get her coat)*: What you need is a little camphor oil. I'll go to the pharmacy.

GREGOR: Really, don't bother.

ERNA: It's what I want to do. Besides, you're sick. You have a temperature. If you're going to Hartford you can't be sick.

GREGOR: If . . . ?

Pause.

ERNA: When. *(Pause)* When. *(Taking a blanket to him)* I'll just be a minute. Keep this over your shoulders.

GREGOR: Erna . . .

ERNA: I said I'll be right back. What do you think, I'm deserting you?

GREGOR *(HE grabs her hand)*: Erna. *(SHE stops. HE gets up and goes to a drawer and takes out a newspaper clipping and a letter. Pause)* Skreta's written my cousin. He's offered me two productions for the season. *(Short pause)* Read this. He enclosed this. *(Hands her the clipping)*

ERNA: Why didn't you . . .

GREGOR: Just read.

ERNA *(Looking at the clipping)*: The party paper? *(HE doesn't respond)* A summary of your career in the party paper? I don't understand. *(Reads)* "Gregor Hasek, director of extraordinary vision." They praise you? *(HE turns away and nods)* They praise you? You leave the country and they praise you?

GREGOR: At the end of the article they say I've been sick for the past months. I'm resting by the Black Sea.

ERNA: You're by the Black Sea?

GREGOR: That's what they say. I've been sick. *(Pause)* Skreta can protect me.

ERNA: No one can protect you.

GREGOR: No.

Pause.

ERNA: But if anyone could, it would be Skreta.

GREGOR: Yes.

Short pause.

ERNA: Two productions?

GREGOR: Do you think we should go back?

ERNA: I try not to think anymore.

GREGOR: Maybe we should.

ERNA: You don't want that. *(Pause)* You have your career in Hartford to think about now. Why are you shivering?

GREGOR: I'm sick. I'm by the Black Sea. *(Short pause)* Wouldn't it make you happy?

ERNA: To be by the Black Sea? I never liked the Black Sea, Gregor. *(Short pause)* I wouldn't mind the mountains.

Short pause.

GREGOR: Tell me what is right. I want to know what will make you happy.

ERNA: Are those now the same question?

GREGOR: Erna . . .

ERNA: Are those now the same question, Gregor?

GREGOR: I want what you want, Erna.

ERNA: That's not true. That's never been true. Sometimes it's been true.

GREGOR: I want you to get better.

ERNA: I'm not the one who's sick. *(Beat)* I'm not the one who's sick.

GREGOR: To tell you the truth I thought you'd be overjoyed.

ERNA: You won't go.

GREGOR: I would—for you.

ERNA: I don't want you to go—for me.

GREGOR: Can't I do something for you? Can you only do things for me? *(Yells)* Can you only do things for me?!!

Long pause.

ERNA: Then let's go home.

GREGOR: Fine.

ERNA: When?

GREGOR: When? *(ERNA goes into the closet)* What are you doing?

ERNA: Packing.

GREGOR: So it really is what you want.

ERNA: Yes.

GREGOR: We just leave.

ERNA: Yes.

GREGOR: You really want me to do that.

ERNA: Yes.

GREGOR: You would do that to me?

ERNA: Yes.

GREGOR *(Stands up)*: I thought you loved me.

ERNA: What?

GREGOR: I thought you loved me. *(HE moves toward the bathroom)*

ERNA: Gregor?

GREGOR: I said—I thought you loved me!!! *(HE goes into the bathroom, slamming the door)*

ERNA: Gregor!!!!

Long pause. ERNA sits on the couch. SHE puts the blanket over her shoulders. SHE shivers, begins to cry. The rain hits the window. The hallway door opens, GREGOR enters with a wet overcoat on and carrying a wet umbrella.

GREGOR *(Entering)*: I found camphor oil. Feel any better? The pharmacy across the street was closed. I had to go ten blocks. *(Takes off his coat)* It's really coming down now. Did you take your temperature? *(HE looks at her)* Erna . . . ?

ERNA: What? *(Turns to him, startled)* Sorry. My mind was wandering.

Scene 16
Erna Recalls Another Scene

Morning, weeks earlier. ERNA *stands by the window with an English-language copy of Chekhov's* Three Sisters *in her hand.* GREGOR, *in his robe, sits on the couch;* HE *smokes, drinks coffee. In front of him is another copy of* Three Sisters *which* HE *is following. Pause.*

GREGOR *(Lighting a cigarette)*: Whenever you're ready.

SHE *nods.*

ERNA *(Reads)*: "One year ago on this very day, May fifth . . ."
GREGOR *(Correcting her pronunciation, as* HE *does throughout the scene)*: Fifth. May fifth, Erna.
ERNA: "May fifth—on your birthday, Irina—Father died. It was bitter cold and snowing."
GREGOR: Cold. And. I'm not hearing the "d's."
ERNA: Cold. And. "At the time, it all seemed more than I could bear; you fainted, I even thought you had died."
GREGOR: I even thought you had died.
ERNA: "I even thought you had died."
GREGOR: It's one phrase. I even thought you had died.
ERNA: "I even thought you had died." *(A beat)* "It's been only a year, we can barely remember it. You're back wearing white; your face glows."
GREGOR: It's—wearing white.
ERNA: ". . . wearing white; your face glows."
GREGOR *(Taking a sip of coffee)*: Bong. Bong. Bong.
ERNA: "The clock struck then too."
GREGOR: You should turn to the clock. See the clock.
ERNA: See the clock?
GREGOR: Yes.
ERNA: I should turn and see the clock here?
GREGOR: Yes.
ERNA: I never turn to see the clock here. Two hundred performances of *Three Sisters* and I never turned here. Olga doesn't move here.
GREGOR: It's better if she turns. In my production she turned.
ERNA: In our production she didn't, Gregor. Skreta didn't want me to turn. You must have seen that production twenty times, why didn't you ever say anything before?
GREGOR: Skreta was the director, Erna. Just try it, you'll see.
ERNA: I'll see what?
GREGOR: That I'm right.
ERNA: So I should turn here.

GREGOR: Yes.

ERNA: Why?

GREGOR: Why? . . . I don't remember why, Erna. My production was ten years ago. I just remember it worked. And that's what we're after.

ERNA: That it works? That's not what we're after, Gregor.

GREGOR: Will you just try it?

Pause.

ERNA: "It's been only a year, we can barely remember it. You're back wearing white . . ."

GREGOR: White, Erna.

ERNA: ". . . white; your face glows."

GREGOR: Bong. Bong. Bong.

ERNA *(Turns)*: "The clock struck then too." *(Short pause)* I turned.

GREGOR: And?

ERNA: And I don't like it. I shouldn't turn there. I never did.

GREGOR: Fine, then just forget it. Forget I said anything! Forget I'm even here! What do I care, it's your audition.

ERNA: It's not my audition, Gregor. I never said I was going to audition. I said I wanted to practice in case I started to think like I might go to the audition, Gregor.

GREGOR: Whatever you say. Though I seem to recall that it was you who asked me to help.

ERNA: To help with my English. I don't need direction. I had a director. Skreta directed me.

GREGOR: And Skreta's a fine director.

Short pause.

ERNA: So I'm not turning here?

GREGOR: Ask Skreta.

Short pause.

ERNA: "I remember them carrying Father away."

GREGOR *(A little hostile now)*: Father! With a "th"!

ERNA: "I remember them carrying Father away." In the Czech it's different. In the Czech it's "taking Father out of our house."

GREGOR: Then say that.

ERNA: But it says in the English . . .

GREGOR: Say what you want to say, Erna.

ERNA: I want to say what Chekhov wanted.

GREGOR: I don't think Chekhov's going to be at the audition, Erna. But if he is, we'll ask him what he likes.

SHE *looks at him. Pause.*

ERNA: "I remember them carrying Father away. The band . . ." *(To* GREGOR*)* Band?

GREGOR: You know what it means. (SHE *mimes a horn player. Short pause)* Keep going.

ERNA: "The band played a march, they fired rifle shots over the grave. For a general of the brigade there weren't many mourners. . . ." Correct me whenever you want, Gregor. *(Pause.* HE *says nothing)* " . . . there weren't many mourners. Well, it was raining hard, rain mixed with snow." Here I turn my head. (SHE *does;* GREGOR *snickers)* What's funny about that?

GREGOR: Don't ask me, I'm not the director.

Pause.

ERNA: Here Irina says . . .

GREGOR *(Reads):* "Why think about it?"

ERNA: That's all?

GREGOR: That's all.

ERNA: In the Czech it's much longer. *(Shakes her head)* Language. *(Reading)* "Now today it's warm. We can even keep the windows open. Though there still aren't any leaves on the birches. . . ." (SHE *gets a small smile on her face and looks out the window)* This is true, no leaves on any birches out there. (GREGOR *just looks at her)* " . . . on the birches. It's been eleven years since Father was put in charge of the brigade . . ."

GREGOR *(Without looking up):* Brigade.

ERNA: " . . . brigade and we all had to leave Moscow."

GREGOR: And we all had to leave Moscow. It's all one sentence.

ERNA: "And we all had to leave Moscow. I remember well, that at this time, in early May, the sun bathes everything."

GREGOR: It's bathes, Erna. Bathes.

ERNA: Bathes.

GREGOR: Bathes. Bathes. God damn it!

ERNA: What's wrong with you? (HE *gets up with the book and moves away. Pause)* "After eleven years, I remember it all as if it were yesterday."

GREGOR *(Quietly):* Yesterday.

ERNA: "Yesterday. Oh God when I woke up this morning and saw the sunshine . . ."

GREGOR *(Pacing without looking at her):* Sunshine. Sunshine.

ERNA: "Sunshine, that golden light . . ."

GREGOR *(Almost shouting now):* That golden light . . .

ERNA: " . . . and smelled . . ."

GREGOR: Smelled!!!

ERNA: " . . . smelled . . ."

GREGOR *(Reading from his book):* " . . . smelled the Spring coming . . ."

ERNA: ". . . smelled the Spring coming . . ."
GREGOR: ". . . it made me so happy . . ."
ERNA: ". . . it made me so happy . . ."
GREGOR: Say it right—it made me so happy . . .
ERNA: ". . . it made me so happy. . . ." Gregor, I'm trying. . . .
GREGOR: Then try harder.
ERNA: You mean as hard as you try?!!
GREGOR: Once I want to hear it right—"it made me so happy, I longed to go home."
ERNA: ". . . it made me so happy, I longed to go home."
GREGOR: Say it—I long to go home. I LONG TO GO HOME!!!
ERNA *(Screaming)*: I LONG TO GO HOME. I LONG TO GO HOME. I LONG TO GO HOME!!!!!

SHE *throws her book at him. Long pause.* ERNA *looks out the window.* GREGOR *looks away.*

(More to herself than to GREGOR, SHE *continues Olga's speech from* Three Sisters *in Czech)* "Every morning it's school, every afternoon and night there's tutoring. It's no wonder I get those headaches. I have started to think like an old woman. Really after four years of this work . . ."
GREGOR *(Quietly)*: In English, Erna.
ERNA: ". . . it feels as if day after day all my strength, my youth is being drained out of me, squeezed, drop by drop. All that grows inside me now is that longing . . ."
GREGOR: In English!
ERNA: ". . . to go to Moscow! Sell the house, leave everything, and to Moscow!
GREGOR *(Screaming)*: IN ENGLISH! IN ENGLISH! IN ENGLISH!
ERNA *(Simultaneously shouting)*: "TO MOSCOW! TO MOSCOW! TO MOSCOW!"

Scene 17
Going Places

ERNA *sits at the table. In front of her is an English grammar book. As* SHE *practices* SHE *covers with one hand the line* SHE *is supposed to figure out.*

ERNA: I will go to the park.
I go to the park.
I have . . . gone to the park.
I . . .

(Checks)

Went? What is this went?

(Short pause)

He will go to the school.
He goes to the school.
He has gone to the school.
He went to the school.

(Short pause)

She . . . will go to the refrigerator.

(SHE *gets up, and moves to the refrigerator*)

She goes to the refrigerator.

(SHE *opens the refrigerator door, looks, closes it, without finding anything* SHE *wants*)

She has gone to the refrigerator.

(SHE *sits back at the table*)

She went to the refrigerator.

(Continues with the book)

You will go to the post office.
You go to the post office.
You have gone to the post office.
You went to the post office.

(Short pause)

We will go to the city.
We go to the city.
We have gone . . .

(Stops. Pause. Then quietly, looking up)

We will go . . . home.
We go . . . home.
We have gone home.
We went . . . home.

(Pause)

Scene 18
Remainders

GREGOR, *alone, sits watching television.*

TELEVISION: "The West German Bundestag, ignoring street demonstrations and warnings from Moscow, voted to proceed with the stationing of American-made, medium-range missiles." *(GREGOR stands and moves toward the television)* "When this was almost immediately followed by the arrival of the first nine of 108 Pershing-2's, Moscow broke off the negotiations in Geneva indefinitely, then announced its own deployment . . . "

GREGOR *turns the sound down.* HE *goes to the phone.*

GREGOR *(Into the phone)*: I wish to make a phone call to Prague, Czechoslovakia, please. Thank you. *(Pause)* Yes. Prague, Czechoslovakia. The number 86-491. Yes. 212-288-5312. Thank you.

HE *hangs up.* HE *goes into the kitchen and opens the refrigerator.* HE *takes out a McDonald's burger, fries, and a shake.* HE *sits back at the table. Opens them slowly, begins to eat. The phone rings.*

(Into the phone) Hello? Thank you. . . . Hello, Erna? . . . Lucie. It is Gregor. I wish to speak to. . . .You don't know when she returns.What is she seeing? Oh. Skreta's *Macbeth*. Tell her I will call. Yes. . . . Wait. Tell her something for me. . . . The critics did not like the production. No. They said it was too European. You are right. She will be very interested in that. Goodbye. *(HE hangs up. Sits for a moment, then goes and turns the television sound back on.* HE *goes back to the table and eats without watching)*

TELEVISION: ". . . Accusing the United States of torpedoing the possibility of agreement in Geneva, the Soviet Union announced a further buildup of nuclear weapons in Czechoslovakia and East Germany as well as aboard submarines off the American coast. Whether intentional or not, the effect was to link the fate of Western Europe with that of the United States. Western leaders reacted calmly. The President said he regretted Moscow's attitude but professed confidence. 'I can't believe it will be permanent,' he said."

END OF PLAY

Cold Air

Virgilio Piñera

translated and adapted by
Maria Irene Fornes

About Virgilio Piñera

Virgilio Piñera was born in the small city of Cárdenas in Cuba in 1912. In 1940 he moved to Havana, where a book of poems and several short stories were soon published. Looking to solve financial difficulties and in search of a richer cultural life, in 1946 Piñera moved to Argentina, where he worked as a clerk in the Cuban Consulate and also as a freelance translator and proofreader. His first novel *La carne de René* was published there in 1952, followed by a book of short stories. In addition to *Aire frío*, Piñera's most important theatre pieces include *Electra Garrigó*, *Jesús*, *Falsa alarma*, *La boda*, *El flaco y el gordo*, *El filántropo*, and his last play *Los viejos pánicos*. Piñera died in Havana in 1979.

About Maria Irene Fornes

Maria Irene Fornes was born in Havana in 1930, and emigrated to New York in 1945. Her many plays include *The Conduct of Life*, *Sarita*, *Mud*, *The Danube*, *Fefu and Her Friends* and *Promenade*. She has been commissioned to write a play for the 1986-87 season of the American National Theater at the Kennedy Center.

Maria Irene Fornes: Plays, a volume containing four recent works, has been published by PAJ Publications. Fornes is currently working on a book of writing exercises she developed while conducting workshops for playwrights at INTAR Theatre in New York and elsewhere. She has held a Guggenheim fellowship, and has recently been the recipient of a National Endowment for the Arts two-year playwriting fellowship, a Rockefeller Foundation grant and an award from the American Academy and Institute of Arts and Letters. Fornes has received six Obie awards, including the Obie for Sustained Achievement.

About the Play

Virgilio Piñera's *Aire frío* was written in 1958 and first performed in Havana in 1962. It has also been produced, in Spanish, in New York and Miami. Maria Irene Fornes's translation/adaptation was commissioned by INTAR Hispanic American Theatre in New York City and supported by a TCG Hispanic Translation Commission. *Cold Air* opened at INTAR on March 27, 1985, under Fornes's direction, and was circulated by TCG's *Plays in Process* series later that year.

Translator/Adapter's Note

When I first saw *Aire frío* at the Cuban Cultural Center in New York in 1976, it deeply moved me. And I thought what a pleasure it would be to translate it. Translating is a singular pleasure. It is re-saying in one language what someone has said in another. It is undoing a work in order to do it again. And hoping that when it is redone it will appear to be exactly the same.

Besides the personal reasons it seemed to me that a translation was an imperative. That the play was not available in English was incomprehensible. It is my hope that after *Cold Air*, other plays of Virgilio Piñera will be translated, as he was a writer of great independence and genius who created an important body of work.

As a public recognizes an author, an author recognizes a public. *Aire frío* was performed in Cuba at the start of the revolution when economy was not a criterion for the production of plays. As the play was done then it was four-and-a-half hours long and had a cast of eighteen. In the United States, today, both the playing time and the size of the cast would create insurmountable obstacles to the play. In my adaptation I eliminated nine characters. Four of them—Laura, Miranda, Don Benigno and Pepe—were important to the play not so much in their presence on stage as in the knowledge and consequences of their existence. I also eliminated five walk-on parts. Close to two-thirds of the lines I cut were repetitions which were true to a popular way of speaking but which would have been meaningless in translation.

Characters

LUZ MARINA, 30.
OSCAR, her brother, 25.
ANA, her mother, 50.
ANGEL, her father, 55.
ENRIQUE, her brother, 33.
NENA, her pupil, 5.
TETE, her pupil, 5.
PEDRITO, her pupil, 7.
LUIS, her brother, 28.
LAURA'S VOICE
LAUNDRYMAN'S VOICE

Except for the children, ages given are at the start of the play.

Time

Place

The living room of the Romaguera family in Havana, Cuba. In the back, to the right is the main door; to the left is the door to the kitchen. Upstage on the right wall is the entrance to Ana and Angel's bedroom. Downstage on the left wall there is a window. Upstage center are double doors that lead to a small inner court. In the court, to the right there is a spiral staircase that leads to Luz Marina's bedroom; to the left there is a door that leads to the bathroom. In the living room there is: up right center, a table with three chairs; to the left of the entrance to the court, a chair; down right, a rocking chair; down left, a sewing machine.

The Play

Cold Air

ACT ONE

Scene 1

November, 1940. Evening. LUZ MARINA *sits left at the sewing machine.* OSCAR *sits at the table.* HE *writes.*

LUZ MARINA: It's so hot. *(Pause)* Is it hot.

OSCAR: Luz Marina, don't start with that.

LUZ MARINA: Should I talk about the cold? – It's November and I'm still roasting. *(Pause)* Maybe in January. . . .

OSCAR: You said that five times.

LUZ MARINA: And I'll keep saying it till my tongue falls. I'll keep saying it till it gets cool. At least cool enough to breathe. – And that won't be till January. And even then it may not be cool enough to breathe. It may be less hot but still not cool enough to breathe. *(Pause)* Let me see. . . . *(Counting with her fingers)* December, January, February, March, four months when the weather may be cool enough to breathe. – April, May, June, July . . .

OSCAR *(Interrupting)*: Luz Marina, will you let me work? If you're so hot why don't you take a shower?

LUZ MARINA: And have a stroke? *(Short pause)* April, May, June, July, August, September, October, November, eight months when you burn alive. – That's right. *(Pause)* There's always a reason why I can't get an electric fan.

Last month it was Father's wisdom teeth. The month before, the laundry bill went up. I'm tired of it. This month I'm getting a fan. Did you hear! I'm buying it! Cash! No installments. A large one. I have my eye on it. Eighteen pesos. I'm not going to sit here and burn. *(Raising her voice so* ANGEL, *who is offstage, can hear)* If someone has to have a tooth extracted, let him pay for it. Or let him go to the public clinic. And if he goes to the public clinic, let him get an infection. *(Pause)* And if he gets an infection, who'll pay for it? (SHE *laughs)* Me. (SHE *sews for a while.* SHE *gets a piece of paper and writes)* Juana owes me six. Elena three. Amalia four. *(Referring to the dress* SHE *is making)* And this one eighteen. *(Adding)* Six plus three equals nine plus four equals thirteen plus eighteen. Oscar. How much is thirteen and eighteen?

OSCAR: Thirteen plus eighteen? . . . (HE *thinks a moment)* Well . . . thirteen plus eighteen . . . (HE *thinks a moment)* Wait a moment. (HE *starts to write)*

LUZ MARINA *(With affection)*: Oscar, you're useless. You can rhyme. But that's all you can do.

OSCAR: I don't rhyme. I write modernist poetry. No one rhymes anymore. Listen to this. (HE *reads)* "The fish from the tower swims in asphalt . . . "

LUZ MARINA *(Interrupting)*: Nonsense. Fish don't swim in asphalt. They swim in water. And even if fish should swim in asphalt, in this heat they would fry. – Papa! How much is thirteen plus eighteen?

ANGEL *(Offstage)*: Thirty-one.

LUZ MARINA: Thirty-one?

ANGEL: Yes thirty-one.

LUZ MARINA: Hm. *(Pause)* For the baker, three. . . . For the milkman, five. . . . For the laundry . . .

OSCAR *(Interrupting)*: Don't forget, I have you down for five.

LUZ MARINA: What for?

OSCAR: For my book. I have twenty-four pesos promised. And I have fifty cents for the raffle.

LUZ MARINA: I'm not getting in that raffle.

OSCAR: Why not?

LUZ MARINA: Because the painting you're raffling is awful.

OSCAR: It's not awful. It's a modernist painting.

LUZ MARINA: I don't like modernist painting. I don't understand it. I don't understand your poems either but I'll give you five pesos for your book. Family's family.

OSCAR: O.K. Be vulgar. Be like the common people who think that modernist art is not art and that anyone can paint a modernist painting.

LUZ MARINA: That's right. Anyone can do it. Even I could paint modern painting like your little friend. *(Pause)* He hasn't come for dinner for a few days. Is he sick?

OSCAR: He left the country last week. He'll soon be in Paris. For his art he's willing to suffer hunger and cold.

LUZ MARINA: Cold? – I wish I were cold. The other day I had to sit on the back seat of the bus and there was hot air under me and hot air above me. Then I came home and what do I find? *(Laughing)* Steaming rice and beans. *(Short pause)* What is a person to do? Thirty years old . . . unmarried . . . clients who don't pay . . . a fan that never comes. . . .

ANGEL *enters from the bedroom with a newspaper in his hands.*

ANGEL: Listen to this. "High heat kills three hundred in Calcutta."
LUZ MARINA: It sounds great. Heat that kills instantly. Indians know how to do things. Our heat doesn't kill you. It just keeps you from being alive. – How's your tooth?
ANGEL: I was just telling your mother that it's hurting me a little.
LUZ MARINA: It's not yet a month since you had two wisdom teeth extracted.

ANGEL *sits in the rocking chair and reads as* ANA *leans out of the kitchen.*

ANA: So what? He has a right to have a toothache. He still has teeth in his mouth. Doesn't he? You want him not to have teeth? Not to have nerves in his teeth?
LUZ MARINA: With our luck he'll need an extraction.
ANA: So.
LUZ MARINA: Good-bye electric fan.
ANA: If he needs an extraction, I'll pay for it myself—with my money.
LUZ MARINA: What do you mean by your money? The money we owe? *(To herself)* Sixty from your retirement and sixty from my sewing, when it's not forty. Not enough. Not a penny from Enrique since he got married.
ANA: Last month he gave me five pesos.
LUZ MARINA: Very nice. Enrique the protector gave you five pesos.
ANGEL: Enough. I'm not in the dentist's chair yet. The pain will pass. I just need some phenol. *(To ANA)* Maybe Laura has some. Would you ask her?
LUZ MARINA: Phenol corrodes the teeth. They turn into shells. Then they'll have to operate.
ANA: You want to scare your father? – His tooth may get better. (SHE *goes to the kitchen)*
LUZ MARINA *(Fanning herself)*: Well. . . . How much is sixty minus thirty-one?
ANGEL: Twenty-nine.
ANA *(Offstage)*: Laura . . . ! Laura . . . !
LUZ MARINA: I have only twenty-nine coming in. *(To OSCAR)* Better sit while you wait for your five pesos. *(Pause)* Sixty and twenty-nine . . . is how much?
ANGEL: Eighty-nine.
LUZ MARINA: How much more to a hundred and twenty?
ANGEL: Thirty-one.
LUZ MARINA: Add four to that.

ANGEL: Thirty-five.

LUZ MARINA: Thirty-five pesos! We cannot think of extractions or electric fans. *(Pause)* I don't have a decent dress to wear. Not for winter.

OSCAR: What winter? The Cuban winter?

LUZ MARINA: Universal winter. Spring, summer, fall and winter. Convinced? *(Pause)*I may roast but I'll not wear summer clothes in winter.

ANA *(Offstage)*: Do you have some phenol?

LAURA'S VOICE: I have oil of cloves. Is that the same?

ANGEL *(To* ANA*)*: Tell Laura not to trouble herself. It doesn't hurt much anymore.

ANA: Thank you Laura, we don't need it. *(Entering)* It hurts but you'd rather be in pain than use oil of clove. I don't want to spend another night like last night.

ANGEL: What happened last night?

ANA: I couldn't sleep with you pacing up and down.

ANGEL: I prefer phenol. I have to go out anyway. I'll stop at the drugstore.

ANA: Laura says they're talking about a shortage of meat on the radio.

LUZ MARINA: In this house we don't hear the news on the radio. We hear baseball.

ANGEL: It's my only diversion. Must I also be deprived of that!

ANA: We don't deprive you of anything. You do as you please. You're going out tonight. Aren't you?

ANGEL: I have a meeting at the lodge.

LUZ MARINA: Mama. . . . (SHE *signals* ANA *to stop)* What did Laura say about meat?

ANA: That there's going to be a shortage of meat in Havana.

LUZ MARINA: Maybe they want to raise the prices. It doesn't matter to me, I don't care much for meat. *(Short pause)* Papa needs meat for lunch and meat for dinner.

OSCAR: The government is sending it to the American army. They transport it in dirigibles.

LUZ MARINA: In dirigibles? Are you crazy?

OSCAR: Alicia told me. She works for the American embassy. She should know.

ENRIQUE *enters through the main door.*

ENRIQUE: Good evening. How's the family. – Have you heard about the meat shortage?

ANA: You can imagine what that means to me. Your father won't eat anything else.

ENRIQUE: He's no fool. Isn't that so Papa? A good steak with fried potatoes, lemon and garlic, pot roast with ham. I don't care what they say, American meals are tasteless. Quaker Oats. Ugh! Isn't that true, Papa?

OSCAR: It's nine already. I have to go. I'm going to a lecture.

ENRIQUE: On poetry?

OSCAR (*Dryly*): On poetry.

ENRIQUE (*To* ANGEL): As I was saying. A good steak . . .

LUZ MARINA: You need money to buy a good steak.

ENRIQUE: Of course. If you have no money, you can't buy a steak.

LUZ MARINA: You can put meat on your table because you have money. But I can't because I don't. That's why I'm quite happy that there is no meat. One less thing to worry about.

ENRIQUE: If you plan right you can stretch your money to last you till the end of the month.

LUZ MARINA: Bravo for the economist. Enrique the economist has a nice salary. So Enrique the economist can do brilliant budgeting. But me, stupid Luz Marina, can't figure out her finances because her finances depend on her clients deciding that they want a new dress. If they don't, stupid Luz Marina doesn't get a penny. This month they decided they didn't want new clothes. So I have a thirty-seven peso deficit. In any case, when you do your brilliant budgeting, why don't you try to include the thirty pesos you promised Mother. You keep forgetting.

ANA: Luz Marina, please.

LUZ MARINA (*Implacable*): The first month you remembered. The second, you contributed only fifteen. The third ten. The fourth nothing. The fifth nothing and this month again nothing.

ENRIQUE: Well, there was the trip to New York . . . Maria's illness. . . . It's not as simple as you think.

LUZ MARINA: What do you expect me to do? Perform miracles? I can't bear these debts. God knows that if I can make ends meet I don't bother you. But I need twenty pesos this month. And you must give them to me!

ENRIQUE: Is that an order?

LUZ MARINA: I am pleading with you. It's only fair.

OSCAR: Don't forget my five pesos, Enrique.

ENRIQUE (*Enraged*): Listen to him! Why doesn't he work! You ask me for money but he can't lift a finger! Why don't you ask him to work? Because he has to write his little verses? (*To* OSCAR) You're not getting five pesos from me!

OSCAR: You're on the list!

ENRIQUE: Remove me from your list! Just remove me! Take me off your list!

LUZ MARINA: Aren't you ashamed to talk like that to your brother? Are you jealous of him?

ENRIQUE (*Laughing loudly*): Jealous of him! He wears my old clothes and comes to my house to ask me for change!

OSCAR: And I'm proud of it. I don't plan to work ever. But don't worry about me. One of these days you'll see me in Paris.

ENRIQUE: That's where you belong!

LUZ MARINA: At least he won't die of the heat.

ENRIQUE: No! He'll die of the cold! Which is worse! (*Pause.* HE *fans himself*) Has it ever been this hot?

LUZ MARINA: Never! I have taken three showers already.

ENRIQUE: If you had bought the electric fan . . .

LUZ MARINA: That's it!

ENRIQUE: What's the matter? I have one. Why can't you have one? I have seen some on sale. Fifteen pesos.

ANGEL: Don't mention that subject. She spends morning, noon and night talking about the fan.

LUZ MARINA (*To* ANGEL): I'm up to here, you hear! Up to here! If I talk about a fan it's because I want to! I work morning, noon and night! And you! What do you do! Drink coffee and smoke! And in the evening what do you do! What do you do!

ANA: Respect your father!

LUZ MARINA: Respect! Respect! You are blind! Don't provoke me or I'll speak my mind.

ANGEL: I'm going to smack you across the face!

ENRIQUE: Enough! Enough! (*To* LUZ MARINA) You're speaking out of turn.

LUZ MARINA: I see! You're scolding me! Of all people you! Scolding me! (*Pause*) If we are poor, we owe it to you! Trips to New York! Going to movies! Meals in expensive restaurants! Clothes! And the family can go to hell!

ENRIQUE: All right, you speak your mind! I'll speak my mind! – Why don't you get married! No man is good enough for you! You're waiting for Prince Charming to take you out of your lethargy! What can you offer him! Beauty! You were never fifteen . . . ! Money! You are as poor as a rat! Youth! It expired a long time ago! Come back to reality! A bird in hand is better than a hundred in flight! Grab the first man you see! You can't have diamonds but you'll get your fan!

LUZ MARINA: If you expect me to have a nervous breakdown because of what you said, you're wrong. For a fan I am ready to marry an undertaker and even sell myself.

ENRIQUE: So be it.

LUZ MARINA: Lay off me. Don't throw more kindling on the fire. It's hot enough as it is. We don't need to make our temperature higher than it is.

ENRIQUE: That's true. (*Pause*) It's a record-breaking heat. This is the third clean shirt I put on. Can you believe it's November?

LUZ MARINA: Well, you won't have any trouble sleeping.

ENRIQUE: What do you mean?

OSCAR: Electric fan! Electric fan! Electric fan is Luz Marina's obsession. Five pesos for my book is my obsession. Enrique, with twenty-five pesos you could dispel these damned obsessions.

ENRIQUE: Cut out the joking. You're too old for that. Get a job digging ditches and earn the twenty-five pesos.

OSCAR (*Looking at* ENRIQUE *attentively*): You will always amaze me brother – much more than a happy verse. Your power of imagination stops at the pick and shovel. (*To* LUZ MARINA) Isn't he amazing? (*To* ENRIQUE) But look, I accept the humiliation and the outrage – just give me five pesos.

LUZ MARINA: You're preaching in the desert. – Your book will be done. My hands will fall off before I give up on your book.

ENRIQUE: Wonderful! Encourage him! He'll end up in the loony bin.

OSCAR: I won't be the first poet who ends up in the loony bin. It's an honor.

ENRIQUE: Oscar in the loony bin! Perfect! *(To* LUZ MARINA*)* And you running around with your tongue hanging out! As far as I am concerned you can jump in the lake if you want to cool off!

OSCAR: Think it over. I won't be offended if you give me five pesos, and if you insist on not giving me five pesos I still won't be offended. You have told me the truth as you see it which does not negate the truth as I see it. You see a social parasite. I see a poet. The poet and the social parasite are not exclusive of each other. . . . They both exist. I am delighted if you feed my parasitism. So long. *(HE exits)*

ANGEL: I'm also leaving. The meeting starts at nine thirty.

LUZ MARINA: Papa. The meeting?

ANGEL: Don't be fresh! You want me to smack you across the face!

ANGEL *exits.* ANA *goes to the bedroom.*

LUZ MARINA: Hm. Do you think in December the weather will change?

ENRIQUE: Who knows! Remember last year? December came in with African heats.

LUZ MARINA: Of course I remember. I spent Christmas sweating over this table. Every client wanted a new dress for Christmas. Why didn't I buy my fan then?

ENRIQUE: You should have followed my advice.

LUZ MARINA: I'm quite willing to follow your advice, but first give me twenty pesos.

ENRIQUE: First I have to figure out my accounts.

LUZ MARINA: I too have to figure out my accounts!

ENRIQUE: Damn it. It's hot. Thirty-two high, twenty low.

LUZ MARINA: I already took three showers. I'll take another before I go to bed, although I don't see the point of that, in two minutes you're drenched again.

ENRIQUE: Leave the window open. It will cool off after midnight.

LUZ MARINA: You should be in my room at three in the morning. An oven. An oven.

ENRIQUE: O.K. I'll be back around the first of the month. So long.

LUZ MARINA: So long.

ANA *appears in the bedroom door.*

ENRIQUE *(Kissing* ANA*)*: So long, Mama.

ANA: So long, son. *(ENRIQUE exits)* I'm going to bed. I don't feel well. Don't stay up too late.

LUZ MARINA *starts cutting a piece of fabric.* SHE *sees a page* OSCAR *left on the table.*

LUZ MARINA *(Reading)*:
> "The fish from the tower
> swims in asphalt.
> He looks for his soul
> in the sewers.
> And I alone,
> standing on the curb,
> see my sister's tears
> roll down her face."

(SHE returns to her cutting. SHE *stops and looks around)* "I see my sister's tears roll. . . . " Maybe he's right.

LUZ MARINA *returns to her cutting. Lights fade to black.*

Scene 2

The following day. It is seven in the morning. OSCAR *is sleeping on a cot down center.* LUZ MARINA *sits at the table. Her hair is uncombed.* SHE *wears a robe.* SHE *spreads butter on a piece of bread.* SHE *fans herself.* ANA *enters with a cup of coffee.* SHE *puts it on the table.*

LUZ MARINA *(Touching the cup with both hands)*: It's hot.
ANA: Try it before you talk. It's lukewarm.
LUZ MARINA: It's steaming Mama.
ANA: Luz Marina don't start. It's too early.
LUZ MARINA: Can't I say the coffee's hot?
ANA: Taste it.

LUZ MARINA *drinks.*

LUZ MARINA: It's not too hot. – It's going to be a day of fire. *(SHE fans herself again. There is a pause)* At what time did Papa come in last night?
ANA: At one thirty. And he smelled of alcohol.
LUZ MARINA: That shouldn't surprise you. He's unemployed but he always has a quarter in his pocket to buy rum. It's your fault. You have always pampered him. I'm tired of it. *(Pause)* This endless heat. The day you least expect it I'll put an end to it. I'll go to New York. *(Pause)* Luis hasn't written in days.

ANA: More than two weeks. I'm worried about him. Something must have happened to him. Oh, how I wish Luisito would find a place for himself in New York!

LUZ MARINA: He's been there a year and he's only sent you twenty pesos. But that's all right. Things never turn out the way you expect.

ANA: You know what your father said last night? That he was going to lie down on the ground and let the dirt cover him till he died.

LUZ MARINA: And you pay any attention to that? He talks like that to torment you. Your life with him has been a nightmare. *(Pause)* And so has mine. – He used to hit us, – insult us.

ANA: That's true. But now he's old, helpless, without work. . . . Still he was not a bad father.

LUZ MARINA: He can't stand me.

ANA: He's used to running things.

LUZ MARINA: What right has he?

ANA: He thinks he's still running the house.

LUZ MARINA: I can't stand it. – The way he talked to me last night. How can he say he's going to hit me across the face?

Pause.

ANA: He cried last night.

LUZ MARINA: So. You know the cause of those tears.

ANA: Lower your voice, your brother may hear. – I could have never imagined . . .

LUZ MARINA: What are you going to do?

ANA: What can I do? I wish I would die.

LUZ MARINA: I don't understand why she even looks at him. He doesn't have a penny. He's old. If she's not getting anything out of it, why does she want to get him aroused?

ANA: . . . To flirt. . . . Or else because she loves him. . . .

LUZ MARINA: You think a fifteen-year-old with a dozen admirers is going to fall in love with a slimy and penniless old man? You are naive. And she's not a flirt. She's a whore. You shouldn't let her come into this house.

ANA: I can't stop her from coming here. She's not a stranger to me. I have a relationship to her. I'm her godmother. And besides, if this thing is out in the open, it is I who will be blamed.

LUZ MARINA: You?

ANA: I will be blamed for it. Gaspar and Marta will blame me. They'll say I'm mentally sick. That I am a jealous woman. – I have no proof.

LUZ MARINA: You should tell the whole world!

ANA: And subject him and myself to ridicule?

LUZ MARINA: Send him out of town! Forbid him to see her ever again!

ANA: He won't part from her. I know he won't. He's obsessed. He slobbers over her. Sometimes he calls me Beba. Do you think he has slept with her?

LUZ MARINA: Please, Mama. You think she's going to sleep with him? She likes to have a man at her feet. That's all.

ANA: Then, she's a monster of evil. *(Pause.* SHE *takes out a photograph from her pocket and shows it to* LUZ MARINA*)* It fell out of his pocket.

LUZ MARINA *looks at the photo, then turns it over.*

LUZ MARINA *(Reading)*: "To my darling Uncle Angel from his loving niece, Beba." I'm going to demand an explanation!

ANA: Don't you dare! If he finds out you know, he may kill himself. He may be an old lecher but he has pride.

LUZ MARINA: You know what? You deserve every bit that's happening to you. You think he doesn't know that you know? – Don't speak to him! Cut off his allowance.

ANA: It would be useless. He's obsessed.

LUZ MARINA: Do as you wish. But don't ever ask me for comfort. You were born a slave and you'll die a slave. My patience has a limit!

Pause.

ANA: . . . I'll talk to him. I'll beg him not to have her in this house again.

LUZ MARINA: Beg! You want to beg! On your knees! Like a slave? It's a good thing I wasn't here when she came. She's not going to set foot in this house ever again.

ANA: I'm sorry I ever told you any of this.

LUZ MARINA: He looks innocent, with his baseball; his despair; the way he threatens to lie down and die; his poor little teeth. He's a jaded old lecher! He's sickening! Scary! The poor old man is in love with his niece. He doesn't care about anything, the honor of the family, your health. And you worship him. Let's not talk anymore about this. My breakfast is a lump—right here.

LUZ MARINA *goes to her room.* ANA *goes to the kitchen.* OSCAR *wakes up and sits up on the cot.* HE's *in his underwear.* HE *gets his notebook and writes something.* LUZ MARINA *enters.*

That's an early start. Is today Friday or Saturday?

OSCAR: Saturday. Listen to this. It's been going around in my head.

LUZ MARINA: I can't think about poetry at the moment. I have other things to worry about.

OSCAR: As you like. I'm going to Muralla Street. I heard about a very cheap printer. A fixed idea is an idea that becomes a reality.

LUZ MARINA: Last night I dreamt about you on a boat. You were going away and you had a flashlight on your head.

OSCAR: The poet goes with his magic lantern in search of a dream. Beautiful dream.

LUZ MARINA: Go to Obispo Street and get me a lottery ticket with a number ending in twenty-three, which stands for boat. And ask them what number stands for flashlight.

OSCAR: I also had dreams last night. You want me to tell you?

LUZ MARINA: No. I'll be tempted to bet on each one of the numbers. (SHE *fans herself*) We can't count on winning the lottery, but on the heat we can always count.

OSCAR *sits at the table.*

OSCAR: Mama . . .

ANA *(Offstage)*: What?

OSCAR: Is breakfast ready?

ANA: Yes.

LUZ MARINA: Can you imagine how many things I could buy with two thousand pesos. To start with: a large fan, not an eighteen-peso fan, a tall one that stands on the floor. Lots of air and very little noise. A musical hum that puts you to sleep. Then I'll buy one for Mama and one for you. Figure this out. Three big fans—one hundred fifty pesos.

OSCAR: They must cost more than that.

LUZ MARINA: Three hundred. The first thing is to get air in this house, from one end to the other. *(Referring to the window)* Here I will hang curtains with a flower pattern: twenty pesos. Two comfortable rockers, not these instruments of torture: thirty. A sofa bed for you: one hundred. Two hundred for a trip to Varadero – I just want to treat myself to that. One hundred to fix the bathroom and the kitchen – no more cockroaches. Two hundred for new clothes. And you know what? I'll open a little notions shop right here by the window.

OSCAR: Don't forget my book. How much should I put down for my book?

LUZ MARINA: That's item number one. Two hundred pesos. Is that enough?

ANA *enters with* OSCAR's *breakfast.*

ANA: Wash up. Your breakfast will get cold.

ANGEL *enters.*

OSCAR: Mama, soon you'll have a fan. (HE *goes to the bathroom*)

ANA *(Going to the kitchen)*: What did he say?

ANGEL: Did you win the lottery?

LUZ MARINA: Not yet. I will this afternoon. If you want to listen to the baseball game you'll have to go to the cafe. I'm listening to the lottery.

ANGEL: Is that how you're going to get a fan?

LUZ MARINA: Yes. Today I'm going to win two thousand pesos. You hear? *(Pause)* Hm! It's eight in the morning and I'm drenched already. At three I'll be roasting.

ANA *enters with* ANGEL*'s breakfast.* OSCAR *enters.*

ANA: We're not a lucky family. In this house nothing turns out right. And it's not just now, or in the last ten years, it's always been so.

ANGEL: I'm lucky at dominoes.

OSCAR: Dominated by dominoes.

ANGEL: And you dominated by poetry! And this one by a fan.

LUZ MARINA: And you, dominated by . . . !

ANA: Luz Marina!

ANGEL: Leave me out of your games. I'm not dominated by anything!

LUZ MARINA: Oh no?

ANA: Respect your father!

ANGEL: She's looking for a beating! *(Gesturing)* I'm going to . . . !

LUZ MARINA: You're not going to nothing. Look in your conscience. It's you who should be beaten.

ANGEL: You are insolent. Damned the day you were born. *(To* ANA*)* As of the first of the month I'm holding the reins of this house again! I'm the head of this house! I'll make ends meet! Things have gotten out of hand here!

OSCAR *(Changing the subject)*: Luz Marina won't you go to the theatre with me tonight? I have two tickets for *A Woman Scorned*.

LUZ MARINA: I would love to. That's the play where the stepfather falls in love with the stepdaughter? *(*ANGEL *is frozen and averts his eyes)* How old is the stepdaughter?

OSCAR: She's not twenty.

LUZ MARINA: And does the mother find out?

OSCAR: Oh, yes. The town sings couplets about it.

LUZ MARINA: And what does the mother do?

OSCAR: She kills the husband. – Those things don't happen anymore.

LUZ MARINA: You think they don't? It happens as much as ever . . . a cousin . . . a niece. . . .

ANGEL *is downcast.*

ANGEL: I'm going back to bed. My tooth is hurting me. *(*HE *exits)*

LUZ MARINA: The older they get the more lecherous they get. And the younger the girls the crazier they get. – What are you waiting for? Go get the lottery ticket. It's almost nine.

OSCAR *(Standing)*: I'm going. "The poet, with his magic lantern, goes in search of his dreams." *(*HE *goes to* LUZ MARINA*'s room)*

ANA: You had your way. What do you gain? To stir the dirt? I am resigned. Why can't you be?

LUZ MARINA: I swear, Mama, if I had any money I'd give it to him so he'd leave . . . go far away.

ANA: If you gave him money, it would end up in Beba's hands. Do you know what happened to the stockings you gave me? He gave them to her. She thanked me for the stockings.

LUZ MARINA: And you still love him. As long as I can remember I have seen you suffering. And worse than that, protecting him so the family doesn't find out. – What we have suffered is not just the days of hunger, the lack of clothes, the electricity cut off, the worn shoes. It is also your despair, the pain of your soul. We spend our lives talking about the heat so we don't have to talk of what is really wrong. And so we die a little at a time.

ANA: A little at a time. . . . He's killing me a little at a time. . . .

OSCAR *enters.* HE *has changed his clothes.*

OSCAR: Let me have the money. *(LUZ MARINA gives him a peso)* What if I don't find that number?

LUZ MARINA: Get any other. With our luck you think it matters? *(OSCAR exits)* If I were you, I would never talk to him.

ANA: How could I?

Pause.

LUZ MARINA: You think of nothing but him. While he thinks of nothing but himself. – Visit Cuba, tropical paradise. Visit the Romagueras on Animas twelve where they live respectably and without a worry.

Lights fade to black.

Scene 3

A month later. It's 8 P.M. OSCAR *is wearing a suit, collar and tie.* HE *is sitting in the rocker looking at a book.* ANGEL *sits at the table reading the paper.*

ANGEL: If the Germans keep this up they'll soon be in Paris. *(To OSCAR)* What do you say about Dunkirk? Your friend must be trying to get out. The Germans must be stepping on his heels.

OSCAR: You talk as if Hitler was around the corner.

ANGEL: He is around the corner. Don't you see how things are tough and getting tougher? During the last war . . .

OSCAR: Please, don't tell me about the cannon Bertha in the battle of the Marne.
  – Luz Marina!

LUZ MARINA *(Offstage)*: I'm coming!

ANGEL: What do you think of Grau San Martin? That's the man.

OSCAR: Papa, I'm not interested in politics. Of course I'm not opposed to your
  getting a job as councilman and putting me on the gravy train. – Luz
  Marina!

LUZ MARINA *(Offstage)*: I'm coming!

ANGEL: One cannot talk seriously with you. You live on the moon. You should
  be like your brother Enrique . . . seriousness . . . persistence . . . self-
  respect . . .

OSCAR: It sounds like an incurable disease.

ANGEL: That's why he is where he is and you are where you are.

OSCAR: That sounds like a riddle. Of course each person is where they are. Even
  you.

ANGEL: I know what I mean. Your brother earns three hundred pesos and you
  earn nothing.

OSCAR: And you?

ANGEL: Don't be disrespectful. I have worked like an ox all my life. It's Luz
  Marina who teaches you that kind of thinking. If I would put twenty pesos
  in your hand you would think I'm the best father in the world.

OSCAR *(Sincerely)*: I'm sorry. I didn't mean to offend you. I am aware of the
  difference between us. You don't work because you can't find work. I don't
  work because I don't want to work. – Luz Marina!

LUZ MARINA *(Offstage)*: All right. *(SHE enters hurriedly, agitated, putting a pin on
  her dress, her bag opened, hanging from her arm)* All right. How do I look?
  Do I look good in red?

OSCAR: Dressed to kill. What a sight.

LUZ MARINA: What about you? A necktie, a jacket . . .

OSCAR: Everything is worn out. It's informal. Look. The tie is frayed. The seat
  is darned.

LUZ MARINA: What do you want me to do? Go naked? Wearing a slip? I'm not
  an intellectual. *(SHE takes a fan out of her purse)* Winter clothes in this horrendous heat. I can see January is going to be like December. *(SHE starts
  putting on lipstick)* What will I be like in 1950? Older? Tired? Wrinkled?
  Roasting in the heat and bored with life.

OSCAR: And in 1960?

LUZ MARINA: I don't even want to think about it. I hope I don't get there.
  – But I know I will. That's how bad my luck is.

OSCAR: How do you like my book?

LUZ MARINA: It's sublime. This is my consolation, better than a fan. We'll send
  a copy to Luis. He'll like to have it. Tell me something: what is the exact
  meaning of *"Profane Games"*? I don't quite understand it.

OSCAR: Games of this world. Games which are not sacred.

ANGEL: You think nothing is sacred!

OSCAR: Nothing is sacred. Everything is profaneable.

LUZ MARINA: How much do we need to pitch in for the party?

OSCAR: A peso a head.

LUZ MARINA: One of us can't go. I only have one peso.

OSCAR: Don't worry, Enrique will be here soon. I told him Mama wasn't feeling well. He's good for one peso.

LUZ MARINA: He'll give you twenty-five cents. That's his top.

ANGEL: Who's staying with your mother? I can't. I have a meeting at the lodge.

LUZ MARINA: The lodge is not going to fall apart because you miss one meeting. Besides, when do I ever go out?

OSCAR: That's true, Papa. Luz Marina spends her life within these four walls. Is it too much to ask you to stay in one night and keep Mama company?

ANGEL: All right. I'll stay. Just so I don't have to listen to her.

ENRIQUE *(Entering)*: How's the family? – Where's Mama? Is she in bed?

ANGEL: Nothing to worry about. She has a headache.

ENRIQUE *(To* LUZ MARINA *and* OSCAR*)*: You're going out.

LUZ MARINA: We're celebrating the coming out of Oscar's book. *(To* OSCAR*)* Show it to him.

OSCAR *hands* ENRIQUE *the book.*

ENRIQUE *(Reading)*: "*Profane Games.*" That sounds important. *(HE looks through the book)*

LUZ MARINA *(To* OSCAR*)*: Do you think it's too much to wear a pin and a necklace?

OSCAR: No. You'd look overdressed even if you didn't wear them. So leave them on.

ENRIQUE *starts laughing to himself as* HE *reads the book.* HE *laughs louder.* HE *shakes his head.*

LUZ MARINA: What do you think?

ENRIQUE: Very modern . . . very . . . modern. . . . *(HE laughs again)*

LUZ MARINA: That doesn't mean anything. Do you like it or don't you like it?

ENRIQUE *(Continuing to laugh)*: I don't know . . . I don't know.

OSCAR: Can't you see he's mentally retarded?

ENRIQUE *(Looking at a poem)*: Incredible! Papa, listen to this: "The archivical notary listens to the sirens shutting his ears with sleeping children." *(Pause)* Can you believe it? *(To* OSCAR*)* I'll pay you one hundred pesos for every archivical notary you show me. And I'll give you a hundred more if he can shut his ears with sleeping children. As much as he tries, a notary could not possibly squeeze a child into his ear and least of all a sleeping child. *(HE puts the book on the table)* Brother, you're crazy. *(To* LUZ MARINA*)* How much did you contribute to this?

LUZ MARINA: Twenty pesos and I'm proud of it.

ENRIQUE: It's not possible. You must be embarrassed by this creation.

OSCAR: Let me have a peso.

ENRIQUE (*Taking a peso from his wallet and giving it to* OSCAR): You earned it. I haven't laughed so much in ages. – I'm serious. You could earn a living reading your poems in public.

LUZ MARINA (*Fanning herself*): Do you think today was hotter than yesterday?

ENRIQUE: Much hotter. High thirty-three in the shade, low twenty-five at 7 A.M. (*Pause*) If things keep on like this, we're going to New York for Christmas.

LUZ MARINA: Before you decide, why don't you pay up last month's twenty pesos and this month's twenty?

ENRIQUE: I'm not sure we're going. I have to figure things out. . . . A little bit here . . . A little bit there. . . . If you hadn't given twenty pesos to this bum . . .

ANGEL (*Jokingly*): Now we'll have to eat sleeping children.

ENRIQUE: Wonderful Papa! (HE *takes out another peso and gives it to* ANGEL) You earned it! (*To* OSCAR) You see? Your book makes people laugh.

OSCAR (*Standing*): Listen to this poem. I dedicate it to you.
In order to save his pretty stool
My brother Enrique covers his ass
With a silver peso.
(*To* LUZ MARINA) Let's go.

LUZ MARINA *and* OSCAR *exit laughing.*

ANGEL: He got you there.

ENRIQUE: What?

ANGEL: Didn't you find it funny?

ENRIQUE (*Standing*): I don't think it's funny at all. I'm going in for a moment to say hello to Mama.

ENRIQUE *exits.* ANGEL *looks toward the bedroom and takes out a picture from his shirt pocket.* HE *kisses it.*

ANGEL: If they think I'm going to stay here they are quite wrong, my little one. You think your papi is not going to see you on your saint's day? (HE *takes out a box from his trouser pocket*) This is your present, a little pin. I hope you like it. (HE *puts the box and the picture back*)

ENRIQUE (*Entering*): Papa, Mama wants you. She's a little dizzy. I'm going to work. Call me if you need anything.

ANGEL: Do you really have to go?

ENRIQUE: Yes, I have to go to work. So long.

ENRIQUE *exits.* ANGEL *stands lost in thought. Then,* HE *goes to the bedroom. The following words are almost inaudible.*

ANGEL *(Offstage)*: Ana I'm going now. I'll be back early.

ANA *(Offstage)*: Where are you going Angel?

ANGEL: I'm going to the lodge.

ANA: I thought you were staying with me.

ANGEL: No, I can't. I have to go.

ANA: I don't feel well, Angel. You can't just leave me feeling like this.

ANGEL: I said I have to go.

ANA: Please Angel, I'm not feeling well.

ANGEL *enters holding a straw hat.*

ANGEL: I don't care! I have to go!

ANA *(Entering)*: But what does it matter, Angel, if you miss one night?

ANGEL: Don't keep asking me! I'm going! I'm leaving! You should have told Luz Marina to stay!

ANA: She has very few occasions to amuse herself. Is it fair that she spends all her time sewing? Everything she earns is for the house.

ANGEL: Let her get married! Let her leave the house! I don't care what she does! I'm going to the lodge!

ANA: Angel, I beg you. I feel very dizzy. I can't stay alone.

ANGEL: I'll call Laura, she'll stay with you!

ANA: Laura is not home.

ANGEL: Well, then stay alone!

ANA: Angel, you're provoking God.

ANGEL: To hell with that! I can't stand your scenes. That's all I needed. We're too old for this!

ANA: But young enough for other things!

ANGEL: What are you insinuating!

ANA: I know what I'm saying!

ANGEL: Speak up! What do you know? You're always seeing phantoms!

ANA: Beba!

ANGEL: What does she have to do with any of this?

ANA: I know! I know. Beba! Beba!

ANGEL: I'm leaving!

ANA *runs after* ANGEL *and pulls the straw hat out of his hands.*

ANA: No! You're not! You love her! You're in love with her!

ANGEL: Mind your business!

ANA: This is my business!

ANGEL: You have spent your life seeing phantoms!

ANA: Phantoms! Do you want me to refresh your memory! . . . Julia . . . Isabel . . . should I continue?

ANGEL: Think what you wish!

ANA: You remember when you kept a house besides this one! I could've complained but I didn't! I was willing to make any sacrifice for my children! But now . . . your own niece!

ANGEL: I love her like a father!

ANA: Hypocrite! You love her like a man loves a woman! When you writhe in bed it's not because of your toothache! It's because you imagine yourself with her! You speak her name and you turn as red as a shrimp because you realize that I heard you!

ANGEL: What are you saying! You're crazy!

ANA: I wish I were crazy!

ANGEL: Beba loves me as a niece loves her uncle! I am her godfather!

ANA: She laughs at you!

ANGEL (*Striking* ANA): You're lying. She . . . (HE *stops himself from finishing.* HE *is disconcerted*)

ANA (*Falling on a chair*): Say it! Say that she loves you! She's laughing at you.

ANGEL: Don't provoke me, Ana!

ANA: You have the devil in you! When this ends how will you face yourself?

ANGEL (*Crying*): I can't bear it. I'm desperate. It's true I have the devil in me. You think it's true she doesn't love me?

ANA: Has she said so?

ANGEL: No. I would be lying if I said she has. But you know that women can say things without speaking.

ANA: She builds hope in you only to laugh at you.

ANGEL: Oh, I feel I'm going crazy. Forgive me Ana. I am worthless. I'm not worthy of the bread I eat in this house. Despise me. Put me out of your life.

ANA: I don't despise you. I love you. You are the father of my children. Put her out of your mind. Promise me you won't see her tonight.

ANGEL: I promise. I will go directly to the lodge.

ANA: You're lying.

ANGEL (*Embracing* ANA): Forgive me Ana, forgive me.

ANA: You'll stay then?

ANGEL: Ana, I beg you, let me see her tonight. I promise you it will be the last time. After that I'll do as you say. Please understand it's a devouring thirst. I'm burning. I have spent all day waiting for the moment I can see her. She's waiting for me.

ANA: She's waiting to laugh at you.

ANGEL: I would kill her if that were true.

ANA: Think of your children. I know I don't matter to you but think of your children. I expect nothing from you, but your children will hate you forever.

ANGEL: I have to go for a walk. I have to be alone.

ANA: You're lying. You're not going for a walk. – Do as you wish but I'm warning you I'll never talk to you again.

ANGEL: Ana, only tonight. I won't stay long but let me see her tonight. I need it. If you want you can come with me.

ANA: You want me to be your accomplice?

ANGEL: Please stop!

ANA: I have suffered this without saying a word when I wanted to put my hands around her throat and strangle her. . . . Always holding back. Always silent. . . . What do you want? You want me to lead you by the hand and take you to her bed?

ANGEL: I have to go. I can't breathe.

ANGEL *exits, slamming the door.* ANA *covers her face with her hands. The lights fade to black.*

END OF ACT ONE

ACT TWO

Scene 1

1950. Evening. LUZ MARINA *sits at the sewing machine.* SHE *speaks to* ANA, *who is offstage.*

LUZ MARINA: Mama, how long ago was Pedro's wedding?

ANA *(Offstage)*: I don't remember.

LUZ MARINA: Was it in 1945?

ANA: I don't remember.

LUZ MARINA: I was remembering the gown I wore for his wedding.

ANA: Do you remember mine?

LUZ MARINA: Of course.

ANA: It was Enrique's present.

LUZ MARINA *(Going to the bedroom with the dress* SHE *has been sewing)*: I knew you'd bring up your baby. The fabric was very showy, but the moment it was washed it shrank.

ANA: I can't remember what year that was. Ask your father. He remembers everything.

LUZ MARINA *(Offstage)*: Stand up. Let's see if this dress has a human shape.

ANA: Who is it for?

LUZ MARINA: Conchita. She's your height, more or less. Madam Conchita who pays two pesos and thinks that her dress should look like a Christian Dior.

ANA *and* LUZ MARINA *enter.* ANA *wears the dress.* SHE *stands center,* LUZ MARINA *starts to pin it.*

This is the fourth time I altered it. The dart isn't right, the cuffs are not right, the hem is not right and besides I have to listen to all her problems. – How are the sleeves? Not too tight? *(ANA shakes her head)* You can take it off. *(ANA exits)* Papa has changed, hasn't he? It's hard to think that we went through such hell on account of Beba.

ANA *(Offstage)*: He's sixty-five and penniless. – He has to change. I feel very sorry for him.

LUZ MARINA: You always did.

ANA *(Entering)*: Leave him alone. He was good to you. He gave you children all you asked for. That's why we never had any savings. He was generous with you.

LUZ MARINA: I understand, Mama. I'm a failure too. I understand. I feel sorry for him too.

ANA: You're still young.

LUZ MARINA *laughs.*

LUZ MARINA: I am an old maid.

ANA: You haven't married because you haven't wanted to. No one was good enough for you. When a woman gets too picky she ends up with nothing.

LUZ MARINA: Maybe I'll end up in a convent.

ANA: May God's will be done.

LUZ MARINA: . . . God's will. . . . And what about the will of the devil?

ANA: That's blasphemy. Everything on earth is the will of God.

LUZ MARINA: I don't need to live on hope. I prefer to know the fact that I'll end up imprisoned in this house. I don't want to deceive myself into thinking that things will change and we will see better times.

ANA: Things can change . . .

LUZ MARINA: They won't. Do you envision a future where our poverty becomes opulence and our hot air becomes cold air? Do you see that?

ANA: Here we go again.

ANGEL *enters from the main door.*

ANGEL: Ana, would you make coffee?

LUZ MARINA: Papa, when was Pedro's wedding?

ANGEL: January 25, 1944. You have the memory of a mosquito.

ANA *exits.*

LUZ MARINA: I wish I did.

ANGEL *(Annoyed)*: You wish you did.

LUZ MARINA: We would be better off if we had no memory.

ANGEL: Maybe for you. But what would become of me if I had no memory? How could I do my work.

LUZ MARINA: Your work?

ANGEL: Yes, my work! The Veguitas lands! The research on the Veguitas lands! The claim on the Veguitas lands! The fortune that is pending on the Veguitas lands: pending on the accuracy of my research: on the accuracy of my memory.

LUZ MARINA: If I were you I would forget the Veguitas lands.

ANGEL: Don't be insolent!

LUZ MARINA: I am speaking the truth. If the government took those lands you can sit and wait for the government to give them back. You're wasting your time. You're not getting those lands back unless there is a cataclysm.

ANGEL: You're too materialistic. That is the reason why the world is the way it is. Materialism. The marquis is entitled to his lands and he's getting them back because I'm helping him get them back. And he's giving me a large commission—ten thousand pesos—and I'm getting a farm with that money. I am starting a chicken farm.

LUZ MARINA: Again!

ANGEL: Again. *(LUZ MARINA laughs)* What's so funny about that?

LUZ MARINA: It's funny. All your business ventures are funny. The hens, the vinegar, the lands of the marquis.

ANGEL: Just wait. Just wait till the money starts coming in.

LUZ MARINA: When!

ANGEL: I don't know!

LUZ MARINA: This century or next century!

ANGEL: Maybe this century! Maybe next century!

ANA *(Offstage; from the kitchen)*: Enough!

LUZ MARINA: Enough . . . and in the meantime we eat dirt.

ANA *enters*.

ANA: Do you remember Mercedez?

ANGEL: Of course I remember. Oscar named her Mercedez after the girl next door. And her father called their goat Luz Marina after Luz Marina.

THEY *laugh*.

LUZ MARINA: I think we were happy then. At least we had a big house.

ANGEL: With a big yard and many hens.

LUZ MARINA: But they all died.

ANGEL: Not the hens, the pullets.

LUZ MARINA: That's right.

ANGEL: I never understood why they died. I did all that was required. Special feed, incubators, heating stoves. – Everything according to science and they still died. It was a curse.

LUZ MARINA: I have no doubt. The Romaguera name is doomed to fail. Things are not any better for me. It is as if we don't know how to strike the right chord.

ANA: I loved that house. But when your father lost his job I started hating it.

LUZ MARINA: Those were hard times. We used to lie in bed to save our energy. And when Papa came home with something to eat we all jumped out of bed.

ANGEL: We were so happy when we sold a bottle of vinegar.

LUZ MARINA: Those were our heroic times. We had no food, but we had hope. Hope for what I'm not sure, but we had it. Today we eat but we have no hope.

ANGEL: I'm going to bed.

LUZ MARINA *sits in the rocking chair.*

LUZ MARINA: Well, tomorrow will be another day. *(SHE yawns)* I haven't finished Nena's dress yet. . . . But I am too sleepy. . . .

LUZ MARINA *yawns.* ANA *yawns.*

ANA: Nena Camacho? Or Nena Salvador?

LUZ MARINA: Camacho the witch. She told me she doesn't sleep with her husband.

ANA: Who does she sleep with? *(SHE yawns)*

LUZ MARINA: With the grocery clerk. Everyone knows.

ANA: I didn't know. *(SHE yawns)* Have you seen Rosita?

LUZ MARINA: No, I haven't. – She's so funny. She says her mother taught her good manners, that she only pees in her house.

ANA: Like your cousins.

LUZ MARINA: They too?

ANA: They say they come from Cardenas already peed.

LUZ MARINA *laughs.*

LUZ MARINA: . . . By the way. . . . Have you any idea how we're going to pay the electric bill?

ANA: No.

LUZ MARINA: Ask Enrique for the money. It's three fifty. We haven't heard from Luis, Mama . . . for more than two weeks. And he hasn't sent any money. I hope he's all right. *(SHE yawns)* Tomorrow will be another day. *(Pause)* Mama, tomorrow, I would like to eat beef stew.

LUZ MARINA *falls asleep. Lights fade to black.*

Scene 2

Three months later. There is an ironing board upstage left with some pressed shirts folded on it. ANGEL *is sitting up center.* HE *is tying his shoelaces.* HE *wears undershorts and a shirt. His pants are on the back of the chair.* ENRIQUE *stands to the right. It is 8* A.M.

ENRIQUE: Papa. I can't wait. I have to go. It's not that I don't want to say goodbye to Oscar, but I have a lot of things to do. – At what time does the boat leave?

ANGEL: At ten. Oscar will be here any minute. *(Going to the bathroom)* I think you should wait for him. Who knows when you'll see each other again. Argentina is very far away.

ENRIQUE: I'll wait five minutes. That's all I can wait. Maybe I can go to the pier later. What pier does the boat leave from?

ANGEL *(Offstage)*: San Francisco. – I'm sure you won't go.

ANA *(Entering from the kitchen)*: Don't you want some coffee? – You should wait for your brother. He went to get the medical certificate. He'll be right back.

ENRIQUE: Do you think I have nothing to do? Yesterday I worked all day. In the evening I had a meeting. Now I have to go in early.

LUZ MARINA *enters from her room.* SHE *carries unpressed handkerchiefs.* SHE *puts them on the ironing board, takes the pressed shirts and walks to the bedroom.* SHE *speaks as* SHE *does the above.*

LUZ MARINA: Always the same story. Why don't you just say that you only have time for your own things. I would like to see you in Oscar's shoes. Eighteen days traveling in third class which is a horror . . . alone and without a penny.

ENRIQUE: Nobody asked him to go. He wants to go – he has to put up with the inconvenience.

LUZ MARINA: Give him some money for the trip. It would help.

ENRIQUE: You think I kick the sidewalk and money grows? *(Taking money from his wallet)* Here, give him this. Ten pesos. O.K.? – Bye. If I can, I'll go see him off. *(HE exits)*

LUZ MARINA: At least with this he can buy fruit and condensed milk. If his stomach were like mine it would be different, but he'll get sick on that food.

ANGEL *(Entering)*: Well, maybe I'm stupid but why does he have to go to Argentina. Why doesn't he go to New York?

LUZ MARINA: Papa, don't you understand that Buenos Aires is Oscar's last resort?

ANGEL: You don't have to give me a sermon. I know Buenos Aires is his last resort, still he could go to New York.

LUZ MARINA: Oscar is a poet. What would he do in a country where they don't speak his language?

ANGEL: Well, he's young. He'll learn. *(HE goes to the bedroom)*

LUZ MARINA: He's not young. He's thirty-five. Do you want to know why he is leaving? He's escaping Cuban hunger and reaching for the Argentinian peso.

OSCAR *enters through the main door.*

OSCAR: They finally gave me the certificate. *(HE looks at his watch)* Luz Marina, did you press my shirts?

LUZ MARINA: Yes, I put them in the suitcase.

OSCAR: Mama could I have some coffee? To think that I paid four pesos for that suitcase. It's made of cardboard. Papa did you give me the letter for the Buenos Aires Masons?

ANGEL *(Offstage)*: Yes, I did.

OSCAR: Where in the world did I put the medical certificate. *(HE looks in his pockets)*

ANA: Calm down. I'll bring you the coffee right away. Don't you think some tea would be better?

LUZ MARINA: Of course. He can't drink coffee in the state he's in.

OSCAR: Neither coffee nor tea. I better not drink anything. (Giving LUZ MARINA *a note*) You can write to me at these stops, Kingston, Barranquilla, Colón, La Guayra, Valparaíso.

ANGEL (*Entering*): Did I ever tell you that when your mother and I got married we almost emigrated to Argentina.

ANA: You could have all been born in Buenos Aires.

OSCAR: So what happened?

ANGEL: I didn't want to leave the family behind.

ANA: I am not sorry we stayed here . . . my house, my people.

ANGEL: You were always practical. You always put the reins on me. You remember when I wanted to move to the country. You wouldn't.

ANA: Of course. How would they have gotten their education?

OSCAR: You could have gone by yourself, Papa.

ANGEL: And leave your mother alone with Enrique only one year old? Literature is your life. The family is mine.

LUZ MARINA: Hurray for the Romaguera family.

ANGEL: To her nothing is sacred. For you the only thing that counts is the pesos. For others, there is the family, affections, sacrifices.

LUZ MARINA: How does all that help. He still has to get into a horrendous third class at the age of thirty-five to go in search of a life for himself.

OSCAR: Please, Luz Marina, I have eighteen days to deal with that. Don't remind me of it.

LUZ MARINA: I'm sorry Oscar but I feel I'm bursting. I have spent my life looking for a way out, a door, a bridge. There must be one, but we will never find it.

ANGEL: The two of you are just dramatic by nature. It may be uncomfortable to travel third class, but it's not the end of the world.

LUZ MARINA: You want to cover the sun with one finger. When you travel third class your whole past is in front of your eyes.

ANA: Luz Marina you are relentless. You are turning Oscar's last minutes here into a nightmare. You'll make him bitter.

LUZ MARINA: He cannot be any more bitter than he is, Mama. His heart is overflowing with bitterness. – Oscar, even if I love you more than anything in the world. Don't you return to this cursed country. Heat, politicians and cockroaches.

ANGEL: Your brother had an opportunity here in his country when he was offered two hundred pesos to write for the radio novels but he chose not to do it.

OSCAR: We are all in the right. You, because you sacrificed yourselves for me. I because I had to do it. Don't think I'm not aware what two hundred pesos a month means to this house. It means, medication for Mama, food for all, a more comfortable house. All these things we lack are a constant reminder of my obsession, my writing. We live in poverty and yet I persist. – Well, consummatum est. I'm going to shut my suitcase. *(To* LUZ MARINA*)* Would you come with me.

OSCAR and LUZ MARINA *go to the bedroom.* ANA *becomes tearful.*

ANGEL: Come on Ana. It is not like it used to be. A trip like this used to take forever. Now it doesn't. Besides, it's only a question of months before the Veguitas estate is settled. I am always told "It's a dream . . . illusions. . . ." But you'll see. One day we'll be swimming in gold.

LUZ MARINA and OSCAR *enter.* SHE *carries a coat and a small suitcase.* HE *carries a large suitcase.*

OSCAR *(Putting the suitcase on the floor)*: Well, this is it. *(Opening his arms)* Mama . . . *(*HE *starts to cry)* Mama . . .

OSCAR and ANA *embrace.* SHE *cries softly.*

ANA: . . . Son . . .
LUZ MARINA *(To* OSCAR*)*: . . . Did you call the taxi . . . ?
OSCAR: . . . Papa . . . *(*HE *is not able to speak)*
ANGEL *(Holding* OSCAR *in his arms)*: You'll be back soon. I'll send for you soon.

OSCAR embraces ANA *again.*

OSCAR: Mama, forgive me. I didn't turn out the way you expected. I have been a bad son. I know I have been.
ANA *(Still crying)*: Son, what are you saying . . .
ANGEL: Let's go. We'll be late. *(To* LUZ MARINA*)* Are you ready?
LUZ MARINA: I'm ready. Let's go.

ANGEL takes the small suitcase, LUZ MARINA *exits.* ANGEL *follows her.* OSCAR *takes the large suitcase and exits. The door is suddenly shut by a strong wind. The lights fade to black.*

Scene 3

A month later. 11 A.M. LUZ MARINA *sits at the sewing machine, which is closed.* SHE *writes the last sentence of a letter.*

LUZ MARINA: Finished. *(*SHE *puts the pen down)* Now I sign it and I mail it and it goes flying to Oscar. . . . Mama. . . .

ANA *(Offstage; from the bedroom)*: I'm here. I'm pressing your father's shirts.

LUZ MARINA: Do you want to write something in Oscar's letter?

ANA: When?

LUZ MARINA: Now. Tomorrow is Sunday. I'm going to the Post Office to cer- tify it. Let me read it to you.

ANA: Go ahead. I can hear you.

LUZ MARINA: "My dear Brother. It was my understanding you were going to take a plane from Valparaíso to Buenos Aires. But I see you had to take a terrible train. Who would have imagined that you were going to spend nine hours stranded in the snow in the middle of the Andes. And you being so sensitive to cold. Although I have opted never to complain about the heat, I must tell you that these last few days we have suffered so much from it that I would have enjoyed being buried in the snow up to my neck." – By the way, did you hear those gunshots last night?

ANA: Yes. I heard that El Colorado killed two a few blocks from here.

LUZ MARINA: Havana, Chicago of the Caribbean. *(SHE returns to the letter)* "Here things remain the same. Papa is in Bayamo expediting the final stage of the Veguitas case. Soon we'll be swimming in gold. – I think we'll be swim- ming in something else. – I hardly ever go out. I'm over forty, but Mama thinks I'll be raped so she doesn't let me go out at night. She says it's not right. What do you think of that? Tell me if in Buenos Aires there are gangsters like here. People here say the government protects them. It must be true because El Colorado comes and goes as he pleases. . . . But Papa still believes in justice."

ANGEL *enters carrying a portfolio.*

Speaking of the devil.

ANA *enters.* ANGEL *kisses her.*

ANA: You came back earlier? Are you all right?

ANGEL *(Sitting)*: I'm as strong as a bull and we'll soon be swimming in gold.

LUZ MARINA: Let's hope, Papa. Let's hope.

ANGEL: I can see all these politicians and thieves running back and forth to no avail. Justice is but one and it is on our side.

LUZ MARINA: Oh . . . Papa . . .

ANA: Should I prepare your bath?

ANGEL *(Putting the portfolio on the table)*: Not now. I have to look up some things. *(HE opens the portfolio and looks among the papers)*

LUZ MARINA: Do you want to write a word to Oscar?

ANGEL: Tell him to get ready to come back. I'll be sending him airplane fare.

LUZ MARINA *seals the envelope and goes to her bedroom.*

(To ANA) Come here, look at this.

ANA: I have to start cooking. It's already eleven.

ANGEL: It's always the same. You're never interested in my affairs. Here everyone thinks I'm crazy, but it's you who are crazy.

ANA: Stop talking nonsense. Right now you are not interested in food but you'll start screaming when you're hungry.

ANGEL: Look at this. These are the old trails, eighty in one hacienda. You see?

ANA: I'm going to start dinner.

ANGEL: Can one talk seriously with any of you? You have never even looked at these maps. You think I'm blind? You say yes, but you don't give a damn about any of it.

ANA: I do. *(Pointing at the map)* Here are the old trails.

ANGEL: That's not where they are. Leave me alone. *(ANA goes to the kitchen. HE looks closely at the map)* Damn it. Where are you. There's no point hiding. I'm going to find you no matter what. *(HE looks in his notebook)* Eighteen degrees northwest. *(Looking at the map)* Where are you? . . . Eighteen degrees northwest. Eighteen degrees northwest, and twelve southwest. I still can't find you. Darn it. Everyone is against me. Just wait. Darn it.

The lights fade to black.

Scene 4

Two years later. 1952. Evening. The only source of light is a kerosene lamp. LUZ MARINA *and* ENRIQUE *are on stage.*

LUZ MARINA: It's your fault that they turned off the electricity.

ENRIQUE: I forgot to pay it. I have too many things on my mind. I'll pay it tomorrow. A night without lights is not going to kill you.

LUZ MARINA: Well, it's a night I can't sew. A night I can't listen to *The Shadows in Her Life*. A night I bump against the furniture.

ENRIQUE: Yesterday Batista took over the government and all you think about is *The Shadows in Her Life*?

LUZ MARINA: Presidents come and presidents go and in the meantime the dirt we eat is exactly the same.

ENRIQUE: You think so? Well, I work in a public office and I'm going to lose my job. That should make a difference.

LUZ MARINA: Of course it makes a difference. Before you helped very little, now you'll help even less.

ENRIQUE: Where is Papa?

LUZ MARINA: He's gone to bed. He's going blind.

ENRIQUE: Don't start. He can see out of the good eye.

LUZ MARINA: He can't see out of his good eye. There's a veil of ashes over his good eye and he can't see anything out of the other.

ENRIQUE: We'll have him examined . . . in due time.

LUZ MARINA: If you're going to take him to the eye doctor, do it now. Losing your sight is not like having the electricity turned off.

ENRIQUE: In due time.

LUZ MARINA: You always manage to enrage me. This is serious.

ANGEL *(Offstage; from the bedroom)*: Luz Marina, who's there?

LUZ MARINA: It's Enrique.

ENRIQUE *(To LUZ MARINA)*: How's Mama?

ANGEL *enters.*

ANGEL: She's coming.

LUZ MARINA: She hasn't tasted food in three days.

ENRIQUE: Everything is happening at once. Now we'll have Batista for ten years.

ANGEL *feels his way along the wall.* HE *reaches the rocker and sits.*

ANGEL: How are you son? They turned off the electricity.

ENRIQUE: How are you Papa? Frankly I forgot. Prio overthrown . . . Batista in power. . . .

ANGEL: Yes, we'll have Batista for a while. Is there a chance you'll keep your job?

ENRIQUE: I doubt it.

ANGEL: Don't you know anyone in the new government?

ENRIQUE: No one knows anything yet. I doubt I'll know anyone.

LUZ MARINA *(Going to the bedroom door)*: What's wrong with Mama? *(SHE looks in the bedroom.* SHE *speaks walking back to her chair)* We should do what everyone does. Have friends in both parties.

ENRIQUE: What a time for this to happen. We owe money to half the world.

LUZ MARINA: We have terrible days ahead. But that's the way it is. I used to worry. . . . But now, . . .

ANA *(Entering from the bedroom)*: How are you son?

ENRIQUE: How are you Mama? We have Batista again.

ANA: I hope they don't cut off the teachers' pension.

LUZ MARINA: Isn't there an honest Cuban who would put a bullet in his head?

ANGEL: We'll have to eat cornmeal and yams. That's what we did with Machado.

LUZ MARINA: When you're fifteen you can eat cornmeal and yams but not when you're forty. – A bottle of Seconal and that's the end of that.

ANA: Don't say that, Luz Marina, not even as a joke.

ENRIQUE: In Cuba each day we have to begin again.

LUZ MARINA: Why don't we buy a big jar of Seconal?

ENRIQUE: Well, tomorrow is another day. I'm going now. Has Oscar written?

ANA: Not for a week. In May it'll be two years he's gone. I think he's managing in Argentina. Don't you think so, Luz Marina?

LUZ MARINA: If you can call living in agony managing, then he's managing.

ANA: What's wrong with him?

LUZ MARINA: The same as with everyone else in the family. Agony. An agony that starts with birth and ends with death.

ENRIQUE: Have you heard from Luis?

ANA: He's fine. He has a new job.

ENRIQUE: That's good.

LUZ MARINA *(To* ENRIQUE*)*: Don't forget to pay the electricity. We should at least get that.

ENRIQUE: I'm going now. We'll see how this turns out. So long. *(HE kisses ANA)*

ALL: So long.

ENRIQUE *exits.*

ANA: Come Angel. Tomorrow will be another day.

ANGEL *and* ANA *go to their room.*

(As THEY *go)* Good night.

LUZ MARINA: Good night.

ANGEL: Good night.

LUZ MARINA *(Standing)*: In view of the gloom . . . *(SHE blows out the kerosene lamp. There is the faint glow of moonlight)* Good night.

LUZ MARINA *goes to her room. The lights fade to black.*

Scene 5

A year later, 1953. The table is now stage left. ANA *and* PEDRITO *sit at it.* SHE *corrects his homework.* LUZ MARINA, TETE *and* NENA *sit stage right.* THEY *sing the alphabet. When* THEY *finish* LUZ MARINA *speaks.*

LUZ MARINA: Tete how many vowels in the alphabet?

TETE *counts with her fingers and shows four fingers to* LUZ MARINA.

No. Think again.

TETE *counts through her fingers repeatedly.* NENA *mouths the word "five" to* LUZ MARINA. LUZ MARINA *puts her finger to her lips indicating to be quiet.*

Tete, how many vowels?

TETE *stares at* LUZ MARINA.

Nena, how many vowels?

NENA: Five.

LUZ MARINA: That's right. Tete, how many vowels.

TETE: Many!

LUZ MARINA: No!

TETE: My mommy's fatter than you.

LUZ MARINA: So what. How many?

TETE *stares at* LUZ MARINA *and says nothing.*

Five!

TETE: Five!

LUZ MARINA: What are they?

TETE: Five!

LUZ MARINA: It doesn't matter. What does it matter. Does it matter if she knows what the vowels are?

ANA *(To* PEDRITO*)*: Two plus three?

PEDRITO *thinks.* NENA *puts her finger to her nose.*

LUZ MARINA: Take your finger off your nose.

ANA: Two plus three?

PEDRITO: Six.

ANA: Two plus two?

PEDRITO: Four.

ANA: And one more?

PEDRITO: Five.

ANA: So. Two plus three?

PEDRITO *stares.*

Five!

PEDRITO: Five.

TETE *(To* LUZ MARINA*)*: Five!

LUZ MARINA: O.K. let's sing.

THEY *all sing the alphabet.*

ANA: Angel spent a terrible night last night. I thought he was going to asphyxiate.

TETE: My mother's skinny and my dad is fat.

LUZ MARINA: Let's sing again.

THEY *sing the alphabet.*

TETE: My mother's skinny. My dad is fat.

LUZ MARINA: Quiet!

ANA: Rita came by when you were out. She wants her dress for tomorrow.

LUZ MARINA: Rita wants her dress. The children have to be taught. The house has to be cleaned. Oscar needs a letter. Papa needs medication. Debts have to be paid and Luz Marina has only two hands.

ANA: I'm getting you a pill. You're in a state.

LUZ MARINA: Could you bring me the dress Mama? Maybe I can do some work on it now.

ANA goes to the bedroom.

PEDRITO: I have to go peepee.

LUZ MARINA: You went already.

TETE: I have to go peepee.

LUZ MARINA starts to take TETE to the bathroom.

NENA: I have to go peepee.

LUZ MARINA: No you don't. You went already.

NENA: I have to go peepee! I have to go peepee!

TETE: She went already.

NENA *(Dancing as SHE sings)*: I have to go peepee! I have to go peepee! I have to go peepee!

LUZ MARINA: Why don't I get an incurable disease and die.

There is a knock at the door. ANA goes to the door and opens it. SHE carries a dress in her hand.

ANA: Who is it?

NENA: I have to go peepee! I have to go peepee!

LAUNDRYMAN'S VOICE: Laundry!

ANA: Luz Marina!

LUZ MARINA *(Offstage)*: What!

ANA *(Walking to the living room)*: It's the laundry! *(SHE puts the dress on LUZ MARINA's chair)*

NENA: I have to go peepee! I have to go peepee!

LUZ MARINA: Tell him to leave the laundry! We'll pay him next week!

ANA *(Walking to the door)*: Leave the laundry. We'll . . .

LAUNDRYMAN'S VOICE *(Interrupting)*: No more! If you don't pay you don't get the laundry.

ANA *(Walking to the living room)*: He can't leave the laundry!

LUZ MARINA *(Entering with TETE)*: Tell him we'll pay him next week.

ANA: I told him already.

LUZ MARINA *and* TETE *sit.*

LUZ MARINA: Tell him again.

ANA *starts to go to the door.*

LAUNDRYMAN'S VOICE: I can't leave it.
ANA *(Returning)*: He says "no."
LUZ MARINA: Tell him "after all these years."

ANA *goes to the door.*

LAUNDRYMAN'S VOICE: No!
ANA: He's left. (SHE *closes the door, gives* LUZ MARINA *the dress and sits)*
LUZ MARINA: Why can't you talk to the man yourself. You know we have no
    money. You know we need the laundry. Why do I have to tell you what
    to say! (SHE *looks at the children)* All right once again.

THEY *sing the alphabet as* LUZ MARINA *sews.*

TETE *(Interrupting)*: My dad has a lot of money and he's going to buy me an
    airplane.
LUZ MARINA: Tell him to pay me what he owes me. Two pesos for last month
    and two pesos for this month. That's four. One, two, three, four. Let's
    hope Rita pays when she comes. Let's finish the song.

THEY *pick up where* THEY *left off. There is a knock on the door.* ANA *opens the door.*

ANA: They'll be right out.
LUZ MARINA: Come on children. It's time to go home.
NENA: I want to go home.
LUZ MARINA: You're going home. Come on, come on.

ANA *goes to the bedroom.* LUZ MARINA *and the* CHILDREN *go to the door.*

Good-bye, see you tomorrow.
CHILDREN: Goodbye. (THEY *exit)*

LUZ MARINA *goes to the inner court.* ANGEL *appears at the door.* HE *waves to the
children.*

ANGEL: Good-bye. . . . Good-bye. . . . *(As* HE *goes to the living room)* Hello. . . .
    Hello. . . . Guess who I met in the street? *(HE goes to the kitchen)* You

remember Benigno? I haven't seen him in years. He's coming for dinner. Where's Ana?

ANA *comes to the bedroom door.*

LUZ MARINA: You asked him to dinner?

ANGEL *returns to the living room drinking a glass of water.*

ANGEL *(To* ANA*)*: There you are. Benigno's coming for dinner, Ana. I haven't seen him in years. (HE *finishes drinking the water and puts the glass on the table)* I'll be back in a while.

ANGEL *kisses* ANA *and exits.* ANA *walks to the rocking chair and sits.*

ANA: What should I make for dinner? I only have some rice and a can of Vienna sausages. Do you have twenty cents so I can buy some eggs?

LUZ MARINA: No, I don't have twenty cents.

ANA: The grocer won't give me credit. I can't just serve rice and Vienna sausages to your father's friend.

LUZ MARINA: Why not! That's what we eat!

ANA: I can't.

LUZ MARINA: You think I kick the floor and money grows? I've had it! You hear! I've had it! Serve him shit!

ANA: Luz Marina, the neighbors!

LUZ MARINA: Damn the neighbors! Tell them we have no money! You're always afraid of the neighbors! Are they going to feed you! So what if they know we have no money! (SHE *goes to the window and shouts)* In this house we have no money! In this house we starve! We starve! We starve!

LUZ MARINA *goes to every window in the house shouting.* ANA *follows her closing the windows.* LUZ MARINA *returns to the windows* ANA *has closed, opens them again and shouts out of them.*

ANA: Luz Marina, why do you say that! They'll believe we don't eat!

LUZ MARINA: We starve! We starve!

ANA: Maybe Laura can lend me twenty cents!

LUZ MARINA *goes to the kitchen.*

LUZ MARINA: Leave me out of this! Leave me out of this! I don't care what you do! Leave me out of this! We starve! We starve!

ANA: Lower your voice! That's all I needed! To hear my daughter talk like that!

LUZ MARINA *starts to go upstairs.* ANA *closes the doors behind her.*

LUZ MARINA (*Offstage*): Luis is in New York, Oscar in Buenos Aires, Enrique is as if he didn't exist, specially now that he's unemployed! And, then what rights do I have! – Every obligation, but what rights do I have! None! The day you least expect it, I'll shack up with someone and leave the house! We starve! We starve!

The doors to the inner court open. LUZ MARINA *enters and goes to the bedroom.*

ANA: Lower your voice! Luz Marina! Lower your voice!

LUZ MARINA: I'm leaving this house! I'm leaving! I can't bear it anymore! (SHE *returns to the living room and opens the window again*)

ANA: Shut up! Shut up! Shut up! I don't want anyone to hear you speak that way! You must go the clinic!

LUZ MARINA: To get Seconal! Is that the only solution for my condition! I'm leaving!

ANA: You're provoking God!

LUZ MARINA: God is always provoking me! Well, now I'm provoking him!

ANA: You must go to confession!

LUZ MARINA *moves to the door.*

LUZ MARINA: Everyone hopes to see me buried in these four walls but I won't give them the pleasure! (SHE *opens the door and exits*) I will give myself to the first man I find! (*Offstage, as* SHE *walks away*) To the first man I find! The first man I find! In this house we starve!

The lights fade to black.

END OF ACT TWO

ACT THREE

Scene 1

A year later. 1954. It is 8 A.M. OSCAR *is sleeping on the cot.* LUZ MARINA *is sitting in the rocking chair.* SHE *drops a spool of thread on the floor.* SHE *looks in* OSCAR'*s direction with concern.*

OSCAR: Don't worry I was awake.

LUZ MARINA: The more quiet I want to be, the noisier I get.

Pause.

OSCAR: He seems like a nice man. How did you trap him.

LUZ MARINA: Out of desperation. One day . . . as usual . . . I was desperate, very nervous . . . unpaid bills . . . worries. Papa came in to tell us that he had met Don Benigno in the street, that he hadn't seen him for a long time and that he had invited him for dinner. So Mama started to worry about how to borrow twenty cents so we could buy eggs to feed Don Benigno because we didn't have anything to put on the table. I went crazy and I started screaming out the window. – I really went crazy. And then I ran out the door screaming "I can't take it anymore. I can't take it anymore. I'm going to go to bed with the first man I see. I'm going to bed with the first man I see." I got on a bus and I sat in the back and I started to cry and the conductor said "Did your daddy die, honey?" and he sat next to me. And that was that. We fell in love.

OSCAR *laughs.*

OSCAR: Has it changed things?

LUZ MARINA: It's the same and it's different.

OSCAR: The same dog with a different collar.

LUZ MARINA: Even the collar is the same. It's just a little looser or maybe a little tighter. – We're as poor as ever. *(THEY laugh)* Things are better in one sense and worse in another.

OSCAR: Do you love him?

LUZ MARINA: In a way.

OSCAR: He seems nice . . . balanced. – Is it true that he takes you to baseball games?

LUZ MARINA: Yes, and we eat out in crummy diners and I ride in the back of his bus to keep him company.

OSCAR *(Guessing)*: And Mama doesn't approve.

LUZ MARINA: Never. *(Pause)* I don't criticize her. . . . Can one criticize someone who gives everything she has? She keeps nothing for herself. Someone who effaces herself . . . who suffers for everyone else . . . never for herself.

OSCAR: You have been devoted to her. Every penny you earn is for her, for the house. You have stayed here to take care of them. . . . I on the other hand . . . I feel there's a finger always pointing at me.

LUZ MARINA: These two years have been very difficult. First, Papa's blindness. Then, Luis . . . his illness . . . and no money to take proper care of them.

OSCAR *stands.*

OSCAR: Where do you get your strength? *(Pause)* Tell me what happened to Luis?

LUZ MARINA: Let's not talk about it. We spend our life in pain and then we spend our time talking about our pain. . . . What are your plans?

OSCAR: My plans? None. I have returned to my point of departure, that's all. – To start again. Tell me about Luis.

LUZ MARINA: Well. . . . One day . . . the young man who lived in a room in the biggest city in the world . . . bought himself a can of lobster soup. And the soup was bad, and he was poisoned. They found him almost unconscious and they took him to the hospital. Encephalitis letargica. The doctor said only one out of a thousand will survive such a thing. He survived but he became deaf. Luis is deaf.

OSCAR *sobs.* ANA *enters.*

ANA: What is the matter?

OSCAR *turns away from* ANA *and dries his tears.*

LUZ MARINA: Nothing.

ANA: Your father is still sleeping.

OSCAR: When a blind man wakes up, does he continue sleeping?

LUZ MARINA: I beg you not to mention blindness in front of him.

ANA: You should know your father's mind is failing.

LUZ MARINA: Let's talk about something else.

ANA: What are you planning to do now?

OSCAR: I have no plans. People like me have no plans.

ANA: Don't you believe in anything? *(*OSCAR *shrugs)* But they say you live for your work.

OSCAR: We live in permanent danger, and what's worse, without any hope of recompense.

LUZ MARINA: Are there cockroaches in Argentina?

OSCAR: And flies and mosquitos and another Luz Marina and another Mama. Everything is the same.

LUZ MARINA: Hurray for sameness.

ANGEL *enters feeling along the wall.* HE *carries a cane.*

ANGEL: Is there room behind the table? – Is the chair there?

LUZ MARINA: There's room, Papa.

ANGEL *walks to the rocker.*

ANGEL: Is this the rocking chair?

LUZ MARINA: Here Papa.

OSCAR *(Helping* ANGEL *into the chair)*: Did you sleep well?

ANGEL: I am a little tired. I got an asthma attack.

ANA: Your father wants you to put his papers in order, Oscar.

ANGEL: You couldn't wait to tell him about my papers! One would think I was waiting for him to arrive to bore him with my papers!

OSCAR: I don't mind . . .

ANGEL *(Interrupting)*: Everyone has to put in their two cents! There is no sense of privacy in this house!

OSCAR: I'm not planning to go out. I can help you with the papers.

ANGEL: Don't trouble yourself now. We'll do it in a few days. Is it true that in Buenos Aires they call blind people "the nonseeing."

OSCAR: Only in ads.

ANGEL: Are blind people a product they advertise?

OSCAR: I mean for preventive advertising. To prevent blindness.

ANGEL: God took my sight away from me.

LUZ MARINA *(Going to the kitchen)*: Papa, do you want your breakfast now?

ANGEL: Don't start besieging me! When I want breakfast, I'll ask for it! I'm not dumb yet!

LUZ MARINA *(Offstage)*: Unbearable.

ANGEL: What!

ANA: Nothing.

ANGEL: What did she say!

ANA: Nothing.

ANGEL: Nothing! If she spoke she must have said something!

OSCAR: Are the papers you want me to look at, Papa, connected to the Veguitas lands?

ANGEL *(To* ANA*)*: You still haven't put the drops in my eyes!

ANA: It's not nine yet. *(Going to the bedroom)* Luz Marina, would you take care of your father's drops? I'm going to lie down a while.

ANGEL *(To* OSCAR*)*: Your mother is not feeling well. But I'm much worse!

LUZ MARINA *(Offstage)*: He'll live to be a hundred.

ANGEL: What was that!

LUZ MARINA *starts making noises in the kitchen.*

OSCAR: Luz Marina, Papa.

ANGEL: Where is she!

OSCAR: In the kitchen.

ANGEL: What is she doing in the kitchen!

OSCAR: I don't know.

ANGEL: In this house no one knows anything!

OSCAR *goes to the kitchen.*

OSCAR *(Offstage)*: Luz Marina, what are you doing in the kitchen?

LUZ MARINA: I'm battling with the enemy!

ANGEL: What did she say!

OSCAR *(Reentering)*: Cockroaches.

ANGEL: What!

OSCAR: Papa. Luz Marina is killing cockroaches!

ANGEL: We don't have a single roach in this house!

LUZ MARINA *enters impetuously.*

LUZ MARINA: Not a roach! You're right! Not one! Ten thousand! You hear? Ten thousand!

LUZ MARINA *returns to the kitchen.* ANGEL *follows her, wielding his cane.* OSCAR *rushes after him to restrain him.*

ANGEL: Where's my whip! Who does she think she is! Instead of making my breakfast, she's killing cockroaches!

OSCAR *(Reentering with* ANGEL*)*: Papa if you want we can look over the papers.

ANGEL: Not now. But if you'd like you could look up something for me in the archives.

OSCAR: I'll be glad to.

ANGEL: The claim to the Veguitas lands is about to . . . *(There is a sound of stamping on the floor and pots falling in the kitchen)* In this house one can't even talk. Who's making all that noise?

OSCAR: At what time do they open the archives?

There are loud noises in the kitchen.

LUZ MARINA *(Offstage)*: You're not going to get away! *(Sound)* Damn it! *(Sound)* There you are! *(Sound)* I got you!

Sound. The lights fade to black.

Scene 2

Two years later. 1956. It is 4:45 P.M. ANGEL *sits in the rocking chair. There is a newspaper on the table.*

ANGEL *(To himself)*: It's a quarter to five and Miranda hasn't arrived yet. He's not interested now that his nephew has a one-thousand-a-month job. The iceman said his eye doctor can bring back my eyesight. He can give me a little ray of light. . . . But my doctor charges me ten pesos just to tell me to continue with the drops. It's almost five and they haven't put in my drops yet. Luz Marina! She must have gone out! She spends the day in the street and Ana spends the day in the bathroom. When I get my ray of light they'll see who's boss here.

ANA *(Offstage; from the bedroom)*: Angel, aren't you going to say the rosary? It's almost five.

ANGEL *(Standing up)*: I'm coming.

LUZ MARINA *(Entering from the street)*: Papa watch for the table.

ANGEL: Just as I thought! You were out!

LUZ MARINA: That's right. Did Mama take her bath?

ANGEL: Can you take me to the clinic tomorrow?

LUZ MARINA: Tomorrow or Saturday?

ANGEL *(As HE exits)*: Don't pretend you are a fool! I said tomorrow! The appointment is tomorrow!

LUZ MARINA *glances at the newspaper on the table.*

LUZ MARINA: I'm not pretending I'm a fool, Papa. *(Reading)* "The Minister of Defense asserts that there are no rebels in the Sierra Maestra." *(Going to the kitchen)* Mama, did you buy the rice?

ANA *(Offstage)*: They didn't deliver.

LUZ MARINA *(Offstage)*: Well, we'll eat potatoes.

ANA: You'll have to get up at six if you're taking your father to the clinic.

LUZ MARINA: All right.

OSCAR *enters from the street.* ANA *enters from the bedroom.*

ANA: Are you doing anything tomorrow morning?

OSCAR: Why?

ANA: Can you take your father to the clinic?

LUZ MARINA *(Offstage)*: I said I'll take him, Mama.

ANA: Did you get the translating job?

OSCAR: No.

ANA: You shouldn't have come back.

ENRIQUE *enters.*

ENRIQUE: How's the family. *(Kissing* ANA*)* How are you Mama? How's Papa?

ANA: From bad to worse. By the way, can you take him to the clinic tomorrow?

LUZ MARINA *(Offstage)*: I said I'll take him Mama!

ENRIQUE: You sound like you can't wait.

LUZ MARINA *(Looking in)*: Still I do it. Not like you . . . *(Returning to the kitchen)* complications . . . obligations . . . Maria hurt her arm. . . . The boss wants you to do this . . .

ENRIQUE *(Going toward the kitchen)*: I do what I can. You take the pleasure out of coming to this house. It seems I only come here to listen to you complain. *(Returning to the table)* I don't have to support you or him.

LUZ MARINA *(Offstage)*: No but you have to support them!

ENRIQUE *(To* OSCAR*)*: You better find work. – Oh, I forgot. You're a poet. You can live on air.

OSCAR: Simpletons are sometimes profound. When you say I live on air you're speaking a truth which is apparent. Look how skinny I am.

ENRIQUE: Great philosophy! But where are the pesos, Oscarito?

LUZ MARINA *(Entering; to* ENRIQUE*)*: I need ten pesos for Papa's tests.

ANA: Yes, Enrique. Your father's cholesterol has gone up.

ENRIQUE: Mama, last week I paid for the electric bill. Maria . . .

LUZ MARINA: Hand over the ten pesos.

ENRIQUE: Blackmail!

There is a knock on the door.

OSCAR *(Opening the door)*: Who is it?

LAUNDRYMAN'S VOICE: Laundry.

LUZ MARINA: Tell him to come back Saturday.

LAUNDRYMAN'S VOICE: If you don't pay today I won't leave the laundry.

LUZ MARINA: Tell him to take the laundry with him.

LAUNDRYMAN'S VOICE: Can't you pay some of it now and more later.

LUZ MARINA: Saturday.

ENRIQUE: That happens when you do things on credit.

LUZ MARINA *goes to the door, gets the receipt from the laundryman's hand and gives it to* ENRIQUE.

LUZ MARINA: Here! Take it! You pay for it! You pay it. It's only eight pesos! What is eight pesos to you! You can pay it cash!

ENRIQUE: You can do the laundry in the house. Why don't you do the laundry!

LUZ MARINA *moves toward* ENRIQUE *as if to attack him.* OSCAR *holds her back.*

LUZ MARINA: Do the laundry!

LAUNDRYMAN'S VOICE: I'll come back Saturday.

LUZ MARINA: Come back Saturday.

LAUNDRYMAN'S VOICE: Give me the bill. I'll come back Saturday.

> LUZ MARINA *puts the bill in the laundryman's hand, closes the door and returns to the living room.*

LUZ MARINA: Are you going to pay for Papa's tests or not?
ENRIQUE *(Giving ten pesos to* ANA*)*: Here is the money. But it's the last time.
ANA: . . . I know son . . . I know . . .
LUZ MARINA: You don't know anything. And you don't have to play up to him. That's his duty.
ENRIQUE: And yours. *(Kissing* ANA*)* So long, Mama.

> ENRIQUE *exits.* LUZ MARINA *goes to the kitchen.* OSCAR *rests his head on his hands.*

OSCAR: One has to cry . . . one has to cry.
ANA: You all drown in shallow water.
OSCAR: Poor Mama. Poor Oscar.
LUZ MARINA *(Entering)*: And poor Luz Marina.
OSCAR: . . . At forty. It is hard to start again. One goes downhill.

> LUZ MARINA *sits down.*

LUZ MARINA: . . . You haven't written anything new?
OSCAR: Oh sure. Treasures. Artistic treasures from my inexhaustible mine. There will always be one more. – We can always eat letters.

> OSCAR *looks at the floor. The lights fade to black.*

Scene 3

> *Two years later. 1958.* ENRIQUE *and* LUIS *place two chairs center stage.* LUZ MARINA *helps* ANA *to the chair on the right.* OSCAR *and* ENRIQUE *help* ANGEL *to the other.* LUIS *places a camera on a tripod down center and looks through it.* LUZ MARINA, OSCAR *and* ENRIQUE *stand behind* ANA *and* ANGEL. LUIS *speaks in a very loud voice.*

LUIS: Get a little closer. *(*THEY *do)* Luz Marina, lower yourself a little. *(*SHE *does)* A little more or your head will be out of the picture.
LUZ MARINA: It would be better for the picture if my head were not in it. *(Leaning over to look at* ANA*)* Mama, do you feel dizzy?
ANA: No, I feel all right.
ANGEL: What did she say?
ENRIQUE *(Leaning down toward* ANGEL*)*: Luis wants us to get closer.

ANGEL: Well, let's get closer.

LUIS: What's going on.

OSCAR *(Speaking with great care to* LUIS*)*: Luz-Ma-ri-na was ask-ing Ma-ma . . .

LUIS: What?

OSCAR: . . . if she was dizzy.

ENRIQUE: Can you believe it, Mama? Fiftieth wedding anniversary.

ANGEL: I know it's our fiftieth wedding anniversary! *(To* ANA*)* You remember our wedding night?

ANA *(Almost inaudibly to* LUZ MARINA*)*: . . . Hurry . . . I need my drops. . . .

LUZ MARINA *goes to* ANA*'s bedroom.*

ENRIQUE *(To* LUIS*)*: Hurry up. Mama is not feeling well.

LUIS: What!

ENRIQUE: Mama – not – well. Hur – ry.

LUIS: Where is Luz Marina?

ENRIQUE: She – went – to . . . *(*LUZ MARINA *enters with a medicine bottle)* Here she is.

LUZ MARINA *goes to the kitchen.*

LUIS: Where is she going now.

OSCAR: Drops. – Drops.

OSCAR *pantomimes the movement of drops. His hand moves very close to* ANGEL*'s face.* ANGEL *moves his hand as if to push away cobwebs in front of his face.* LUZ MARINA *enters with a glass of water with the medication in it.* SHE *gives it to* ANA *and takes her place in the group.*

LUZ MARINA: I'm not photogenic.

ENRIQUE: Come on.

LUIS: Be still now. Is everyone ready?

ANGEL *(To* ANA*)*: Do you remember the little dog?

ANA *(Feebly)*: . . . What dog . . .?

ANGEL: The little dog we had.

ANA: . . . Oh yes. . . .

ANGEL: Sultancito. *(*HE *barks)*

LUIS: Be still.

OSCAR: We're ready. Be quiet.

LUZ MARINA: Voices don't show in pictures.

OSCAR: But the mouth comes out crooked.

ANGEL: What did he say?

LUZ MARINA: Oh, God!

ANGEL: Oh, God! I heard you. Hypocrite.

ANA *begins to sway.*

LUIS: Mama is going to faint.
ENRIQUE: Come on Luis.
LUIS: Ready!
ANGEL: What was that?
LUIS: Ready!

LUIS *sets the camera and runs to stand next to* LUZ MARINA. EVERYONE *is still. The sound of the camera is heard.* ALL *start moving except for* ANA, ANGEL *and* LUIS.

Did the camera go off?
LUZ MARINA: Yes.
OSCAR: Yes.
ENRIQUE: Yes. *(To* ANA*)* Well, Mama, you are immortalized.
ANA: . . . Immortalized. . . .
ENRIQUE: Should I help you to your room?
ANA *(Smiling)*: . . . Yes, I want to lie down . . .

ENRIQUE *picks* ANA *up in his arms.*

ENRIQUE: Papa, I'm carrying your bride for you.
ANGEL: What?
ENRIQUE: Your bride. – Mama. – Are you coming?

ENRIQUE *takes* ANA *to her bedroom.*

ANGEL: Where is my cider?
LUZ MARINA: I forgot. *(SHE goes to the kitchen)*
ENRIQUE *(Offstage)*: Luis, help Papa.

LUIS *doesn't hear* ENRIQUE. OSCAR *goes to* ANGEL.

OSCAR: Do you want to go to the bedroom?
ANGEL: Yes, but I want my cider.
OSCAR: Come Papa. I'll bring it to you.

OSCAR *and* ANGEL *go to the bedroom.*

LUZ MARINA *(Offstage; from the kitchen)*. . . Fifty years. . . . Fifty years, my God. . . . Fifty years.
LUIS: What?

The lights fade to black.

Scene 4

Seven days later. July, 3 P.M. ANGEL is sitting in the rocking chair. LUIS reads a newspaper at the table. LUZ MARINA is offstage.

ANGEL: Luz Marina! *(Pause)* Luz Marina!

LUZ MARINA *(From the bedroom door)*: Yes, Papa.

ANGEL: Luz Marina!

LUZ MARINA *(Going to ANGEL and touching him)*: Here I am, Papa. Did you want something?

ANGEL: What are you doing?

LUZ MARINA: Tea for Mama.

ANGEL: Where is Enrique?

LUZ MARINA: He'll be right back. He went to get his fan.

ANGEL: His fan?

LUZ MARINA: Yes, Papa. His fan. To cool off Mama's room. – It's very hot.

LUIS: What's the matter?

LUZ MARINA *(Mouthing the words)*: The fan.

LUIS: Have you told Papa?

LUZ MARINA *(Indicating not to let ANGEL know)*: No.

ANGEL: Who was just talking? Was that Luis?

LUZ MARINA: Yes, Papa.

LUIS *(To LUZ MARINA)*: What did the doctor say?

LUZ MARINA *(Mouthing the words)*: Very bad. *(SHE goes to the kitchen)*

ANGEL: Luis . . . ! *(HE waits)* Of course. He can't hear. I can't see. Luz Marina!

LUZ MARINA *(Offstage)*: Yes, Papa.

ANGEL: Tell your brother that I'm talking to him.

LUZ MARINA *(Going to ANA's room with a cup in her hands)*: In a moment.

LUIS *follows* LUZ MARINA.

LUIS *(Reenters)*: Enrique is taking forever . . . and Mama is asphyxiating.

ANGEL: Is that you, Luis? Is that you? *(LUIS goes out the main door)* I always forget. The blind talking to the deaf. We might as well not exist.

LUIS *enters.*

LUZ MARINA *(Entering)*: Luis, Pa-pa wants to tell you something.

LUIS: Papa?

LUZ MARINA: Pa-pa wants to tell you something.

LUIS: I understand.

LUZ MARINA: En-ri-que doesn't want to tell him about . . . *(SHE points to the bedroom)*

LUIS: He doesn't?

LUZ MARINA: No.

LUIS (*Loudly*): I think we should tell him. If she dies . . .

LUZ MARINA *puts her hand over* LUIS*'s mouth to silence him.*

ANGEL: Luis. . . .
LUZ MARINA: He's calling you . . . Papa is calling you. *(LUIS goes to ANGEL)* Here is Luis.
LUIS: Papa it's me, Luis. What do you want?
ANGEL: When are you going back to New York!
LUIS: What did he say?
LUZ MARINA (*Mouthing the words*): When are you going back to New York?
LUIS: Papa, as soon as Mama gets better!
ANGEL: You think she'll get better!
LUIS (*Looking at* LUZ MARINA): Mama?
LUZ MARINA: Do you think she will get better!
LUIS (*To* ANGEL): Do you think she will get better?
ANGEL: That's what I just said to him! You just can't talk to a deaf person.
LUIS: What did he say?
LUZ MARINA: That he's tired. Tir-ed.
LUIS: Oh . . . tired. . . .

ENRIQUE *enters carrying a fan.*

ENRIQUE: Here it is.
LUZ MARINA: Finally.
ENRIQUE: Is she worse?

ENRIQUE *goes to the bedroom.* LUZ MARINA *and* LUIS *follow him.* LUIS *reenters.*

LUIS: Mama needs an injection! *(HE holds* ANGEL *by the shoulders)* Papa!
ANGEL (*Starting to stand*): Who's that?
LUIS (*Making him sit*): Sit down!
ANGEL (*Annoyed*): It must be Luis!
LUIS: Papa . . . !
ANGEL: Everyone here is crazy! Where's my whip!
LUIS: Papa, Mother is . . . !
ANGEL (*Calling and crying*): Ana! – Ana! – Ana!
LUIS: Mama is very bad.
ANGEL (*Crying*): Mama! Mama!
LUIS (*Shouting*): Yes! Mama is very sick!
ANGEL: Very sick! Very sick!

OSCAR *enters.* HE *goes to* ANGEL.

You're driving me too far. You can't live with a deaf person.

OSCAR *(Holding* ANGEL*)*: It's not his fault if he's deaf.

ANGEL *(Angrier)*: Who's talking to me?

OSCAR: Me, Oscar.

LUIS: Tell him that Mama is very ill.

OSCAR: Papa . . .

ANGEL: I don't want to talk. Leave me alone.

LUIS: What's the matter with him?

OSCAR *(Calming* ANGEL*)*: Good Papa. Good.

ENRIQUE *(Entering from the bedroom)*: What's wrong with Papa?

OSCAR: He doesn't like to talk to Luis. They don't understand each other.

LUIS: Tell Papa that Mama is very sick.

ENRIQUE: No!

LUIS: Why not! Papa is the head of the family.

ENRIQUE *(To* OSCAR*)*: Did you bring the Coramine?

OSCAR *(Walks to the bedroom)*: Did you bring the fan?

LUIS *(To* ENRIQUE*)*: How did you find her?

ENRIQUE *(Mouthing the words)*: Very bad. She's dying.

LUIS: Dying . . . ? *(Pause)* Will they give her more medication?

ENRIQUE: She – can't ab-sorb it.

LUIS: What?

ENRIQUE: Ab . . . sorb . . . *(Pointing to the place where the vein is in his arm)* Ab . . . sorb. . . .

LUIS: I see. . . . I see. . . . Poor Mama.

LUZ MARINA *(Entering)*: I'm very nervous. I haven't slept in three weeks.

ENRIQUE: Don't start Luz Marina. I also haven't slept and I worked all morning.

LUZ MARINA: But it is I who has to deal with everything. As always. *(To* ANGEL*)* Papa, come . . .

ANGEL: Is it you Luz Marina?

LUZ MARINA *takes* ANGEL *to the bedroom.*

LUZ MARINA: Yes, Papa. Mama is better. You can rest awhile.

OSCAR *(Entering)*: She looks very bad. She didn't recognize me.

ENRIQUE: The doctor said she won't survive the evening. We have to arrange for the funeral.

OSCAR *(Very excited)*: Enrique, she's still alive. Don't bury her while she's alive. This is not the first time she has a seizure like this. We should not be her undertakers.

LUIS *(Speaking loudly)*: What's the matter? Is Mama worse?

ENRIQUE: You live in the clouds and you can spend your life being sentimental but I have to take care of the affairs of this house—the unpleasant affairs.

LUZ MARINA *(Entering)*: I heard you! I heard you! You're thinking of burying her already. Mama is here! Still breathing! And you want to put her in her grave!

ENRIQUE: You two are floating in the air but I have my feet on the ground. Besides, it's I who have to pay the bills.

LUIS *(Speaking loudly)*: What's happening! Explain to me what's happening!

LUZ MARINA *(Mouthing the words)*: En-ri-que . . . you un-der-stand En-ri-que.

ENRIQUE *(To LUIS)*: We have to make arrangements for the funeral.

LUIS: The funeral? *(To LUZ MARINA)* Mama's funeral? Is that what he's saying? Is she dead? *(HE gets pencil and paper from his pocket and gives them to OSCAR)*

ENRIQUE: We have to make arrangements. We don't have a family lot.

LUIS: Write it down!

OSCAR *writes.*

ENRIQUE: Maria is trying to get room for her in her family lot. Their cousin died only three months ago so they can't take her out. But I said that they could take Pancho out because he's been dead two years, almost three.

LUZ MARINA: Will you shut up!

ENRIQUE: Don't you speak to me like that!

OSCAR: Don't you speak that way about the one who is expiring her last breath in that room! Don't you speak that way! Don't you think of burying her while she's alive! Don't you dare!

LUIS: What's the matter?

ENRIQUE: I have decided . . .

LUZ MARINA *(Interrupting)*: You have decided! And us? We don't exist! Mama told me she wants her wake here in this house.

ENRIQUE: That can't be.

LUIS: What is happening? *(To OSCAR)* Write it down.

LUZ MARINA *(To ENRIQUE)*: It will be as she wants it. I'll tell her what you're doing.

ENRIQUE: This house is too small for a wake. I can't bring the president of my company here.

OSCAR *(Giving LUIS the paper)*: Please stop. Luis is very upset.

LUIS *(To ENRIQUE)*: It's a shame that you want to deny Mama her last wish.

ENRIQUE: Ve-ry s-mall. The pla-ce . . .

LUIS: It's her wish! Her wish.

OSCAR: If Mama wants . . .

LUZ MARINA *(Interrupting)*: Oscar it's useless.

LUIS *sits at the table facing front.*

ENRIQUE: Do you think we can bring anyone to this dilapidated place?

LUZ MARINA: In this dilapidated place your mother lived. Why now do you want to change it. You are realistic and so am I. Did you buy her a refrigerator when she was alive! Did you buy her furniture so she could live in a more pleasant place? No! Let her be mourned where she lived!

ANGEL *(Coming out of the bedroom)*: It's too hot here. Turn up the speed on the fan. She's suffocating. *(HE and* ENRIQUE *go to the bedroom)* Poor Ana . . .

There is the sound of the fan. ENRIQUE *enters.*

ENRIQUE: God. It's so hot. It's a good thing the fan is powerful.

LUZ MARINA: You brought it when it can no longer do any good. In this dilapidated place, in this heat, she has spent the last twenty years of her life.

OSCAR: It's terrible to fight like this while Mama is dying.

LUZ MARINA *(Crying)*: It's true. I am beside myself . . . I'm going in. *(To* ENRIQUE*)* You have taken care of her funeral! Have you taken care of him! What is going to become of him!

ENRIQUE: What do you mean?

LUZ MARINA: I mean Papa! Have you decided where he's going to live once this is over!

ENRIQUE: We'll think about that after.

LUZ MARINA: I'm telling you right now. That is not going to fall on me.

ENRIQUE: Don't worry. Papa is not going to a home.

LUZ MARINA: Maybe you'd let him go to a home. Not me.

ENRIQUE: Make up your mind.

LUIS: What are you talking about?

LUZ MARINA: About Papa!

LUIS: Oh!

OSCAR: Please stop arguing. We sound like savages. Do you forget that poor Mama is there . . . dying? *(Pause)* Well, do as you want.

OSCAR *goes to the bedroom.* LUZ MARINA *and* ENRIQUE *follow.* LUIS *puts his head on the table. Slow fade.*

END OF PLAY

About TCG

Theatre Communications Group is the national organization for the nonprofit professional theatre. Since its founding in 1961, TCG has developed a unique and comprehensive support system that addresses the artistic and management concerns of theatres, as well as institutionally based and freelance artists nationwide.

TCG provides a national forum and communications network for a field that is as aesthetically diverse as it is geographically widespread. Its goals are to foster the cross-fertilization of ideas among the individuals and institutions comprising the profession; to improve the artistic and administrative capabilities of the field; to enhance the visibility and demonstrate the achievements of the American theatre by increasing public awareness of the theatre's role in society; and to encourage the development of a mutually supportive network of professional companies and artists that collectively represent our "national theatre."

TCG's centralized services today encompass some 30 programs, including casting and artist referral services; management and research services; publications; literary services; conferences; and a wide range of other information and advisory services. These programs facilitate the work of thousands of actors, artistic and managing directors, playwrights, literary managers, directors, designers, trustees and administrative personnel, as well as a constituency of over 250 theatre institutions across the country.

TCG gratefully acknowledges the generous support of individual contributors and the following corporations, foundations and government agencies: Actors' Equity Foundation, Alcoa Foundation, Atlantic Richfield Foundation, AT&T Foundation, Chevron, USA, Chubb & Son, Citicorp/Citibank, Columbia Pictures Industries, Consolidated Edison Company of New York, Dayton Hudson Foundation, Equitable Life Assurance Society of the United States, Exxon Corporation, The Ford Foundation, The William and Mary Greve Foundation, Home Box Office, Japan-United States Friendship Commission, The Andrew W. Mellon Foundation, Mobil Foundation, The Mabel Pew Myrin Trust, National Broadcasting Company, National Endowment for the Arts, New York Life Foundation, New York State Council on the Arts, The Rockefeller Foundation, The Scherman Foundation, Time Inc. and Xerox Foundation.